I0121012

Succeed!™

Your Essential Guide To Business Growth

Douglas J. Hammel
MBA
Business Development Specialist

Muse Exuberans

Published by
Muse Exuberans Publishing
825 W Sims Way
Port Townsend, WA 98368

Printed in the United States of America
First Edition 2024

Library of Congress Cataloging-in-Publication Data
Hammel, Douglas J.
SUCCEED!™ your essential guide to business growth / by Douglas J. Hammel.

Includes index
1. Business — Handbooks, manuals
2. Entrepreneurship
3. Management

ISBN 979-8-218-34966-0 (Paperback)
LCCN 2024900664

Contact the Author and Download Free Spreadsheets:
www.douglasjhammel.com

Dedication

For my wife of many years
Dr. Deirdre Wilson

Introduction

This book is for entrepreneurs **already in business** who want to maximize their profits and create exceptional results for themselves, their family, and their employees. You might be the owner of a service-based company bidding on one project at a time, an artist with creative product outputs, or a manufacturer with forty employees ready to create a new profit center, but you are not a large enterprise. You are like millions of Americans who chose to start a business because you have a technical skill or an interest in something you thought you could develop into a living, and like most entrepreneurs you left out the planning and opened your doors believing your enthusiasm would be enough. You gained a certain level of prosperity through hard work and determination but now face increasing difficulties and need effective methods for managing your effort.

You may have purchased this book because you feel these difficulties undermining your success but see no clear path to a stable future. You may find yourself in a crisis, a marginally profitable concern, or an expansion. If you're in a crisis, you may be heavily in debt, short of cash, and losing customers to the competition; if you are in a marginally profitable period or an expansion, you may be uncertain what actions will assure success. The workshops and books entrepreneurs choose as a solution for their difficulties are usually business-planning guides that are well intentioned but present problem solving in absolutely the wrong order, an order that may slow the progress of your existing business.

Business-planning books assume you are not in business yet. This book assumes you *Are*.

Once you start seeing customers, your methods must change, even if it's your opening day.

With that in mind, *SUCCEED!*™ begins with measures designed to have an immediate and positive effect on your cashflows and then leads you step by step through efficient problem-solving activities and on to the long-term planning that will keep your company healthy. *SUCCEED!*™ is structured to improve the performance of any business; the sequence is the same for crisis management, profit improvement, recession recovery, or expansion and is a result of observing what works in the real world and improving on it with good, basic practices. If you are ready and willing to look closely at your business with the *SUCCEED!*™ approach, you should be able to make steady and significant progress and transform your firm into your personal vehicle for success.

This book has been developed to solve problems in a logical sequence. You may want to read the entire book without too much attention to detail, then go back to the beginning and start to make changes — and don't skip around! The order is important.

Each Chapter in *SUCCEED!*™ is organized as follows:

- An OUTLINE of SUBJECTS to get you oriented
- ALL of Us, a highlighted real story included to illustrate entrepreneurs who have discovered challenges in an operating enterprise
- HOW-TO INFORMATION to get you solving problems today
- EXAMPLES from my advising experience to show you how other entrepreneurs used these methods to become more profitable
- PRINCIPLE and WHY, highlighted boxes like the one below to help you remember valuable concepts

> PRINCIPLE:
> If you have an existing business, Business-planning may harm your company.
> WHY:
> Business-planning solves problems in the wrong sequence for an existing firm.

- LEADERSHIP LESSONS placed throughout the text to build your skill and insight for managing your teams
- TASK ASSIGNMENTS at the end of each section you will need to complete before moving on

TASK: Complete Project Costing System

Measured, steady progress is the key and remember that you are not the only entrepreneur who wants to recover from your mistakes and maximize your profits; and it might be comforting to know that big business managers make the same mistakes entrepreneurs make, and for the same reason — lack of skill. The only difference is the size of the financial consequence. To improve your *skill,* you will need self-motivation and dedication to lead your organization and the people you employ. The transition to increased profit will be time consuming; but things *will* get better, and, at some point, you will be working smarter, not harder, and become the successful entrepreneur you want to be.

Stay focused, keep your spirits up, and get to work.

Best of luck,
Douglas J. Hammel, MBA
Business Development Specialist

Acknowledgements

My list of acknowledgements is short but significant. Many thanks to:

- Deirdre Wilson ED.D. *Licensed Mental Health and Family Therapist*, Mindful Solutions, for overall editing.

- Mikko Mead BA, for her perspective as a young entrepreneur and editing.

- All my clients who over the years have enriched my counseling techniques with their own insights and hard work.

Table of Contents

Table of Figures

CHAPTER 1: The *SUCCEED!*™ Method

The *SUCCEED!*™ Method
Why Not Business Planning?
The Right Time for Strategic Planning
A Word About Business Books

<u>All of Us</u>

Don and his family were doing well. They started their business in a garage and six years later occupied a 10,000 square foot warehouse that employed 15 people. * Their creativity and energy were their greatest assets and they had used them to outpace their competition and gain a loyal customer base. Sales had expanded from $10,000 their first year to $1.2 million in their sixth year.

With little warning, they found themselves short of cash and struggling to pay their vendors. They received a bank loan and line of credit but quickly used up this cash too. Their product was still selling well and they showed a profit on their Income Statement, but they were behind on fulfilling orders and customers were beginning to complain.

How, they wondered, could they be running a profitable business that was functionally bankrupt? They needed to change something but didn't know what questions to ask or where to start.

* All examples in *SUCCEED!* are real entrepreneurs. To maintain confidentiality, names, and industries have been changed.

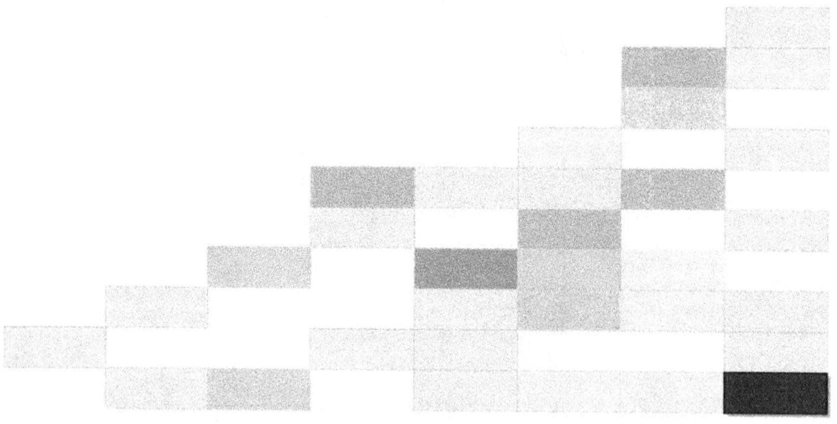

The *SUCCEED!*™ Method

Your own story as an entrepreneur is unique but your problems are not. All entrepreneurial efforts have a startup, an expansion, and, usually, a crisis. Likewise, the skill set for success in business is well established. Not well understood is the best method for improving an existing business, meaning, an orderly, effective, problem-solving sequence. The most important question you can ask yourself is:

- Which problem should I solve first, that is, which problem, when solved, makes all the remaining problems easier to solve?

While faced with the daily press of managing a business, helping customers, and creating products and services, entrepreneurs must address a complex set of old threats, inefficient systems, and long-term planning *and* not become sidetracked by new threats, new information, and new opportunities.

This book will give you:

- A practical point of attack for your business development
- A sequence of problem-solving activities that build your skill, efficiency, and profits with maximum effectiveness, and
- Exceptional results for you, your family, and your employees

SUCCEED!™ begins with measures designed to have an immediate effect on your cashflow and leads you step by step through efficient problem solving activities. It concludes with the long-term planning that will keep your business healthy.

Figure 1 illustrates the **Problem-Solving Sequence** in brief. The complete sequence of activities that fulfills this diagram can be found in **Appendix A**: The *SUCCEED!*™ Outline, and will be covered systematically as we move through each Chapter.

The first three Boxes in the diagram are the most important. They focus your work on solving problems that are the prerequisites for solving all other business problems, including the "Hot Button" issue that may have compelled you to purchase this book, and will create information, increase your cash flow and productivity, and start you on the long process of becoming an effective leader.

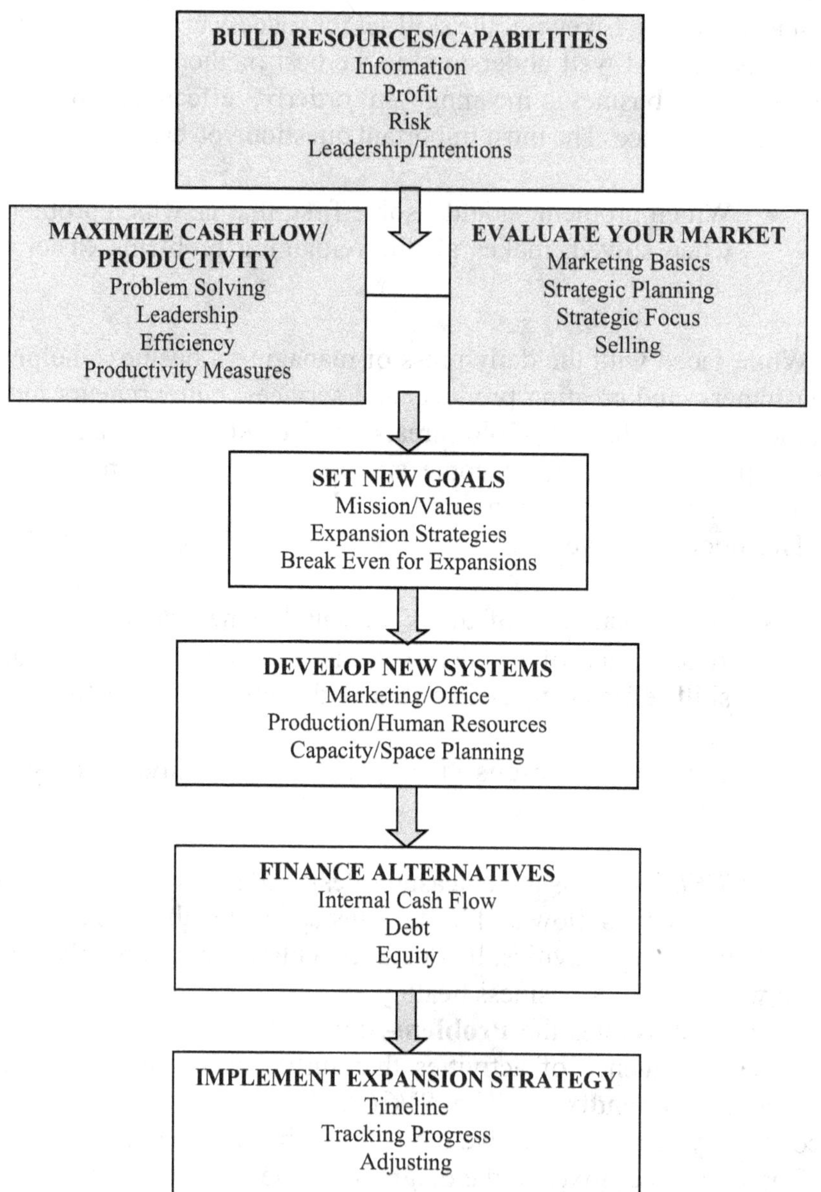

Figure 1: The *SUCCEED!*™ Problem Solving Sequence

As you move through each step in the **Problem Solving Sequence**, the *SUCCEED!*™ Method removes limitations to your success and achieves results by fulfilling the goals illustrated in Figure 2 when you:

- **Create** Information and Short-term Wins that increase cash flow and buys time
- **Invest** in Long-term Skill Development to maximize efficiency and improve problem solving
- **Make** Strategic Decisions as Information and Skills Accrue

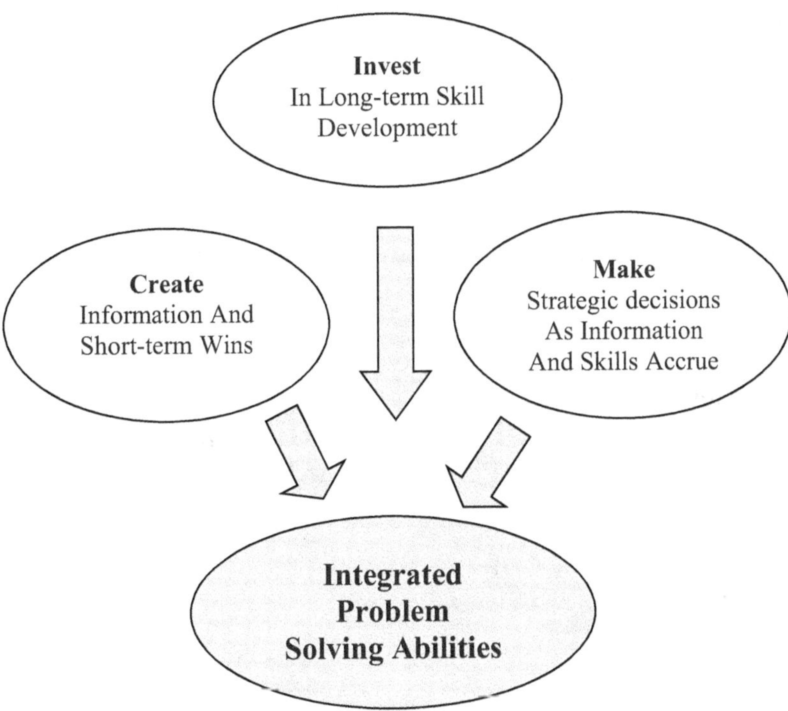

Figure 2: The *SUCCEED!*™ Goals

The outcome is Integrated Problem Solving that becomes the backbone of your success. I have proven these results through my observations and experimentation over 30 years of counseling and consulting with more than 3,000 clients, and it is the **most efficient process** for improving your business and maximizing your profits.

SUCCEED!™ also incorporates the broad strategy of solving problems in the right order, that is:

- Pricing
- Efficiency
- Volume

Pricing is free money just for thinking about it and getting it right. Efficiency is also free money but takes longer because it requires systems development. Volume is last, because adding volume to poor pricing and inefficiency just reduces your profits faster.

If you start your work anywhere but in the First Box of the **Problem-Solving Sequence**, Figure 1, you will waste valuable time working on problems that you cannot solve until you have addressed the activities higher in the diagram. Each Chapter will take you, in detail, through the problem solving and skill development you need to succeed.

At this point, you might be tempted to rush forward to the next Chapter before hearing the case I want to make for this method, but please bear with me because I want to tell you why Business Planning and Strategic Planning methods fail.

Why *Not* Business Planning?

Business Planning uses the sequence of activities illustrated in Figure 3 to create a new business.

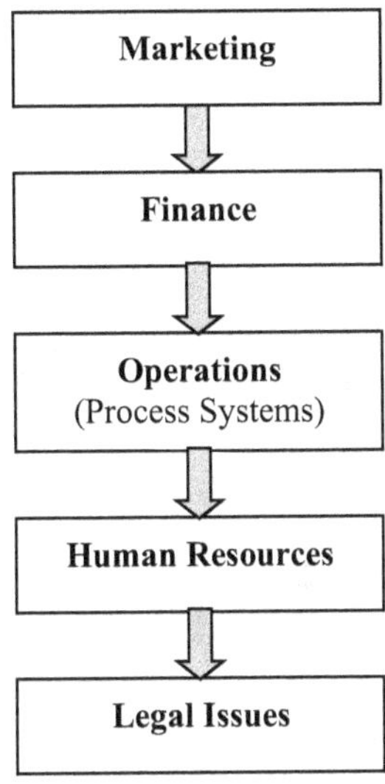

Figure 3: The Business-Planning Model

This sequence makes sense for a new business because you must first research your market to determine the feasibility of your company. If your business is feasible in your market, you move on to the next step, Financing. If your business is not feasible, you need go no further. There is no point in financing a business that is not feasible. You can research a different location to see if your business is feasible there, but you must stay on the first step, marketing, until you are certain your business will work in your location. Likewise, successfully completing each step is a prerequisite for continuing to the next step. If you have a feasible market, you can try to finance your business. If you can finance your business, it makes sense to build the operations (process systems).

Unfortunately, if you solve problems with this sequence, you may harm an existing business. Let me give you an example.

If you want to expand your business, Business Planning would tell you to implement the marketing first but if you create new sales before creating efficiency in Operations (systems), you will over burden those systems and may harm your business due to inefficient production processes, excessive personnel expenses, and increased use of cash. I have helped many clients return to profitability after they created a cash crisis by placing marketing activities before systems in their existing businesses.

PRINCIPLE:
If you have an existing business, Business Planning will harm your business.
WHY:
Business Planning activities are in the **wrong sequence** for solving problems in an existing business. You will waste valuable time working on problems that you cannot solve until you have addressed the activities higher in the diagram.

The Right Time for Strategic Planning

Strategic Planning uses the sequence of activities illustrated in Figure 4 to diagnose problems and reveal opportunities and threats in an existing business.

Strategic Planning and Strategic Management present activities in this theoretical format to create structure with the least amount of confusion. This model organizes your work as a marketing activity that weds distinctive competencies to the most lucrative market opportunity. The goal is to:

- Provide an overview of how well the business is functioning
- Describe the company's finances and systems
- Determine the most profitable market focus
- Create action plans that will fulfill the market focus through productive activity
- Create a written plan that tracks progress and improves management decision making

Unfortunately, Strategic Planning makes you aware of unresolved problems but gives you no direction on where to begin your work.

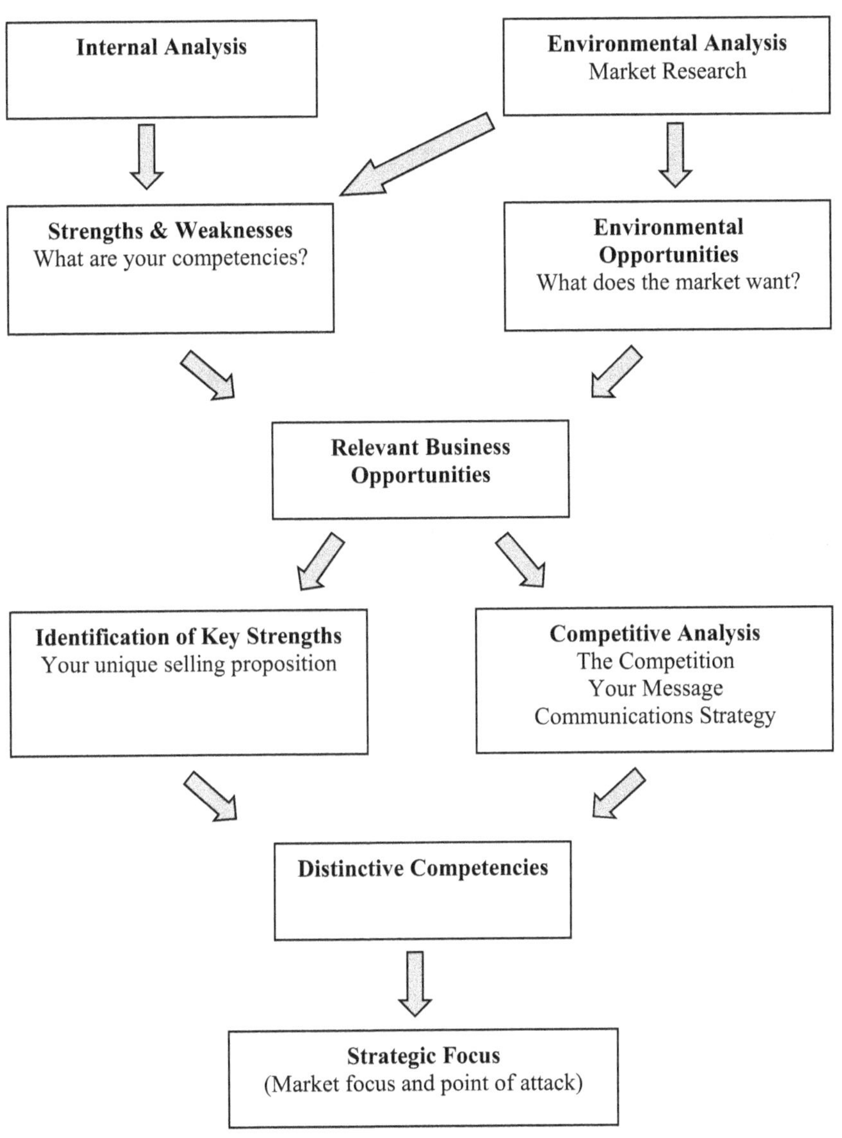

Figure 4: The Strategic Planning Model

This model fails to prioritize fundamental activities that are prerequisites to Strategic Planning itself! It does not ask you the essential question; with what problem-solving sequence will you obtain the maximum efficiency in resource use and the minimum time for results? Your business can fail due to a lack of cash flow before finishing even your Internal Analysis.

Strategic Planning needs implementation at the right time in the development of your business to succeed.

PRINCIPLE:
If you have an existing business, Strategic Planning will harm your business if implemented at the wrong time.
WHY:
Strategic Planning does a good job of outlining a sequence for **diagnosing** problems in an existing business but is the wrong sequence for **solving** problems. Implement Strategic Planning at the right time.

The *SUCCEED!*™ Method provides the following benefits unique from Business Planning and Strategic Planning:

Why It Works
The *SUCCEED!*™ Method:

- Maximizes the effect of each activity by solving prerequisites first
- Improves your skill in the most efficient sequence
- Focuses on the source of problems rather than their symptoms
- Avoids going to diffusion as you discover multiple problems
- Obtains results in the shortest time
- Buys the maximum time to solve problems in a crisis

When It Works
The *SUCCEED!*™ Method is also a comprehensive process that integrates:

- Organizational Development
- Organizational Change
- Turnarounds and Expansions
- Strategic Planning
- Recession Recovery

If you are beginning any of the above, you are beginning an isolated initiative that is NOT integrated with your entire business problem solving process.

A Word About Business Books

Some Self-Help/How-To business books are very good, but many are filled with gimmicks, management fads, and buzzwords that tend to oversimplify the work required for your success. They also tend to focus on narrow subjects such as management, marketing or the other functional areas of business and offer no integrated approach to problem-solving with an effective practical point of attack.

College Textbooks are long on theory and short on practical problem solving, good for students but not for entrepreneurs. They, again, have a narrow focus without integrated problem solving or a practical point of attack. Examples are mostly related to big business and not useful to most business owners and managers. Almost all textbooks will either misdirect an entrepreneur into solving the wrong problems or overwhelm them with too much detail.

Unlike big business managers, most entrepreneurs lack significant resources in personnel, cash, bank funding, and time.

All of Us

Earlier in **Chapter 1,** you met Don and his family who had lost control of their business because their rapid expansion had gobbled up cash as all expansions do. They paid their vendors for production materials sometimes months before they received cash from sales, creating a "cash gap." The faster they expanded, the larger the gap became and the less cash they had. If they had created a Cash Flow Projection, they would have understood the looming crisis and taken focused action to either slow their expansion or finance their cash gap. As it was, they used up all their debt capacity and sent their business into a crisis.

They implemented three immediate solutions to bring their business under control: creating cash flow projections, slowing the rate of expansion, and financing the cash gap. Over time, they applied the *SUCCEED!*™ Method and became a prosperous business.

Moving Forward

In **Chapter 2,** you will begin with your Financial Review and then continue to take focused action by creating information and short-term wins in the First Box of the Problem-Solving Sequence: **Build Resources/Capabilities**.

CHAPTER 2: Build Resources/Capabilities

Information
Profit
Risk
Leadership Lesson 1
Intentions
Practical Point of Attack

All of Us

Claire had created a wonderful service business. She had started as a Sole Proprietor with nothing and after ten years paid herself $80,000 per year. Her eleven employees were also well paid and dedicated to their work. She had solid profits beyond all expenses and carried no debt but suddenly all her cash had gone. She needed to purchase software and equipment and give her employees raises but worried she didn't have the resources to do so. Slow Collections had always been an issue, but the level of Accounts Receivable had not changed, and she could not understand where the cash had gone.

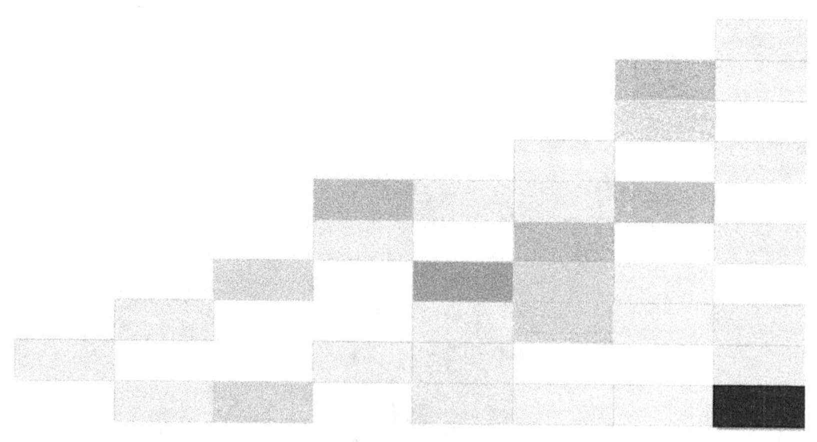

Build Resources/Capabilities

Information:

Financial Review/Embezzlement
Project Costing System (Bid Sheet)
Cash Flow Projections
Price Increases/Retail (Merchandising)
Collections/Construction Liens
Software/Information System
Accounting/Planning Notebook/Cash Management

Profit:

Cost/Profit/Volume
Price Ceiling/Higher Profit Margin Products & Services
Overhead Allocation to Profit Centers/Product Strategies
Up-selling/Easy Cost Reductions/Clutter

Risk:

Timeliness in Invoicing/Contracts
Insurance/Legal Structure/Control/Ownership
Intellectual Property/Handling Procedures/Image

Leadership Lesson 1

Personal Goals/Educating the Whole Organization
Facilitation/Making Transitions
Communication/Training/Delegation

Intentions

Intentions/Assumptions
The Entrepreneurial Problem
Thinking Patterns/Personality Types
Wellness Issues/Commitment to Change

Practical Point of Attack: Tasks for This Section

Practical Point of Attack/Interim Financing

Figure 5: Build Resources/Capabilities

Build Resources/Capabilities is the First Box in the Problem-Solving Sequence because completing the activities in this box is the prerequisite for solving *ALL* other problems in your business. That is a strong statement and I say it with purpose. My experience has taught me that these activities contain the **Practical Point of Attack** and the **Prerequisites** for solving most business problems.

It will be tempting to skip ahead to your "Hot-Button" issue because it is either:

- Long-standing or
- Immediately threatening the existence of your business

If you start anywhere but in **Build**, you will waste time and resources as you find you cannot solve your Hot-Button issue without completing the essential activities outlined in this first important step.

Your business is like a Swiss cheese. The solid parts of the cheese are the things you do well, the holes are the things you do not do well. You may not be aware that some holes even exist. You may have completed all, some, or none of these activities in the development of your business. Your job is to fill in the holes in the most effective sequence making sure the solid parts really are solid and creating new structures that you will not have to fix later.

Build activities (Figure 5) focus on:

- Information
- Profit
- Risk
- Leadership
- Intentions
- Finding the Practical Point of Attack

Completing all of these activities will:

- Create information for decision making
- Increase cash flow
- Reduce risk
- Begin the process of controlling your finances
- Prepare you to work more effectively with your employees

The activities are listed top to bottom in the order they need to be completed and you may ask at this point, how long will it take? To complete all the activities in this guide might take you two years but that is not as long as it sounds given that this is your career. The objective is not to work fast, but to work effectively, and give yourself time to learn new skills and absorb changes.

Let's start with your first assignments under Information Resources: Financial Analysis and Project Costing System.

Information

Financial Review

We do not begin with a rigorous financial analysis or instruction in accounting. That is for later, but I do want you to know your profit margin as a benchmark. If you use Quickbooks, you can go to Reports > Profit and Loss Standard. In the Compare Another Period window, choose Percent of Income and then Run Report. The percent next to your Net Income is your Profit Margin. Make sure you have subtracted a reasonable owner's draw before you calculate net income.

If you do not have an accounting system, subtract total expenses from total sales for the year to find your Net Income. Divide Net Income by Total Sales. This is your Profit Margin. If you are in trouble, it is probably less than 5%.

Now look on the Balance Sheet. Is your Cash less than your Accounts Payable? Is your Cash less than two months expenses? If so, you are cash poor. This simple analysis is a reality check so you know where you are beginning as you work through the activities that will begin to improve your position.

Embezzlement

Embezzlement is your first short-term win and deserves to follow your financial review because of its prevalence in our culture and its importance for increasing cash flow. There are many ways for cash to disappear from your business, through either the cash register or the accounting/check writing function. It is a result of poor financial procedures and lack of skill in understanding accounting and financial statements (Profit and Loss, Statement of Cash Flows, Balance Sheet). Too often entrepreneurs turn over the responsibility for cash handling and accounting to unqualified employees, business managers, or bookkeepers before they understand these critical areas themselves. Business counselors catch embezzlers every year when they examine a client's books and find cash drains that need explanation. The clients sometimes have perfect accounting records prepared by a CPA or a bookkeeper.

The worst case of embezzlement I have seen was a client whose material costs as a percent of sales had gone from 15% to 35% over a three-month period but he did not know how to read his Profit and Loss Statement. His bookkeeper had been paying fictitious companies and then cashing the checks. She had accounted for all the transactions perfectly. His accountant had taken the bookkeeper's data and faithfully completed a Financial Analysis but had not looked at it closely. The percentages identified the embezzler within a few minutes. My client had lost $30,000 that he never recovered, all due to lack of skill and inattention to detail. This is the worst case because to this entrepreneur $30,000 was everything he had. I have observed embezzlements in greater amounts, but many entrepreneurs had the reserves to absorb their losses.

Later in **Chapter 2** I will talk about accounting and the skill you will need to manage this aspect of your business, but for now take these measures to stop any embezzlement that might be in progress:

Embezzlement Checklist:

- Lock up checks and credit cards
- Take back the responsibility for signing checks
- Make deposits yourself
- Open bank and credit card statements yourself
- Balance your checkbook and credit cards yourself
- Stop payments to vendors out of the cash register

Then check for the following to see if:

- Checks are missing or out of sequence
- Cash register Z Tape or Point of Sale System (POS) does not match the deposit slip for the bank
- Pay rates for employees have been increased
- Credit card limits have been increased
- Checks and credit card charges are to invalid vendors
- Expense items (as a percent of sales) have increased
- Credit cards are missing

The embezzler is always someone with access, usually someone you trust: a business partner, bookkeeper, office manager, or family member. Ending an embezzlement is straightforward and makes all other activities easier to accomplish. The results will alter your understanding of your finances. You will find a complete Internal Control Questionnaire in **Appendix B**.

TASK: Complete Embezzlement Checklist

Project Costing System (Bid Sheet)

Many entrepreneurs in services, trades, or construction must submit bids for approval before work can begin. This is not a complicated process but seems to be one with which new businesses have trouble. The problem arises from leaving out or underestimating key cost elements that turn many bids into unprofitable ventures. Sometimes this takes the form of a major unexpected cost overrun but it is more likely that the bid process is flawed, and small amounts of cash leak away over time. The small leaks eventually catch up to you and create a cash crisis. To avoid this, you need to create a standardized project costing system (bid worksheet) that identifies *all* the costs and then, after the job is complete, compares actual costs with bid costs so that the bid sheet becomes a tool for improving your bidding process and assumptions, and educating yourself about all the components of profit. The increased cashflow from accurate project costing will become your second short-term win.

Remember you do not show this bid worksheet to your customer; this is for you, to help manage your business. No customer wants to see overhead and profit on the bid. Create an estimate for your client that embeds these two items in the labor charge. Refer to Figure 6 as I explain the Bid Process.

The Bid Worksheet includes four Cost Items: Direct Labor, Direct Materials, Overhead (OH), and Profit; and three columns: Bid Cost, Actual Cost and Variance. Create a spreadsheet like Figure 6 or download the Project Costing System spreadsheet from www.douglasjhammel.com (all spreadsheets download at once) and place all your projected costs in the Bid Cost column. You can automate the math by creating separate cells for hours and labor rates per hour and write a formula for the Bid Cost column that will recalculate every time you enter new data. You can do the same for any Material Item.

Cost Item	Bid Cost	Actual Cost	Variance
Direct Labor			
3 hours X $25/hour	75	100	(25)
5 hours X $6/hour	30	25	5
Total Labor	**105**	**125**	**(20)**
Direct Materials			
25 ft X $.20/ft	5	10	(5)
10 ft X $5/ft	50	60	(10)
Total Materials	**55**	**70**	**(15)**
Overhead			
Labor hrs X OH Allocation			
8 X $2	**16**	**18**	**(2)**
Subtotal All Costs	**176**	**213**	**(37)**
Profit 25%	59	**22**	(37)
Total Bid	**235**		

Figure 6: The Bid Worksheet

Labor and Materials are easy to understand but understanding Overhead and Profit seem to be difficult for many entrepreneurs. Refer to Figure 7 as I explain the difference between Direct Costs and Overhead for a construction job.

Direct Costs include any cost you can assign to a *specific* job. You can see under Direct Costs in Figure 7 that each of the expense items can be assigned to only one job.

Overhead includes all costs you cannot directly assign to a specific job, costs that you still have without *any* jobs. A portion of your Total Overhead must be allocated to each specific job so that the job accurately reflects its share of these costs.

Direct Labor is *not* an easy item to estimate. You know the price of various skill levels in labor, but you can make several mistakes.

Direct Costs	Overhead
Carpenter Labor	Management Salaries
Cleanup Labor	Clerical Labor
Wood	Software
Concrete	Computer Repairs
Sheetrock	Equipment Repairs
Permits	Small Tools
Gasoline to Job Site	Gasoline for Management
Employment Tax Carpenters	Employment Tax Management
Sales Tax	Depreciation

Figure 7: Direct Costs versus Overhead

The full hourly cost of labor must include all taxes and benefits the company pays in addition to the labor rate, or you will underestimate the total hourly cost; but the biggest mistake is underestimating the time it takes to complete the job and then not supervising the job closely enough to accomplish the work within the Direct Labor Bid.

A client who had several crews installing all aspects of new landscaping, and had well defined bidding and well documented systems, continually lost money on jobs. I asked him to park his van near each job and observe his crew with binoculars. He found employees taking two-hour lunches, leaving the site to buy materials that should have been in their supply truck, using coins instead of wrenches to tighten pressure couplings because they hadn't brought the right tools, and the crew chief installing a stereo in his car with the company credit card. Cost overruns beyond the bid were guaranteed.

Direct Materials are usually the easiest item to estimate. If you have planned your materials list well, it is a simple matter of multiplying the number of Units times the price per unit. You can reduce your risk by using Allowances for some items, such as, a $1,500 Allowance for lighting fixtures. If the customer spends more than the Allowance, they must cover the additional costs themselves. Be careful because overuse of Allowances can inflate a bid beyond the price ceiling of your customer. They are not substitutes for knowledge of your market or careful and accurate bidding.

The easiest way to allocate Overhead is by using Direct Labor

Hours as a proxy. Refer to Figure 8 as I explain how to create an Overhead Allocation. The Total Average Overhead per month for this business is $200 (the total of all costs that you cannot assign to a specific job.) The Available Direct Labor Hours, in this case for carpenters and Other on the job labor, is 100. Divide Monthly Overhead by Available Direct Labor Hours to get the Overhead Allocation per Direct Labor Hour. This means, for every Direct Labor Hour you must assign $2.00 in Overhead. Figure 6 shows 8 hours of Direct Labor multiplied the $2.00 Overhead Allocation to get $16.00 in Overhead for this job.

Data	
Total Average Overhead Per Month*	$200
Available Direct Labor Hours Per Month	100
Overhead Allocation	
Overhead Allocation Per Direct Labor Hour	
$200/100 = * You can also use annual figures	$2.00

Figure 8: Overhead Allocation

You may find that only one type of Direct Labor is the best estimator for an allocation. Cleanup labor may not be representative because it varies, but carpentry labor really does represent how much of the company's resources have gone into the job.

The last item to estimate is Profit. Some entrepreneurs believe they are making a Profit because they receive pay for their labor, but a company cannot sustain itself without Profit for the *whole* business. I believe any well-run business can create a 20% Profit Margin but bid in at least 10% to start. For this business, we take the Subtotal for all Costs including Overhead and divide it by 1 minus the entrepreneur's desired Profit Margin of 25% (1 - .25) to get the Total Bid:

Total Bid = $176/(1 - .25) = $235*

*Rounded to nearest dollar.

The Profit is also the Total Bid minus the Total Costs:

Profit = $235 – $176 = $59

So far, the bid process looks like bottom-up pricing, that is, adding costs and profit to arrive at a retail price but you are not finished. You now need to compare your total Bid to the market Price Ceiling, that is, the maximum the average buyer will pay for this kind of job. If you have no competition in your market, the buyer will either accept or reject your bid based on their perception of value. If you have competition, they will be able to compare prices. Remember that pricing drives efficiency into your bid just as it drives it down through a distribution chain, so look for ways to become more efficient.

Experience will be your best guide as you become an expert at bidding but for now, if you find yourself losing bids, you are probably over the price ceiling because you are inefficient at completing the work. There are many opportunities to create efficiency within each cost item. A bid sheet for a custom-built house can be a spreadsheet 25 pages long.

One of the most effective ways to create efficiency is to communicate the bid to your employees. Tell your employees how long their work should take and maintain oversight throughout the project to stay on-bid. Also, create Change Orders in triplicate so any additional work your customer requests is bid, approved, and paid for.

When the job is finished, complete the Actual Cost column to see where your assumptions were wrong. In our example in Figure 6, you can see many items were underbid, leaving negative numbers (in parentheses) in the Variance column. The result was less Profit, $22.00 instead of $59.00. With this information you should be able to make better estimates, drive efficiency into the bid process and improve your next bid.

In summary, to complete a Bid effectively you must:

- Create a Standardized Bid Sheet
- Estimate costs effectively
- Compare your Total Bid to the market Price Ceiling
- Drive efficiency into the various costs
- Communicate the Bid to your employees
- Maintain oversight throughout your project to stay on-Bid

- Create Change Orders in triplicate and get paid
- Compare Bid Costs to Actual Costs post project
- Improve your Bid Sheet and your next Bid

Consider this example:

Construction

A custom home construction firm started by two carpenters had been in business for several years. They had grown slowly and been successful in most of their work but had lost $100,000 on each of their two most recent projects due to cost overruns. They created a Standardized Bid Work Sheet with all their employees present and uncovered many wrong assumptions regarding costs.

Results:

Profits:	$200,000 in new Profit in the first year
Cost Overruns:	Eliminated
Customers:	Increased Customer Satisfaction

The spreadsheets Bid Sheet and Project Costing System can be downloaded for free at www.douglasjhammel.com.

TASK: Create a Bid Sheet in Excel

Cash Flow Projections

Creating a cash flow projection is probably the single most important activity you can complete to improve your business. Your accounting system looks backward in time and is like the rear-view mirror in your car. A cash flow projection looks forward in time and is like turning on your headlights when you drive at night. Yes, you *can* drive fast at night without your headlights on but turning them on means you can be sure you won't hit anything. Your task is to get control of your finances in the shortest amount of time by creating a month-by-month projection of all your cash inflows and outflows for the next year.

First, go to www.douglasjhammel.com, Download Free Spreadsheets and open Excel file: Cash Flow – Simple. You will use this spreadsheet to create your own cash flow. Refer to Figure 9 as I explain the cash flow projection, how to create it, and how to use it to make decisions.

1) A cash flow projection starts with all sources of Cash Inflows for at least twelve months. This could be from sales, loans, your personal capital, sales of old equipment, etc., anything that brings cash into the business. The largest monthly inflows will probably be from sales with occasional large lump sum inflows from loans or investment of your personal capital. Adding all these inflows together gives you the Total Cash In, Figure 9.

2) The next section lists all the Cash Outflows: Rent, wages, materials, etc. Your projection will include many more categories including all regular monthly expenses, loan payments, owner's draw, and capital expenditures for large purchases of equipment.

3) The last section is a summary that turns your inputs into useful information. Net Cash Flow is the Total Cash In minus the Total Cash Out. If the Net is positive, it adds cash to your business; if it is negative, it subtracts cash from your business. Your Beginning Cash is the cash you had in your bank accounts on January first. When you add the Net Cash Flow to the Beginning Cash, you get the Ending Cash. Note that the Ending Cash for one month is the Beginning Cash for the following month.

You can see in Figure 9 that this business has, month-by-month declining Cash In, flat Cash Out except for materials, negative Net Cash, and a growing negative Ending Cash. Clearly, this entrepreneur needs to act before they run out of money. They may not understand what is causing the cash crisis, but they can at least see it before it arrives.

Using Cash Flow – Simple, change the titles for Items in Column A to match the categories you use in your business. The cells in blue are unprotected. Input the Cash In for each Sales category. Do not include other sources of cash from loans or investments at this point.

Next input Cash Outflows for all expense items. Assume at this point that nothing in the business will change. The summary calculations will be automatic. This is your baseline cashflow projection and shows you how much cash you will have to work with over the next twelve months. Initially you may find negative Net Cash Flows in some of the months and a declining Ending Cash, but at least you know what you're up against. You will have to cover these shortfalls but don't go out and get a loan. Activities for increasing cashflow will be addressed shortly.

	Jan	**Feb**	**Mar**	**Apr**	**May**
Cash In					
Sales	100	100	100	75	50
Investment					
Loans	50				
Total Cash In	150	100	100	75	50
Cash Out					
Rent	50	50	50	50	50
Wages	50	50	50	50	50
Materials	25	25	25	18	12
Total Cash Out	125	125	125	118	112
Net Cash	25	(25)*	(25)	(43)	(62)
Beginning Cash	10	35	10	(15)	(58)
Ending Cash	35	10	(15)	(58)	(120)

Figure 9: Cash Flow Projection
*Negative numbers are in parentheses (standard accounting practice)

Remember, this is just the first draft of a tool you will revise repeatedly as you input new information and test new assumptions about your business. In addition, there will be mistakes in the first draft that you will correct as you revise. If you are creating your cash flow with paper and pencil, you should start learning how to operate an electronic spreadsheet like Excel that will speed up the calculations and make the whole process much easier. Classes are available at your local community college. With a well-constructed cashflow spreadsheet that links all the months with simple equations, you get a powerful tool for cash management. Changing one input, say for wages in March, changes the entire cash flow projection.

As you progress through *SUCCEED!*™ you will find your baseline cashflow an invaluable tool for testing your assumptions and creating scenarios. If you have negative cash, as in Figure 9, you can test the effectiveness of price increases, cost reductions, and other interventions. If you want to purchase equipment next summer or raise wages for all or some of your employees, you can input the data to the appropriate month and see the result. Each of these decisions will have cashflow implications. Try out the changes in your cash flow *before* you make a decision that may cost you actual cash and see if the changes improve the results in the summary. Input cash to the loan line to see if you can solve a shortfall with an investment.

You may find that you will have to invest more cash now to get a better result later or you may reduce some costs for an immediate savings; but the main advantage is that you will become aware of the possible result of any decision before you spend your time and hard-earned money.

TASK: Create a 12-month Cash Flow Projection

Price Increases

Price Increases are your third short-term win. You may have uncovered deficits in your projections and raising prices to market level is something you can do TODAY that will have a positive effect on your cash flow, so do not wait. Many entrepreneurs are timid about raising prices because they initially made an entry in the marketplace by undercutting their competition. They wrongly assume they will lose customers. Most people buy products and services based on other critical factors and will not react negatively to the increase. If they do, they will not find a lower price at your competition. Raising prices is the quickest way to increase your cash flow. Get over your timidity about pricing now.

This activity requires research and experimentation and the only one who knows the answer is the customer. A specialized consultant, a client, wanted to provide post project research services to engineering firms. She didn't know what to charge as a day rate for her services and wanted to ask her potential clients if they would pay $500.00 per day. She had been advised to rephrase the day rate question as follows:

- What is the maximum you would pay for this service per day before you stopped buying? Check the appropriate box:
  □$400 □$600 □$800 □$1,000… □$1,800 □$2,000 □ $2,200

- At what price level would this service sound suspiciously cheap?
  □$400 □$600 □$800 □$1,000… □$1,800 □$2,000 □ $2,200

Her customers said they would pay $1,800 per day and that any price at or below $1,000 per day sounded suspiciously cheap. Her own bias about her value would have caused her to vastly undervalue and underprice her services. She may not have signed *any* clients because her initial price range fell below the suspiciously cheap level.

Another client was advised to stand in front of the competition's store and complete a pricing survey on *their* customers as they made an exit. Still another client asked a similar business in a nearby city if she could complete market research on his customers and share it with him. He set up a table for her and she spent three days completing her research and they both received important feedback. Asking customers about pricing is essential in determining the Price Ceiling. Consider the following example:

<u>Electrical Contracting</u>

A busy electrical contractor with a high demand for his services came into counseling behind on his bills and in danger of defaulting on his vehicle loan. He was constantly leaving job sights to service emergency clients and could not work enough overtime to satisfy everyone. The market rate at that time for electrical services was $65 per hour but he charged $55 an hour as a customer incentive. We raised his hourly rate to $65 that day and implemented a charge of $90 per hour for emergency services.

Results:

Regular Services:	$19,500 additional <u>profit</u> per year
Emergency Services:	$10,000 new <u>profit</u> per year
Time Management:	Less overtime
Customers:	No loss of customers

The customers appreciated this client's work and had no incentive to go to his competition only to pay the same market rate. Their emergencies also became less urgent, and many were willing to schedule appointments rather than pay the additional charge.

Make sure you charge extra for emergency service and rush orders. This encourages your customers to plan before they use your services and will decrease this highly inefficient use of your time. Then if you do go out on an emergency call or provide a rush order, the higher price will pay for the inefficiency.

Another example is to drive home these points:

Retail Shop

A well-established retail shop with lots of customer traffic began suffering after one partner bought out the other. The remaining partner had borrowed money for the buyout and paid too much, resulting in an excessive debt burden and a cash shortage. The more fundamental problem was that they had not raised prices in ten years. Because the entrepreneur was in a crisis, they were willing to try something new. We raised prices 20 % on all their products that day.

Results:

Profits:	$89,000 additional profit per year
Cash Crisis:	Eliminated
Customers:	No loss of customers

Note that a price increase adds pure profit. There are no additional costs related to raising your prices.

If you are already at market level or in a Recession, price increases are not an option, and you will have to move on to the next activity to find a short-term win but let's consider pricing in more detail to determine if there are opportunities you have not considered.

The first thing to understand about pricing is that it is a top-down process. This means starting with the highest retail price that customers are willing to pay (the price ceiling), and then backing out the markups in the distribution chain to find the maximum manufacturing cost per unit.

You may be any of the participants, but you must start at the retail price and work your way down to find out what you can charge at your position in this chain. Figure 10 illustrates the process of backing out the maximum manufacturing cost for a product.

Retailer Price to Retail Customer (Price Ceiling)	**$100.00**
Retail Markup (100%)	50.00
Distributor Price to Retailer	**50.00**
Distributor Markup (25%)	10.00
Manufacturer Price to Distributor	**40.00**
Manufacturer Markup (10%)	3.64
Max Manufacturing Cost Per Unit	**36.36**

Figure 10: Pricing and Markups

The retail price for this product is $100. We find the retail price ceiling by asking customers the maximum price they would pay for this product before they stop buying or experimenting with different prices and watching how much of the product sells at various price levels. Also check your competition's price but don't take this as the price ceiling. They may not know anything about pricing and may have unreasonably low prices. The retailer's markup is always 100% (key-stoning) and means they need to buy it from the distributor for $50 so they can add another $50 (their 100% markup, $50 X 1.00 = $50) on top of the distributor's price to end up with the $100 price to the retail customer.

We find the distributor's markup by asking all the distributors that carry the product and choosing the average markup. In this case the distributor's markup is 25% and means they need to buy it from the manufacturer for $40 so they can add another $10 (their 25% markup, $40 X .25 = $10) on top of the manufacturers price to end up with the $50 price to the retailer.

The manufacturer determined that they need a 10% markup per unit on their manufacturing costs to cover overhead and profit and means they need to produce the product for $36.36 so they can add $3.64 (their 10% markup, $36.36 X .1 = $3.64) on top of their manufacturing costs per unit to end up with the $40 price to the distributor.

If you are the retailer, you will not buy this product from the distributor unless they can sell it to you for $50 because if you buy it for anymore, you will not be making enough profit to run a viable business. The retail customers will not buy it if the price goes over

$100, so how can *you* pay more than $50? The same is true for the distributor. They will not buy it from the manufacturer unless they can obtain it for $40. So, what happens if someone cannot make the profit needed at his or her point in the chain? Either:

- The manufacturer finds a less expensive way to produce it so that the retail price ends up in the right range after all the markups
- Everyone in the chain becomes more efficient
- The product dies (no one will carry it)

That is capitalism in brief: the pricing process drives efficiency down through the distribution chain. Your inefficiency, covered in **Chapter 3**, may be a hidden threat. The spreadsheet Markups and Margins can be downloaded for free at www.douglasjhammel.com.

TASK: Research the Price Ceiling and Markups
TASK: Raise Prices

Retail: The Merchandising Experiment

For retail businesses the next activity after raising prices is to implement the merchandising experiment. In retail you have a limited amount of space that must turnover products regularly to create a profit. Each industry has a different inventory turnover rate, and you must research this to get it right. Every square foot of space needs to produce profit by moving products off the shelf and into customers' hands. In women's retail apparel the turnover rate is 4 times per year, meaning four separate items moved through that space.

As a retailer you must experiment every month to discover the set of products with the highest turnover rate so your average sales meet or exceed the norm. If a product does not "turn" in 90 days, you must put it on sale, get your money out of it, and perform another merchandising experiment with those dollars and that square footage.

You can make this easier by using the Open to Buy spreadsheet that calculates how much inventory you should buy each month. Refer to Figure 11 as I explain Open to Buy. The formula is:

Planned Sales + Planned Markdowns + Planned end of Month Inventory – Beginning of Month Inventory = Open to Buy

You can think of it as:

Everything You Need – What You Have = What to Buy

	Everything You Need			What You Have	What to Buy	
Month	Planned Sales	Planned Markdowns	Planned End of Month Inventory	Beginning Of Month Inventory	Open To Buy	Whole-Sale Cost 50%
JAN	15000	1000	20000	25000	11000	5500
FEB						
MAR						
APR						

*All values are at retail prices except wholesale cost

Figure 11: Open to Buy

Assume it is the first day of January. Figure 11 shows you have estimated Sales for the month of $15,000 but need to Markdown $1,000 of current Inventory. You also need to have an End-of-Month Inventory of $20,000 to be ready for February Sales. You currently have a Beginning Inventory for January of $25,000.

15,000 + 1,000 + 20,000 – 25,000 = 11,000

You are Open to Buy $11,000 of Inventory at retail prices. Your actual Wholesale Cost for the inventory is 50% of $11,000, or $5,500. This is assuming you have been "key stoning" like many retailers, that is, doubling the wholesale price to obtain the retail price.

When you take your next inventory, you need to mark down all the products that have not moved in the last 90 days, get rid of them, and replace them with other products you believe will sell. It is a continuous experiment so don't be disheartened when it doesn't work as well as you want. Keep experimenting and you will eventually find a stable set of products that provides you with your main monthly sales and a set of experiments that change every month. This is especially true during the holiday season when you may carry products for only a short time.

Download the spreadsheet Open to Buy for free at www.douglasjhammel.com.

TASK: Begin the merchandising experiment.

Collections

If you are in a cash crisis, collect everything that's owed you NOW! Don't wait to write letters. Call everyone. Anyone who has owed you money close to ninety days needs to know you are not willing to wait any longer for payment. If you have regular customers that buy supplies from you monthly but are getting too far behind in their payments, place them on a cash basis for all future purchases with the understanding that when they pick up and pay for new supplies, they will also have to make a payment on the past due amounts. Anyone who is not a regular customer who has owed you money for *more* than 90 days needs to know you will submit the bill to collection by the end of the week. Most entrepreneurs make the mistake of thinking they will alienate good customers if they try to collect receivables too vigorously. The people who have owed you money for more than 90 days are NOT good customers. They are people who use your products and services for themselves and let you finance it.

It is unpleasant to call someone and collect, but it is a basic activity that adds an increment of cash flow you need to address before it becomes untenable. Just take a deep breath and dial their number. Be calm and non-threatening, but firm. Set limits. Some will ask for more time. If you make a deal for them to pay overtime, make it short — a week or two, but no more. And make sure they know the bill will be placed immediately into collection if they fail to adhere to the arrangement.

From this point on set a firm credit policy of all payments due in cash unless your customer has passed a credit check, then offer only

30-day terms, no exceptions, and enforce it. If you are short of cash don't offer credit to anyone until the business gets back on its feet. (This does not mean refusing credit card purchases. Credit cards *are* cash.)

If you have decided to offer 30-day payment terms, get your invoices out *immediately* after the service has been provided. Your customers will have 30 days from the date of the invoice, so if you wait too long to mail it, you may not get your money for an additional 30 days.

When customers do not pay your invoice on time (30 days), send them a collection letter on day 45. On day 60 send them another more demanding collection letter. On day 75 call them and tell them the bill will go into a collection agency at the end of the week if they don't pay. You must do this because the likelihood that you will collect anything on the bill goes almost to zero after 90 days.

And don't listen to any hard luck stories. People make decisions every day about how they spend their money, and they are deciding not to spend it on you! If you think bill collecting or setting firm credit policies are unpleasant activities, remember that you are doing this for your family so that you and your loved ones will be stable in a changeable world. Going bankrupt is a lot harder than collecting. You *will* get over feeling uncomfortable.

Charging cash for your services is always the first choice but many of your customers or clients will not expect to pay you immediately after you provide them service or will have "forgotten" their checkbooks when you ask for payment. Practice these sample phases with your spouse, business partner, or a friend so you are prepared if this happens:

- We've found that it doesn't work for our business to defer payments. It builds up an unmanageable accounts receivable and undermines our relationships with our clients
- I understand, but we cannot finance your purchase and you will have to drop off a check
- We won't be able to schedule any more service/appointments until the bill is paid in full

For businesses that ship at a distance, email your invoice as an attachment and receive payment BEFORE the products are shipped; or take their credit card number over the phone and get payment immediately. Your accounting system should have this feature. If you ship without payment, offer a discount for early payment. This typically is a 2/10 Net 30 discount which means your customer can take a 2% discount if they pay within ten days, otherwise the whole bill is still due in thirty days. Do not discount too much. The object is to get your customers to pay early not to radically reduce your revenue.

Collections is a system, and you *can* create policies, procedures, collection letters, and a relationship with a collection agency now. We will talk more about additional systems in **Chapter 3**.

Remember you need to take each activity to completion before moving on so that you embed permanent improvements in your business and develop new skills in yourself. One client related to me that one activity per week, equal to about single page in this book, was a fast but sustainable pace. Set your own pace but keep going.

TASK: Collect all Accounts Receivable, Set Credit Policy

PRINCIPLE:
Create information and cash flow first.
WHY:
Information gives you an accurate view of your business; cash flow buys time to solve problems.

Construction Liens

For people in the building trades there is a special collection device called a construction lien. If a homeowner, building owner, or general contractor fails to pay you for completed work, you can place a lien on the property through the court system in most states. This is true even if the person who hired you is not the person who owns the property. Typically, just the threat of the lien gets amount due paid to you, however, there are many cases where the subcontractor went all the way to foreclosure and sold the property to get their time and money out of the job.

There are some time limits to be aware of that vary from state to state. Generally, you have a limited period to file the lien, three to six months, and another limited period after you file to go to foreclosure. Check with a lawyer or the agency that administrates contractor licensing in your state.

Create a construction lien package with all the required documents for each job so you are not learning about the process while trying to submit your first lien. Place a lien clause in your contract. When you must lien, inform all parties that could influence payment that you intend to lien. If a homeowner hears from you that the general contractor is causing you to place a lien on his house, he or she will have a few strong words with the general contractor that will get you paid in a hurry.

TASK: Create a Construction Lien Package

Software/Information System

A Software/Information System is the combination of basic computer applications required to run any business and is the heart of a service business. It coordinates and connects contacts, appointments, documents, processes, and billing. An uncomplicated business can use an office suite like Microsoft Office with word processor, spreadsheet, data base, and presentation functions; but a Portal System may be necessary for your more specialized operations if you are a lawyer, manufacturer, or electrical engineer. Many portal systems include all the functions of an office suite, including an accounting system, but better handle the integration of information for your specialty, like manufacturing, service, or retail. If you are using an office suite, you may need to add Quickbooks for your accounting and inventory. If you need to track many customers for individual sales contacts, you may need a customer relationship management system (CRM.) There are many systems you can buy and download to your computer.

If you are changing software systems, be sure to allow enough time for the transition. The biggest mistake entrepreneurs make is not training employees on the new software before implementation. Give them all the time they need to get comfortable, pactice, and ask questions. Having a demo model or a dummy file set up on the application gives your team members enough experience to weather the frustrations they will encounter in learning a new system. Many managers lose their best employees because they mismanaged these critical transitions.

If you have all your applications and information reside on a server, you can grant access to employees and increase your efficiency but give yourself and your employees enough time to choose the *right* software. Choosing the right software will be effective, choosing the wrong software will be a nightmare.

You also need to address prerequisites that connect to the new system for a successful implantation such as: filing systems, naming of computer files and inventory items, space, and other required equipment. In a complete process you should:

- Explore demo software
- Vet basic functions with employees
- Train employees
- Practice with dummy files
- Complete prerequisite activities

TASK: Implement the right Software

Accounting

Accounting

You need useful information about your business to make better decisions and that useful information comes from your cash flow projection and your accounting system but acquiring accounting skill seems to be the most daunting activity many entrepreneurs encounter because accounting has an arcane terminology and a logic unrelated to almost all other disciplines.

This is the hard part — the part no one likes but one that is essential for running a profitable business. Saying you don't want to learn accounting is like the pilot of your commercial jetliner saying he doesn't want to learn how to put the wheels down for landing. He might get the plane up safely, but he is certainly going to endanger everyone aboard when he tries to land.

Accounting is also a long-term project for most entrepreneurs, so don't expect to take a weekend seminar and have this part finished. Six months would be a reasonable amount of time, with help. Invest time into learning accounting while you are working on other areas of your business.

How you obtain the skill is up to you. I have provided a graphical explanation of accounting in **Appendix C** that should get you started but you will need a professional who can answer your questions.

Some entrepreneurs take an accounting course at their community college; some hire a business consultant as their guide and instructor. My preferred technique is to give my clients a one-hour workshop based on Appendix C then help them input transactions in their accounting system using the logic they absorbed from the workshop. Their skill grows with each transaction until *they* are explaining accounting principles with perfect logic. This process helps them understand financial analysis until they can perform this task on their own with confidence. How long this transformation takes is hard to estimate: one client became an expert within a few weeks; another took two years with weekly appointments and instruction. Both had the same skill in the end, and both ran successful businesses.

At some point your new skill leads to feelings of accomplishment and confidence in your decision making.

TASK: Read **Appendix C**: Accounting Explained

Financial Analysis

Along with basic accounting you need to learn how to create and read financial statements (Income Statement, Statement of Cash Flows, and Balance Sheet). Don't expect your bookkeeper or accountant to analyze your financial data, most don't. Sometimes they don't even get the basic documents in the correct order. There is a wide range of skills in the accounting field, and you need to ask what their background is, how much education they have, and whether they have passed any certification exams. Even a good education in accounting doesn't mean they know how to manage a business and the entrepreneur who is expecting management advice from a bookkeeper or accountant is gambling with his/her own assets.

But please don't be discouraged. You can get help with this and any other business concept and get it for free. The best kept secret in the Federal Government is The Small Business Development Centers (SBDCs). They are a network of business counselors that will give you FREE one-on-one counseling. You may have heard of SCORE counselors who are volunteers that give free counseling through the Small Business Administration (SBA) but it is rarely mentioned that an organization of highly professional paid counselors is also funded by the SBA in every State — the SBDCs. The Small Business Administration funds SBDC programs to hire counselors at selected colleges in each of the States, Puerto Rico, and the Virgin Islands for the sole purpose of helping you, the entrepreneur. I have been one of them. Go to www.asbdc.org for a list of all the SBDCs in the country. Go to your State SBDC website and find the closest SBDC to you. It is probably located within easy driving distance. If you live in a medium-sized city or larger, it is probably located in your town at one of the local colleges.

This is a free service, so the hours any counselor can spend with you are limited. You may need a business consultant to continue with in-depth business counseling. Consultants also have various skill levels, so gauge their knowledge against the concepts in this book and get a recommendation.

Your local Economic Development Council (EDC) also provides advising, referrals, business development classes, funding, and much more. Call them and see what they offer. Consider this example for trades:

Trades

A trade business that accomplished its work for residential customers always seemed to have minimal profits. The entrepreneur had more demand than he could service with his three trucks but did not understand accounting or financial analysis. A quick review of his accounting uncovered pilfering of supplies and use of the company trucks for personal errands and unauthorized work; value that went directly into the hands of his employees.

Results:

Profits:	$50,000 in new Profit in the first year
Customers:	Customers were unaware of the changes

I have provided a short explanation of financial analysis in

Appendix D to get you started.

TASK: Read **Appendix D**: Financial Analysis

TASK: Hire a consultant or take an accounting class to begin the long-term process of learning Accounting and Financial Analysis. Your local college, EDC, or SBDC may offer Workshops or Classes

PRINCIPLE:
An understanding of finance is the core of your success.
WHY:
Your accounting system looks backward in time, your cashflows forward. Without these financial maps you will not understand the results of your decisions. Do not skip the hard work of becoming competent.

Planning Notebook

It may seem that I am addressing this book to small business and to elementary skill development, but I have counseled clients with more that 30 million in sales and they all have skill deficits, missing systems, inefficiencies, and ineffective approaches to problem solving. I started with the practical points of attack that I have found relevant to *all* businesses, no matter the size.

So now that you have created some useful systems and information for decision-making and experienced the impact of short-term wins, it's time to organize your current and future work and prepare for the long-term effort.

The Planning Notebook

If you do not organize a Planning Notebook with supporting computer files, your good work will become scattered and useless. You will waste valuable time trying to find important spreadsheets, documents and systems that have disappeared into the labyrinth of files on your computer or the disorganized clutter on your desk. You will lose focus and momentum and repeat already completed work. Many of my clients have made this mistake and still feel regret.

Get a three-ring binder with 8 dividers and label them according to the outline below.

- The *SUCCEED!*™ Outline
- Leadership
- Marketing
- Finance
- Operations
- Human Resources
- Legal Issues
- Appendix

This list looks like Business Planning, but it is not. If you were planning a new business, you would complete all the sections of the business planning model in the order given in Figure 3, **Chapter 1**. For an existing business, the *SUCCEED!*™ Outline leads you through the problem solving sequence with maximum effectiveness — the other sections are where you place your finished work. You *do* end up with a business plan, but you have solved problems in the right order.

Create a Word file (Microsoft Word or another word processor) called Development Plan and get this outline on your computer. If you don't already know how to operate a word processing program now is the time to learn. Creating your planning document on computer will save you much time and effort and will encourage you to revise without cumbersome rewrites on a typewriter. If you don't have a computer, find one that you can use on a regular basis. A personal computer is one of the most important tools an entrepreneur can learn how to use, and much of your success will rely on your ability to operate word processing and spreadsheet software. Without these skills, you will be at a great disadvantage.

It is possible to improve your profits without a computer if you have a very simple business, but the more complex your business becomes the more you will need one. If you want to succeed, now is the time to get comfortable with a computer.

Again, it may sound like I am speaking only to small business managers, but I often find, even with clients who have millions in sales, that these basic skills and systems are absent.

Remember this planning notebook is a way to organize all the information about your business but it is not the order in which you will implement these activities. In a business development, an expansion, or a crisis you should follow the sequence outlined in this book. Review **Appendix A** for the full sequence.

Place finished work in your notebook according to the following:

- Leadership: Effectiveness issues, wellness issues that are hindering your motivation, and business skill training needs for yourself
- Marketing: Target market, customer profile, product list and features, pricing, market strategy, critical motivators, market literature (brochure, business card, stationary), re-marketing plan, location analysis, competition, and market strategy
- Finance: Cash flow projections, income statements, balance sheets, cost estimates, accounting system details, bid worksheet, bank accounts, credit policies, and dealer bulletins
- Operations: Major operational systems/procedures, equipment lists, and space plan
- Human resources: Organization chart, job descriptions, job tasks and processes, redesign process, and training requirements
- Legal Issues: Legal form of business, corporate documents, permitting, zoning, and regulatory issues
- Appendix: Internal control forms and processes, sales manual, personnel policy manual, sources of supply, and anything else that is better organized at the end of your planning notebook

Get your planning notebook organized now and your problem solving will flow more smoothly.

Naming and Organizing Computer Files

Computer files become disorganized simply from the constant creation of new information. Without a system of naming files, they become lost. You already have a document titled Development Plan. In your Documents file create a file folder called Business and place your Development Plan and spreadsheets there. If your plan becomes too large for a single document, create file folders that match the sections of your planning document and place the appropriate files within them.

Time Management

Every entrepreneur is extremely busy. New activities focused on your business development must be planned; otherwise, they will always take second place to your daily tasks. It is helpful to work on development first thing every day. Take thirty to forty minutes in the morning before the phone starts ringing and before you open your doors. Make it your religion. Get this activity into your schedule and keep it there. At certain times your business will get the better of you and you will miss a day or even a week, so use your planning notebook to stay on track. Mark your place in the *SUCCEED!*™ Outline where you left off and make it easy to resume your work.

Write down ideas, new information, and edits in your planning notebook in the right section of the *SUCCEED!*™ Outline so that it is placed in an effective sequence. You may have a great idea, but make sure you solve the prerequisites first. Many of your best ideas will be lost if you rely on memory alone. Few entrepreneurs can keep the organization of their business completely in their head. If you don't have your notebook handy, write your idea on a sticky note so you can paste it easily into your notebook later. It is helpful once a week to type all your notes into your Development Plan and print out a clean copy of your updated pages. If you get behind on this activity, you will become distracted by the clutter. The notes will pile up, you'll forget where you are in the process, and your new level of organization will be lost.

Staff Meetings

Staff Meetings will become essential when you move into Maximize Cash Flow and Productivity in **Chapter 3** but for now use staff meetings to communicate the *SUCCEED!*™ process to your employees and track your progress. See the Staff Meeting Agenda at the end of **Appendix A**.

TASK: Create your Development Plan in Word
TASK: Create Planning Notebook
TASK: Rename and reorganize computer files

Cash Management

As your profits improve you will need to manage the disbursement of cash. Many businesses find themselves behind on payables and taxes but require investment capital for equipment, employee raises, and lease payoffs. You may also not be able to obtain a loan or line of Credit (LOC) to ease your cash requirements, so management of cash is essential. Try to minimize payments on old debt and build a cash reserve to increase your safety. This will reduce the effect of unexpected economic shocks such as: reduced sales, unforeseen expenses, and personal needs. You must be your own bank until you can prove to a commercial bank that you are a good risk for their depositor's money.

Profit

To maximize your profit, you must understand the Cost/Profit/Volume relationship. We have already covered Pricing as an isolated component of profit and Project Costing Systems as an integrated way to incorporate this concept into Bids, but you now need to explore the underlying structure.

Cost/Profit/Volume

The following formula defines the Cost/Profit/Volume relationship:

Profit = Sales – Costs

More accurately the formula should be:

Profit = (Price X Units) – (Cost X Units) – Fixed Costs

You should read the formula: Profit = Price per unit X Units, minus Cost per unit X Units, minus Fixed Costs. Cost per unite X Units is Your Cost of Goods Sold (COGS). Fixed Costs is Overhead and appears as Expenses on a Profit and Loss Statement. There are three big opportunities for maximizing Profit: Pricing, Costs (efficiency) and Volume (number of units) as indicated in the diagram below:

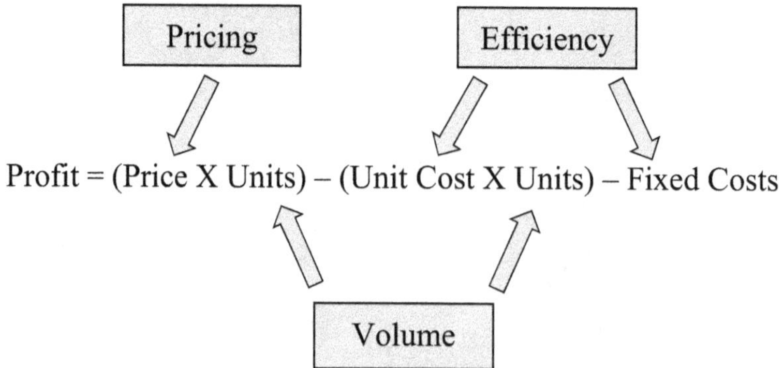

You drive each opportunity to its maximum according to Figure 12 below and in the right order.

Opportunity	Driven By
Pricing	Knowing and Charging the Price Ceiling Higher Profit Margin Products/Services Profit Centers (best combination) **(Chapter 2)**
Efficiency	Systems Redesign in Group Problem Solving **(Chapters 3)**
Volume	Basic Marketing, Strategic Planning Strategic Market Focus Profit Centers (expansion) **(Chapter 4)**

Figure 12: Maximizing Profit

You can see each opportunity is covered in-depth in a logical sequence by chapter and you will not have the full effect of all your work until after **Chapter 4**, but you can obtain the quickest results possible by staying in the *SUCCEED!* Process and completing all the activities in the order outlined.

Higher Profit Margin Products/Services

Each business has a unique set of products and services but each offering in this set does not have the same Profit Margin (PM). One service may have a Profit Margin of 40% and another of 2%, or worse a negative -10%. Entrepreneurs create a mix of Profit Margins by adding products or services without any analysis. Now is the time to analyze your products and services and choose the most profitable mix.

What you want to know:

- Products: Profit per square foot
- Services: Profit per Direct Labor Hour

The results should show you which products/services return the most profit for your effort. For simplicity we will use Gross Profit in our calculations, that is, profit before Overhead is allocated. First, some definitions:

- Cost of Goods Sold (COGS): What it costs you to buy the products that went out the door with your customer. This can be COGS for your entire business or just one product/service
- Gross Profit (GP): Sales – COGS. This can be GP for your entire business or just one product/service
- Square Feet: Sq Ft
- Direct Labor Hour (DLH): Labor hours that you can assign to a specific job

These numbers should be available in your accounting system or point of sale system (POS). If not, you need to improve your knowledge of accounting and set up your accounting system to track this data. Many of my clients create detailed spreadsheets to analyze COGS and this is where some of the hard work begins. You may still be working on developing your accounting skills so take your time and do not skip ahead.

Products

For each product calculate the following:

- GP = Sales – COGS
- GP per Square Foot = GP/Sq Ft

Example: Product A

Data: Product A	
Sales A =	100
COGS A =	50
Sq Ft A =	2
Calculation	
GP A = 100 – 50 =	50
GP per Sq Ft A = 50/2 =	**$25.00**

Example: Product B

Data: Product B	
Sales B =	200
COGS B =	75
Sq Ft B =	4
Calculation	
GP B = 200 – 75 =	125
GP per Sq Ft B = 125/4 =	**$31.25**

Product A has a GP per Sq Ft of $25.00; Product B has a GP per Sq Ft of $31.25. If you had to make a choice about placing a product on your last square foot of shelf space, you would choose Product B because you make more profit per square foot. Make a spreadsheet of all your products and automate the calculations. With this information you should be able to select a mix of products that provides the variety your customers want while maximizing your profit per square foot.

I call this the merchandising experiment: Experimenting with new products to find the most profitable mix as the market and your customer's interests change. It can sometimes be daunting but without making calculations it is impossible.

Consider this example for a product-based business:

Book Store

An independent bookstore had 10,000 volumes on their shelves but only a cash register to record sales. They had no idea which books sold better than others and could not make choices about which books to stock except by intuition. They installed a Point-of-Sale system that tracked each volume by bar code.

Results:

Before: No information available to choose the product mix
After: Perfect information about profits per square foot by author and category of book
Profits: Increased

Services

For each service calculate the following:

- GP = Sales – COGS
- GP per Direct Labor Hour = GP/DLHs

The calculation is the same as for products except that some Services like consulting may have no COGS except wages; others like landscape maintenance have costs for gasoline, wages, material, equipment, etc.

Consider this example for a service-based business:

Landscape Maintenance

A landscape maintenance entrepreneur had many faithful customers and excess demand. We analyzed the profit per direct labor hour for each customer and found that it varied from $9/hour to $52/hour. Only three of his customers were in the $9/hour range, the rest were all near the highest profit range. He raised the prices on the bottom three customers. Two of them said they knew they were getting an incredible deal and did not complain. The third customer left but was replaced by a new customer at the higher rate.

Results:

Profits:	$10,000 in new Profit in the first year
Customers:	One customer lost; one customer gained

TASK: Complete Profit Margin calculations for each Product/Service

Profit Centers

Allocation of Overhead to Profit Centers

Just as you allocate overhead to each job in your project costing system you need to allocate it to your various profit centers to understand how much they contribute to total profits. Refer to Figure 13 as I explain the allocation process. I've made the numbers simple for this example.

The input data must come from either your accounting system or an accurate cashflow projection. We must use a proxy for allocating overhead and use the percentage of direct labor hours as we did in the project costing system.

	Total P&L	Center 1	Center 2	Center 3
% Hours		50%	40%	10%
Revenue	200	140	50	10
COGS:	60	42	15	3
Overhead Alloc.	120	60	48	12
Profit	20	38	(13)*	(5)

*Negative numbers in parentheses

Figure 13: Overhead Allocation to Profit Centers

The results show that Profit Center 1 is profitable but Profit Centers 2 and 3 are not, and you may be tempted to drop 2 & 3 right away, but the analysis is not finished. We must next create a cashflow without Profit Center 2 and reimagine the cost structure of the business.

Figure 14 shows the remaining profit centers with reduced and reallocated overhead. Some of the overhead for Profit Center 2 will disappear because it no longer requires labor, but much remains that did not change.

	New P&L	Center 1	Center 2	Center 3
% Hours		84%		16%
Revenue	150	140	0	10
COGS 30%	45	39	0	3
Overhead Alloc.	65	55	0	10
Profit	40	46	0	(3)

Figure 14: Overhead Allocation Without Profit Center 2

Profit Center 1 is more profitable. Profit Center 3 is still unprofitable, but it was the project-based part of this business and could be improved with a project costing system. It also contributed to covering overhead by using space that Profit Center 1 did not need. Don't forget that even if Profit Center 3 was only at breakeven it would still contribute to covering overhead costs.

Opportunities for Sales in Profit Centers

If you are running a severe deficit, you may need to expand sales volume before your systems work (Systems Redesign, **Chapter 3**.) With a deficit, you have excess capacity in square footage, labor hours, and systems that can be used to create profits, but if you have enough cash flow, be careful not to employ new profit centers before you complete your Systems Redesign activities. You will undoubtedly burden inefficient systems and destabilize your business.

Refer to Figure 15 as I explain Profit Centers. I will use a Product example but it is the same for Services.

	Old Product	New Product
Old Market	Old Product Old Market	New Product Old Market
New Market	Old Product New Market	New Product New Market

Figure 15: Profit Centers

You have only two choices for Products: Old or New; and two choices for Markets: Old or New. Combinations of Products and Markets give only four choices for Profit Centers:

- Your old products competing in the old market
- Your old products competing in a new market
- Your new products competing in the old market
- Your new products competing in a new market

There is an appropriate time to use each as a strategy for greater profit. These strategies apply well to entrepreneurs who *create* products and services and don't simply buy at wholesale to sell at retail, but it works for everyone.

If you have not been consistent in marketing to your current customers and you have excess capacity, remarket your old product/service to the old market first and get your existing customers back. If you are at capacity do not create any new marketing efforts.

If you are in a recession, market your old products and services to a new market first. All your competitors are marketing to the reduced number of customers in the old market and you cannot gain market share there. You already have the products so you might as well get the full potential from them before creating something new.

If you have tough competition and limited market venues, you need to innovate and sell new products in the old market.

If you have completed your *SUCCEED!*™ Development Plan and are ready to expand, use the best combination of all four Profit Centers but always maximize your old product sales first before creating something new.

An example will help. I had a client who sold specialized seafood to high end restaurants in large cities all over the United States. They had great systems and efficiency but had not done a good job of marketing and didn't really understand their customer base. The following is how they staged the use of Profit Centers. They:

1) Created a market survey and met every existing customer to increase sales of the old product in the old market
2) Sourced new customers for the old product in the old market
3) Found a new market for the old product in Japan and the United Kingdom
4) Created a new seafood product for both the old and new markets

Their sales increased dramatically, and their systems were ready to support the volume. Remember not to create any new marketing efforts until you have completed **Chapters 3** and **4** unless you are running a deficit and have excess capacity.

TASK: If you have excess capacity, remarket Old Product/Service to Old Market

TASK: If you are in a Recession, market Old Product/Service to New Market

Product Strategies

Remember that in **Chapter 2** you are beginning the process of building resources and capabilities; but I am proposing some short-term strategies. Pricing, Profit Centers, and Product Strategies, at this point, are short-term measures designed to stabilize your business and build cash flow. A serious reorganization of your marketing is covered in **Chapter 4**. I will refer to Phillip Kotler, *Principles of Marketing*, (Upper Saddle River: Prentice Hall, 2010) as we move into marketing strategies.

The Merchandising Experiment

As mentioned earlier, retailers must experiment with new products monthly. Without this experiment, your product offering becomes out of date. Styles, prices, and customer interests change over time and you must keep up with market trends. The goal is to find a core set of products that sell well all the time and then experiment with new products to see if they can be a part of that core.

You need to have enough cash to purchase new products for your experiment but don't waste it. If the products do not move off your shelves in 90 days reduce the price in a sale and get rid of them, even if you must reduce the price to your original cost. The goal is to get your money back and find a new profitable product for the next experiment.

Some of your experimenting will uncover fads: A one-time product that sells quickly and is never purchased again. Investing in fads is risky because you may get stuck with inventory you don't want when the public's interest dies out.

Bundling

Bundling means reducing the price of individual products if they are purchased together. Combining complimentary products in a bundle that you know the customer needs or wants will stimulate a larger purchase that might not have been made at that moment. Consider buying your child soccer gear. You need cleats, shin guards, socks, and maybe clothes and a ball. You have other interests and needs competing in your mind for the money in your pocket. You may choose to buy the minimum to get your boy or girl started (cleats, socks, and chin guards) but bundling will tempt you to buy all the products because you will get the best price if you don't wait. This works especially well if the bundle is a one-time offer at the beginning of the soccer season.

This is effective for most businesses. For example, at a deli counter when you can buy the sandwich with chips and a drink for less than the total if bought separately. The caution is that you must have inventory on hand to complete the bundle. This is an investment risk, and you may not have the cash on hand to stock your shelves at this point in your development.

Product Lines

Creating product lines means extending the reach of any product in two ways:

- Different Features
- Different Prices

Usually, these two issues go together. As the number of features increase, so does the price. Retailers can experiment with products to understand which features in a line suit their customers. Manufacturers can create new profits by creating a line from existing products. This requires market research and should not be attempted until **Chapter 4**.

Up Selling

Up selling means making additional sales to the same customer at the time of purchase. This could mean asking them if they need knee pads when they purchase a soccer ball, replacing a plumbing valve that looks rusty after you've cleared a drain, or making a follow-up appointment for additional service. Do not sell your customer products or services they do not need, rather, fulfill a need they might not be aware of. "Hard Selling," forcing a sale through manipulation, will always lose customers.

Up-selling means training your employees to assist your

customers. For example, a retail client with a mall location ran a deficit each month. When I observed her clerks, I found them reading behind the counter as customers browsed the store, avoiding customer interactions, and eating on the job. We trained her clerks in customer assistance, upselling, and complementary product combinations. Her sales increased by 30%.

TASK: Experiment with Product Strategies
TASK: Train employees how to up-sell

Easy Cost Reductions

When a business is in trouble, entrepreneurs intuitively begin to reduce costs, but it requires a thorough examination of all costs to create a substantial long-term benefit. Major cost reductions come from efficiency in systems covered in **Chapter 3**, but some easy to implement solutions are available. The following is a short list of cost reductions you may not have considered.

Rent

Ask for a rent reduction from your landlord. What do you have to lose? One of my clients reduced their rent from $6,000 per month to $4,000 simply by asking. This was in a recession with the occupancy rates dropping and the landlord had the choice of reducing the rent or having my client move out. Some heated words were exchanged but the landlord did reduce the rent.

If you are in a service business like mental health counseling, graphic arts, or hair styling where customers come to your office for service, you are probably using your space only one third of the available time. Search for another person like yourself to share the space in your off hours. Make sure you get along with the person you will be subletting to and be the lease holder, so you have control of the space. If you sign a joint lease, you cannot force the other renter to leave when you have a disagreement about their unpleasant habits.

Discounts

Eliminate contractor discounts, customer discounts, and giveaways like buy 10 get one free. You are losing more than you know. Discounts may be a part of your marketing strategy, but have you really analyzed the cost and whether it is having the intended effect?

Consider this example of eliminating a discount:

Retail

A retailer with a product that cost her $50.00 each and sold for $100.00 each, sold 700 of them each year but gave away one for every 10 sold. By eliminating the give-away, she saved $3500 in additional costs: 700/10 = 70 giveaways, 70 X $50.00 = $3500 saved

Results:

Cost Savings:	$3,500 per year
Profits:	$3,500 in new Profit in the first year
Customers:	Customers were unaware of the changes

This may not sound like much, but if you are offering this on many products it could add up quickly. And remember if you are running a marginally profitable business your increased profits and your higher standard of living will be found in all these seemingly small savings. They add up. $3500 is a weeklong get-away for you and your partner, and if you are like most entrepreneurs, you haven't had a vacation in the last ten years — and you need one.

You may not give discounts, but you may be able to obtain discounts from *your* suppliers by paying them quickly or by purchasing in volume. It could be an additional 2-4%. You need cash to accomplish this, and a Line of Credit (LOC) is the ideal choice if you do not have your own reserve. The charge for the LOC will be smaller than the savings from the discount. If you cannot pay your LOC off at the end of the month or the end of your sales season, do not use this method. You will just increase your debt and decrease your cash flow.

For businesses that buy supplies from industry wholesalers like plumbing and electrical supplies, go to some of the big discount retailers and make a price comparison. Most of the time, the retail price of basic supplies at these discount outlets will be one half the wholesale price at the wholesale supplier.

Non-value-added

Eliminate non-value-added activities, that is, activities that your customers don't care about but cost you money. One convenience store client gave away baseball caps and Frisbees with a beer purchase. When asked what they did with them, the customers said they gave the Frisbees to their dogs and threw away the caps.

Phones/Data Charges

For the young, a Smart Phone is an entertainment center but for a business owner it needs to be a productive asset. Ask yourself what productive work you can accomplish on a cell phone. What are the useful features? And don't pay for anything you can't use.

Get rid of data charges and downgrade to something less than a Smart Phone unless you always need internet access. Most entrepreneurs don't unless they travel. For a sole proprietor this $30 per month data charge would amount to $360 per year; for a business with 30 employees, it would be $10,800.

Likewise, get rid of land lines unless they are a critical piece of business equipment. Most cell phone companies have unlimited calling for the same price and land lines are redundant. If you must have a land line use VOIP (Voice-over Internet Protocol) that connects to the internet through your computer. It is one tenth the cost of regular phone companies.

Switch to radio communications if you are in a trade and need to communicate with your office for service call updates. There are communications companies all over the country with radio communication towers for local service. Many of them also run specials for the first-year service that could cut your communications costs in half.

There is also an incredible amount of competition for regular long-distance service since the deregulation of telephone companies, but it is very hard to compare long distance carriers because they rarely give you enough information. There are, however, companies that provide the service of analyzing your phone records and recommending a carrier.

Employees

Take an initial look at the number of employees you have. This will be covered more thoroughly in **Chapter 3** under Efficiency in Existing Systems, but you can use a simple method for discovering inefficiencies today. Take an unannounced tour of all the work areas of your business at three different times in the week. Pick random times on different days and simply count the number of employees who are not busy with the productive, core activities of the business. If you find people standing around, taking uncalled for breaks, not attending to their machinery, or three people repairing something that one could handle on their own, you probably have too many workers. Do not be rash and fire people because you first need to understand the systems they operate within and know that you have planned to retain critical skills before you change personnel.

I had one client who used this quick method and found they needed only three of the five employees on staff. After redesigning the job tasks the savings from reducing the staff amounted to $2,400 per month, $28,000 per year! This does not mean you should skimp on the number of employees it takes to effectively run your business. For instance, you might need five employees during the lunch rush at a sandwich shop, but you can send four of them home as soon as the rush is over.

Consider also that there are many local programs at Community Colleges and State level agencies that will sponsor interns to work in your business. The College or agency typically pays half of the intern's wages in exchange for on-the-job experience. You get an employee for half the cost while evaluating them for future employment. When the internship is over you have the opportunity, but not the obligation, to hire your intern. Interns are available to fill many functional areas: office management, accounting, marketing, industrial design, electronics, and much more. Check with your local colleges and state agencies.

Insurance

You may have large hidden costs if you haven't reviewed your insurance policies recently: Property, auto, health, and liability.

One client reduced their property insurance from $3,387 to $1,010 per year by changing insurance companies. They also cut their auto insurance in half.

You may be able to reduce health insurance costs for you and your existing employees by applying to a State supported health insurance plan. In the State of Washington where I live the Basic Health Plan will provide insurance at subsidized rates based on your income level. Check with your State's Department of Social and Health Services. Many states have State supported health plans that will subsidize health insurance for you and your employees if you can prove a need. If you are in a crisis or in the early stages of your Development Plan your financial situation may qualify you. A small business with three of four employees could save $500 or more each month by applying for this assistance.

Large businesses have an even greater opportunity to reduce costs because they can negotiate with insurance companies but the reason for overpaying is always the same: lack of a regular review of costs.

Advertising

Any advertisement, including Yellow Pages, that does not pay for itself should be reduced, canceled, or moved. By paying for itself I mean that it brings in as much income as it costs. I will talk about this in much more detail in **Chapter 4** but you may be coming up to renewal time for your current advertisements and need to make a decision. First call a business similar to yours in several cities other than your own. Tell them who you are and where your business is located and that you are not in competition with them. Then ask them in what section of the Yellow Pages they place their advertisement and how many customers call them because they see the advertisement. If all the businesses you call place the advertisement in the same section that yours is in and they do not pay for themselves either, then cancel the ad and reduce it to a one-line listing or try a different section. If they place the advertisement in a different section that gets results, change your advertisement to that section. One client in construction who worked mostly on remodels from insurance claims for fire and water damage, received no calls when the add was placed under "Restoration" but received ten calls per month and $50,000 per year in additional income when it was placed under "Carpet Cleaning". People who need renovation work, after a flood or fire, want their carpets cleaned first! Place the advertisement in the right section. Again, this is a short-term solution. A more thorough look at your marketing strategy and the message you create in your Yellow Pages advertisement will be covered later.

The internet is so powerful you may not need Yellow Pages at all. Many of my clients find consulting services through Google search. A one-inch advertisement in the Yellow Pages will cost you several hundred dollars per month; hosting a website will cost you $6.00 per month through Laughing Squid.

One enterprising client with a mail-order business calculated the cost of postage, paper, and ink for each page of his print catalogue. If the product on that page didn't cover the cost of the page, he dropped the product. He was mailing 30,000 catalogues and each page represented a substantial investment.

Vehicles

Downsizing your vehicles can save both on running expenses and monthly payments. There is no point in maintaining two full size pickup trucks if you really need a mini-pickup and a van. See if you can trade them in for what you really need and get these costs in line. If you have vehicles, you are not using at all, get rid of them. Their value is depreciating by letting them sit, and licensing is an unnecessary expense.

Safety

Safety is another concern. It may not be costing you anything right now, but an accident that creates a Workman's Compensation claim could be very expensive. Your rate payments to your state agency will increase for all existing employees and could cause inspections and fines. Make at least the most obvious improvements to your workspace, work rules, and work processes currently. Invite your employees into a safety dialogue in your Staff Meeting. They know which parts of their work are unsafe. Later in **Chapter 3** I will discuss process redesign that will contribute to your efficiency and safety.

Waste

Start looking at some of your costs as revenue opportunities. Selling or reusing your waste could be one of these. One client used old motor oil from oil changes to heat his auto repair shop. Another client who shredded thousands of documents per week found a recycler who paid for and hauled the paper. LEAN principles for reducing all types of waste will be covered later. A summary is provided in **Appendix F**.

Assets

Take a quick look at all of your assets and decide if they are critical to the functioning of the business. Sell anything that is either unproductive or not in use. Hanging on to something because you think you might have a use for it some day is just another way of tying up useful capital and valuable space.

Old Inventory

Inventory is your main asset if you are a retailer or manufacturer and creates costs for materials, labor, and square footage. Anything that has been on the shelves for over 90 days sell at cost. It is just taking up space. You can recoup the cash you have tied up in that inventory and invest it in products that move more quickly. What are those products? Ask your customers or invest time in the merchandising experiment. Ask them what they want that they haven't found and stock the best-selling items. Go to your competition and find out what they carry that has a high turnover. This can easily be accomplished by sending a friend. One clever business owner subcontracted some work to his competition but insisted he inspect their books and management procedures to "assure" himself that they could perform on the contract. In one meeting he even obtained a list of their sales by category, which was highly beneficial.

If you find that you are ending up with a lot of empty shelf space that cannot be filled with saleable products, rent out the extra space. Consolidate your shelving and sublet to someone who has complimentary products and can set up their own business within your space. There are many entrepreneurs who are moving their home-based businesses out of their houses for the first time and would jump at the chance to rent a small manageable space with low overhead without having to be the lease holder.

If subletting is not possible you may need to reduce your square footage costs by relocating. But this is a long-term decision that should not be taken lightly, and be considered only after you have tried all other measures.

Past Due Taxes

It may be difficult to pay your taxes on time at this point in your business development but try to make this a priority. The interest and penalties for late payment are usually the worst of any creditor you may have. This is also true for non-sufficient funds (NSF) charges from overdrawing your bank account. A late charge from a supplier might be 1% per month but the penalty and interest on excise taxes could be from 5-20%. NSF charges could be 200% (a $10 check with a $20 NSF charge equals 200 %.)

If you owe taxes to the IRS or one of your state taxing agencies, get in touch with them immediately. Many entrepreneurs are literally afraid to contact these agencies and so put off the inevitable, hoping a little more time will get them clear of the problem. This is absolutely the wrong approach. When contacted in good faith and told that you are having a problem paying your taxes, these agencies will try to work out a payment schedule with you; but when you avoid them and don't answer their letters and phone calls, they become more aggressive, especially for employee taxes like social security and unemployment.

Make sure you complete your cash flow projections (outlined earlier) before you agree on a monthly payment. Find the right amount to pay: the one that still leaves you with a cash balance every month.

Answer any letters from these agencies immediately. If you wait, your response will be in the mail just as they are sending out their next notice and the communications will get complicated. Always include your tax number on your letter and the control number printed on the agencies letter. That way they will know which document you are responding to.

Pay all trust fund taxes such as employee social security, income tax deductions, and sales tax first. These taxes will not be forgiven in a bankruptcy. Make a note on your payment coupon and check stating which taxes and which time period you are paying for so that your payment doesn't get applied to the wrong one.

Personal Expenses

Consider that you probably need to reduce your personal expenditure also so that you can reduce your personal draws on the business. In the last recession one client reduced their annual family expenses by $16,000 by eliminating telephone land lines, refinancing their mortgage, and shopping for better home and auto insurance.

Original Purchase Price: Did You Pay Too Much?

One of the problems you may have encountered is the burden of paying off a previous owner for the purchase of your business. The size of the monthly payment may make it impossible to pay other bills in a timely way and may reduce your profits to a discouraging low level. If this is true, it could be that the purchase price was unreasonably high. This happens frequently in small business because the buyer and the seller have no knowledge of financially sound valuation methods and so use ad hoc methods like "triple the net income" or adding the value of assets to some dreamed up number called "blue sky". At this point in your development, you need to go back and determine if the price you paid was reasonable; and if it was not, to try and renegotiate the terms of the deal. The seller will obviously be reluctant to take less and will need to be convinced that the valuation method you are proposing makes sense.

You do have some leverage. If the monthly payment to the previous owner is killing the business, and if you do not have personal collateral tied up in the deal, you can threaten to walk away from the business and throw it back in the seller's lap. Faced with that alternative, they may come around. If they decide *not* to renegotiate the price, you will have to decide how big a problem this monthly payment is, and if your development activities will raise profits enough to compensate.

You will need professional help to accomplish a valuation, but I have provided a short explanation of business valuation methods in **Appendix G** to get you oriented.

Clutter

Clutter can be expensive, especially if it causes accidents and Labor and Industry injury claims in your state. It is a symptom of inefficiency and addressing it is a prerequisite for systems redesign in **Chapter 3**. Garbage, parts on the floor, dusty workspaces, and unsteady shelving are hazardous. Unfiled paperwork covering your desk is confusing, time-consuming, and inefficient. Many managers use Sigma 6 (S6) which stands for: Sort, Safe, Straighten, Scrub, Standardize, and Sustain. Apply these principles now and you will save yourself headaches later.

TASK: Reduce all possible Costs and declutter your workspace with Sigma 6 (delegate some of this work to employees)

PRINCIPLE:
Always solve problems in this order: pricing, efficiency, and volume.
WHY:
It is the most efficient sequence for building profits. Any other sequence wastes time and money.

Risk

Many entrepreneurs live with continuing risks that can be easily eliminated and thereby avoid unexpected shocks to their cash flow. Many clients have claimed they did not have the time to address these issues until they created an economic disaster.

Timeliness in Invoicing

Business owners compound their collections problem by waiting to invoice completed work. There are only two reasons you are waiting to invoice:

- Too many problems are distracting you
- The invoicing process is inefficient

Nevertheless, this is a priority for improving cash flow and you need to attend to it now. Working more service hours will not help you with your cash flow if you never invoice and never collect.

Set aside some time at the beginning of the day (time management) so you can complete the previous day's invoices. The beginning of the day is better because you will be fresh and less likely to avoid the task. Make it your practice. Better yet is to set up your accounting system to create invoices as you speak to your customers. A daily routine will get invoicing back in order.

TASK: Invoice Daily in your Accounting System

Contracts

The object of a contract is to protect yourself, as best you can, from issues that will hurt your cash flow. Remember every way you have been harmed in the past, and place that issue clearly in your next contract. You may need legal help with phrasing and to make sure you have covered all the relevant clauses. A few suggestions for contract items are as follows:

- Scope of Work
- Payment Schedule: down payment, milestones, retainer
- Copyright: Designs, systems, specifications, materials
- Travel and Lodging: customer pays in advance
- Disputes: use binding arbitration
- Liens for collections

Remember that a contract is a negotiation. Never sign any contract someone else gives you without a thorough review. Ask for clauses that will harm your business to be removed or modified, such as monetary penalties you will have to pay if your project is not completed on time.

If you are working on lengthy projects, you must have a contract that protects you from the poor behavior of your customers and, at a minimum, outlines how much cash is given to you up front to begin the work and when additional payments will be made as more work is completed (milestone payments). In construction or engineering this means getting enough at the beginning of the project to cover materials and design work and insisting on regular payments throughout the project, hopefully once per month. In service work where you may be writing reports or performing a service that has no materials involved, this means getting the entire fee in advance as a retainer. Never give a customer a final report without full payment. In retail, all special orders must be paid for in advance. In the special situation where you must work for a customer before you can estimate what the charge will be, such as auto mechanics, don't give them back their car, VCR, or anything else you have worked on without payment. Service businesses should copyright their designs so the customer cannot take it and have it fulfilled by another service provider.

Customers who find it difficult to pay you up front for a service or product are probably not going to pay you at all, so do not waste your valuable time on them. You may think you will drive customers away, but my experience is that entrepreneurs waste many hours providing services that are never paid for and then waste more time trying to collect the debt. It is more realistic to know who the paying customers are by requiring them to pay in advance and spend the time you have saved marketing to more of these valuable people. Be willing to say no to those who will not pay you.

Many basic legal documents can be purchased from Nolo Press (www.nolo.com) or other internet providers. I have included a simple contract in **Appendix E**: Sample Service Contract.

TASK: Create a Service Contract with help from your lawyer

Insurance

Insurance is an essential protection against risk but is undoubtedly costing you more than you think. Most managers address this issue in a crisis when they are under financial pressure, but you can reduce costs now, and gain some cash flow by looking into the details.

Review *all* your insurance policies. Make sure you have the insurance you need but are not paying for unnecessary benefits.

One client reduced their property insurance from $3,000 per year to $900 per year without losing any coverage. They also cut their auto insurance in half with a simple internet search.

Brick and mortar insurance agencies that have a local presence may feel safe because you know the owner/agent personally, but it is more expensive for them to own that building and you cover the costs. There are many national companies with excellent coverage and services that cost less, and they process claims perfectly well. You don't need a local representative to file a claim.

TASK: Review insurance policies and reduce costs

Legal Structure/Control

If your business is designated as a sole proprietorship in your state, your personal assets are at risk for lawsuits and bankruptcy. You may not be running much risk for this now, but circumstances change, and you may wish later that you took the simple step of becoming an S-Corp (Small Corporation) or an LLC (Limited Liability Company.)

Apply through your state agency that grants legal status to corporations. Specific rules for reporting activity in your business can differ state by state, but in general the LLC has less annual reporting. This separates your personal assets from your business assets.

Apply to the IRS to be taxed as an S-Corp, which means you do not pay an additional corporate tax. You fill out a corporate tax form (1120S) but the Net Income on the 1120S is reported on your personal tax form (1040) as business income. You get the limited liability of a corporation while avoiding the corporate tax.

You need a Partnership Agreement for a partnership, or By-Laws for a corporation that spell out how you will deal with control issues like voting rights, quorums (the minimum number of Board members present to carry a motion), intellectual property rights, and sales of stock. A Buy/Sell clause is essential so that you don't get trapped in your business entity with no way out. If you issue stock, you need a Subscription Agreement that spells out the rights, responsibilities, and limitations for stockholders.

One client's Buy/Sell agreement, between two partners, each with 50% ownership, stated that if Partner A offered to buy out Partner B and B said no, then *B* had to buy out A. It may seem extreme, but it worked for them when it came time to part ways both partners were satisfied with the outcome. They also defined the method for valuing the business so there were no arguments at the time of sale and the price made financial sense.

TASK: Change your legal structure to avoid risk

Ownership

I have been speaking mainly to business owners, but *you* may be a manager and employee of the business wanting to buy out the current owner. It is often the case that an aging owner brings in a younger manager to continue the business while the owner steps back to retire or take time off. This manager could be a relative, a son or daughter, or someone with the technical skill to move the business forward.

This at first seems like an opportunity but you quickly realize the continued health of the business depends on you, and you are spending valuable career years working for less pay than if you owned the business. You may also be a better manager than the original owner creating expanding profits, and more profit makes the business more valuable with every passing year.

You then face the choice of buying the current business that you, by your own efforts, have made more expensive to purchase, or the task of starting and financing your own business. At some point there is no reason to invest your management skill in a business you will not own.

Valuation methods are covered in **Appendix G**, and I will not address them here, but some cautions are in order. The real value of a profitable business is its future profits. The owner will speak of "blue sky" and the value of their name, but the *only* value is the right to own those profits. Getting the buyer and seller to understand the logic of valuations can be difficult with the seller having an inflated sense of value for all the years they put in and the buyer needing a reasonable rate of return on their investment.

There will be many objections from the seller as they realize the business is worth less than they believed. There are risks on both sides, but you can always walk away if you cannot get a reasonable purchase price. A qualified valuation expert is helpful during the negotiations and in developing a reasonable price.

TASK: Secure ownership rights or start your own business

Intellectual Property Rights

If your business depends on intellectual property, you need to secure those rights against infringement. Intellectual property includes:

- Trade secrets and design specifications
- Patents and patent infringement (www.uspto.gov)
- Non-disclosure agreements…

Other Risks

Other risks in:

- Supply chain reliability
- Loss of key personnel (key person insurance)
- Computer and bank security
- Identity theft
- Going to comfort after success, that is, feeling less ambition and giving less attention to your business

---

PRINCIPLE:
Address basic business risks early.
WHY:
Lingering risks can emerge at any time to combine with current problems and undermine your success.

Setting Critical Policies

Setting a critical policy means deciding on a way of behaving that is essential for the success of your business. As you implement policies you will either add or subtract a small increment of profit because *every* decision you make affects profits. These small increments add up to the one big profit number that everyone focuses on, the annual Net Income. If you set a critical policy and do not enforce it, you do *not* have a policy! And you have given up a piece of your success. Please make these critical policies *firm* policies by enforcing them.

That does not mean you cannot change them. If you find a policy does not function because it no longer contributes to your profits, change it.

Many entrepreneurs have trouble with the *firm* part of policies because they cannot see the direct connection to profits, so think of our ancestors who hunted for their food. They set policies to get the maximum return (profit) from your efforts such as: always have *sharp* arrows, never running in *front* of the stampede, and never wasting an ounce of the precious resource. They would not dream of changing these rules because it would just make it harder to eat.

Be clear regarding policies.

From this point on, document your policies and place them in the appropriate section of your Development Plan.

Handling Procedures

Many businesses that suffer poor profits have slack cash, check, credit card, and inventory handling procedures, which invite employees to pilfer or embezzle and customers to shop lift. The best employees and customers would not consider stealing from you under any circumstances, the worst will do it at every opportunity, and the marginal ones will be tempted when it becomes too easy to ignore. You need to make it difficult to take cash and products.

Cash

Immediately stop all uses of cash from the cash register that are not sales related. These include advances to employees, borrowing for you, and paying vendors. Start writing checks for everything — it leaves a permanent record.

In addition, implement these policies:

- Employees must have their purchases checked through the register by some other employee, not themselves
- The person who operates the cash register must not be the person who balances the cash drawer at the end of the day
- Make each cashier responsible for their own till, i.e. don't have more than one person operating the same till

- Give door keys only to opening and closing managers and change the locks once a year. If you are uncertain how many keys are out, change the locks now.

Checks and Credit Cards

Credit card machines, blank credit stubs, check machines, and postage meters should be locked away every night. Business checks should always be locked up. All credit card transactions should be coded to identify the employee who serviced the transaction.

The credit cards that you use to charge expenses for the business should be under strict control and the monthly statement should be reviewed by you personally. If employees must have access to a credit card for daily purchases of gasoline, supplies, tools, and other consumables, make sure the card has a low credit limit that will automatically reject extraordinary charges.

Inventory

For inventory the policy is KEEP TRACK. The only way to know if your products are still on the shelf is to count them. This is a major responsibility for retailers but is essential for good management for two reasons.

- To know your cost of goods sold
- To see what is missing from pilfering or shoplifting.

Taking inventory once a year is not enough. Once a quarter is better, but once a month is ideal. It catches problems in a relatively short amount of time.

This means developing a system that removes the burden from taking inventory. The first step is to create a list of the inventory by department or shelf position, so it is easy to match list items with actual products. The next step is to track sales by item so you can compare what is left with what should be left. There are point-of-sale inventory systems that integrate with your cash register and accounting system that will do this for you, but it isn't that hard to do it manually or on a spreadsheet like Excel or a database like Access.

If you transfer inventory between stores attach a routing slip detailing the items signed out by the employee at the shipping site and checked in by the employee at the receiving site. The goods may be disappearing on route with the driver, and this will stop it. Seal the shipping baskets or containers with shrink wrap if possible.

Computer Files

Back-up computer files offsite at the end of every day. This can be accomplished automatically and takes very little time to establish. It could save you from months of reconstituting data when your computer crashes, your building burns down, or employees sabotage your network.

Keep in mind that you may not have all the problems I am outlining, but you may develop them if you do not increase the reliability of your methods. Please consider every issue I touch on. It is not often the case that a business has just one big problem to solve, rather, it is the compound effect of many small problems that cost time, energy, and cash.

> TASK: Create and Document Handling Procedures. Place in Operations section of your Development Plan

> TASK: Implement inventory tracking in your accounting system or setup a point-of-sale system for your retail business

Image

The visual impression you leave on customers is your first and sometimes only chance to make a sale. Clean up your location now. Get the fingerprints off the door, repaint the exterior and signage, and wax the floor. Two gallons of paint will cost you $90.00 and a weekend of work. You may not be aware of how shabby you have become just from continued exposure to dust, fingers, and feet. The new paint will also draw the attention of new *and* old customers. You may have faded into the visual background of your community simply because everyone looks at the same row of stores every day. People literally screen out old information. An inexpensive new exterior (paint, awning, and sign) puts you back on the radar.

Store window displays are also one of the best and most

economical forms of marketing available to retailers so do not waste this valuable resource. Most window displays fade into the background just like your store front. Keep displays fresh with new products, new colors, new photographs, and new approaches. Window displays are noticed only when they change. Everyone has had the experience of noticing a store in their hometown only when the old poster that has been taped on the window for years finally falls. That is not the optimum use of window space as a resource.

There are likewise inexpensive solutions for your interior that will improve your image without a major renovation. Replace light bulbs; clean lighting, fixtures, and blinds, and add new lighting to brighten up dark corners. If your space is small, you may be able to find a new carpet remnant that covers the whole floor for less than $100.

Rearrange products on the shelves to shake up the old look and give customers a sense that something is different. It also makes customers look at products they normally do not see because they are looking in the same old place for the same old product and finding something new.

For service businesses, stock your trucks neatly, repair cracked windshields, dress in new uniforms, polish your shoes, and look professional. Even wash your car before appointments.

TASK: Improve the visual appearance of your physical assets

Leadership Lesson 1

To succeed in any organization, you need to be a student of Leadership. As an entrepreneur, Leadership *is* your career and you will have to read, absorb, and practice as you proceed. I will refer to readings from the list of books in **Appendix I:** Resources, Management Reading List, to deepen your knowledge. Your reading will provide you with valuable information as you proceed through this book. It will be worth it.

There are many books on leadership theory and much debate about what leadership is and who can become an effective leader, but I will suggest only the practical reading I believe is valuable from *The Leader's Companion: Insights on Leadership Through the Ages,* J. Thomas Wren, Editor, and *Communicating for Results*, by Cheryl Hamilton. These fine books present leadership concepts in short and to the point chapters without overwhelming you with academic concepts.

Beyond the assigned reading, the best way to develop your leadership ability is by facilitating group problem solving in Systems Redesign. The opportunity is there in the Redesign moment to practice all your skills while at the same time transforming your business. In **Chapter 3** you will redesign your first system but before you begin that effort, you need your first Leadership Lesson. The issues essential for you to understand in Leadership Lesson 1 are:

- Personal Goals
- Educating the Whole Organization
- Facilitation
- Making Transitions
- Communication
- Delegation

Personal Goals

What is it you really want out of your business and your life? Do you want to be the next Microsoft? Do you want to have fun doing something you love? Do you just want to cover your bills and have more time off? If you are not clear on what you want, you will be directing your business toward the wrong goals and end up somewhere you don't want to be. This manual can help you get your business on track, but you must decide where you want to take it and be assured it will fulfill your personal needs.

So ask, will working in *this* business every day for many years satisfy you? If your answer is no, your motivation will be low, and you should think about making a transition into something else. If the answer is yes, continue with your Development Plan and create a business that will meet your financial and psychological needs. Your goals will translate into clear objectives and then tasks, so make sure you are pointing your efforts to the life and business you want.

You may feel that the question of satisfaction is irrelevant; that you are stuck in your business for better or worse because all your assets are committed to its success. But you always have a choice. You could walk away from your business, allow it to close, write-off your assets, and start something new. You could sell it at a discount and pay off your debts. You could work through the *SUCCEED!*™ development process and sell it at a profit. You can choose a satisfying life, one in which you enjoy your work and are willing to work hard for your success.

Frustration, fear, anxiety, and doubt all contribute to your feeling of being depleted but each activity you complete will help replace these feelings with a more positive outlook because you will be getting results.

Before you decide to sell your business, you should read the rest of **Chapter 2** and discover other issues that may influence your choices.

TASK: Define your personal goals. Place in the Leadership section of your Development Plan

Educating the Whole Organization

From this point forward you must begin to educate your whole organization. Your employees must read what you read, and you will need to lead them through discussions of their readings in staff training. This may sound too academic for your entrepreneurial spirit, but it is essential to create open dialogue in your business and bring the skill of your whole organization to an effective level.

I ask all my clients to imagine that their business is a ship in the open sea and to decide who they are on the ship. Many may say they are the captain, the engineer, or the helmsman but they are missing something fundamental in their thinking. They are the *designers* of the ship. You will design your ship so that it is the most efficient, capable ship in your market. You will create the environment and structure for your teams just as I am creating the structure for business development with this manual. You must train yourself and your staff through dialogue to be critical thinkers so everyone can contribute to the design of your excellent ship.

Staff trainings focused on open communication and skill development are a prerequisite for both efficiency and solid decision making and essential practice for changing the group dynamic that may be impeding success in your organization. The process will help you and your teams learn a new vocabulary, a new way of communicating, and prepare staff for group problem-solving. I will outline the reading for you and your employees in task assignments and help you stay organized by giving you discussion questions to use as you lead your training.

A caution: be wary of workshops, internet videos, books, and consultants who break this process into two-minute sound bites that make business development sound easy. They may be promoting enthusiasm as a replacement for skill.

The following list of additional readings may be helpful to you in learning more about leadership. They take only a few minutes to read.

TASK: Read *The Leader's Companion: Insights on Leadership Through the Ages*
Selection 22: What Leaders Really Do
Selection 8: What Is Leadership?
Selection 9: Historical Views of Leadership
Selection: 11: Rulers and Generals Are History's Slaves

Facilitation

Changing how people solve problems and relate to each other (the group dynamic) is your goal in facilitation. In every facilitation you need to create trust and openness and focus the group on solving fundamental problems in your business systems – without blaming any of the participants. This is called a Systems dialogue that we will cover in detail later in **Chapter 2**. In this chapter each group and everyone in the group will go through a transition as they learn new communication skills and create a more effective group dynamic. When you are facilitating a group, you must be aware of group members as they:

- Defend positions and territories
- Use assumptions instead of facts
- Employ unexamined intentions (Chapter 2)

(You will write the above on a whiteboard before each facilitation and ask everyone to point out when the group falls into these traps.)

At the same time, you must:

- Keep it cordial
- Use humor
- Teach effective listening
- Teach an understanding of intentions
- Surface and suspend assumptions
- Model openness and fairness
- Assign everyone one the role of the critical evaluator after the group has reached a productive cohesion

Although group problem solving is the most effective process for improving your business, you are always the final judge in any decision and will become more confident with each meeting.

Before you lead your first discussion, you need to alter the habits of your team members. I accomplished this using a card game called *Wamerjam! The Conversation Game*, developed by Galen Radtke, breaks into old communications patterns and sets the stage for change. The game begins by choosing a subject to discuss. Each card states the kind of communication you must use, such as: clarify, expound, translate, mediate, challenge, etc. You can only play the cards you hold so it makes it impossible to fall into old perceptions and responses and creates many opportunities for insight. Open groups will get it right away and dive into the exercise, closed groups will struggle for about 30 minutes to adapt their communications and then start laughing. The transformation is fun to watch and will give you some initial information about each of your employees and yourself. You can purchase *Wamerjam!* online at: www.thegamecrafter.com/games/wamerjam.

Explain to your employees that you want to explore communication because you want to improve your business and need to create better communication before moving forward.

Again, this may not be easy for you. We all have habits instilled in us by our families, neighborhoods, and cultures. If you need help practicing communication yourself or facilitating discussions, hire a trained professional, preferably a Psychologist with a PH.D. but don't be afraid to be a novice. Let your employees know you are attempting something new and will make mistakes. To prepare for your first facilitation, create Training Notebooks with these tabbed Sections:

- Leadership
- Communication
- Lean Principles
- Systems Redesign
- Marketing

TASK: Create training Notebooks for each of your employees

Use the following questions in your first *Wamerjam!* session. Practice with friends and family first, then move on to your employees.

Discussion Questions for your family, partner, or living group:

- How effective is our communication?
- How do we make decisions?
- How should we make decisions?
- How do we deal with conflict?
- How should we deal with conflict?

Discussion Questions for Your Staff Meeting:

- How effective is our communication?
- How do we make decisions as a business?
- How should we make decisions as a business?
- How do we deal with conflict?
- How should we deal with conflict?

> TASK: Break into old communication patterns by playing *Wamerjam!* at home and then at work with your employees

Making Transitions

Whether you feel it or not, you have begun a major life transition because you are implementing change. Transitions can be disruptive and confusing, but they are normal and necessary. As William Bridges outlines in his book, *Transitions: Making Sense of Life's Changes*, there is a difference between change and transition. Changc is situational, transition is psychological; and you need to understand both and how they will affect you.

Change occurs because you act or something in your environment is altered. You may change jobs, lose your savings in a recession, move to a new town, or simply grow older. *Transition* occurs as you progress through the psychological process of accepting and integrating change. If you are working through this manual, you are creating change and will experience transition, so you need to be prepared with some basic concepts to assist you.

Bridges identifies three Stages in the transition process:

- Ending: a time where external changes have progressed far enough for us to accept that our old identity is no longer useful or relevant. Bridges discusses "five aspects of the natural ending experience: disengagement, dismantling, disidentification, disenchantment, and disorientation."
- The Neutral Zone: a time of confusion and distress where we surrender to the process. Individuals feel "stripped of the old reality."
- Beginning: a time where we feel a renewal, an "inner alignment," and "resonance," and can achieve a "reintegration of our new identity with elements of our old one."

This seems like an elementary concept, but it is a profound experience that should not be taken lightly. Think about your own transition from adolescence to adulthood; how fraught it was with disruptions and how long it took to settle into a new concept of yourself. Implementing change in your business will create a similar transition both for you and your employees.

Your organization can only absorb so much change over any period because it is filled with individuals absorbing that change and making their own transitions. This is a major reason why businesses need a well-defined sequence for solving problems: to limit the number of activities that create change. Too much change from too many competing initiatives will overwhelm the people inside your organization.

Bridges explains how to take care of ourselves and understand "what undermines our resolve." He has made a lifelong study of transitions and explains the process far better than I can, so begin your study of management by reading *Transitions*. It is an easy read at only 194 pages, and I will refer to Bridges' concepts as we move forward.

After getting comfortable playing *Wamerjam!* you and your employees will read *Transitions* and you will facilitate a discussion of the book.

PRINCIPLE:
Change needs to be implemented in small increments.
WHY:
Employees can only absorb so much change before becoming overwhelmed, unproductive, or quitting.

TASK: (For you and your employees) Read William Bridges, *Transitions: Making Sense of Life's Changes*

Outline for Your First Facilitation

A. Introduction:
Explain that you will be implementing change in your business and change creates psychological transitions for all the individuals. An understanding of transitions will create a new vocabulary and help everyone manage the change.

B. Discussion Questions:
1) What is the difference between "change" and "transition?"
2) Think of a time in your life where something major ended, a watershed moment that seemed to change everything. What was it? How long did it take to let go of the old way of living and thinking before you felt settled in your new life?
3) Can you identify the Neutral Zone? How did it feel?
4) What helped support you psychologically in the Neutral Zone?
5) Can you identify the new Beginning in your transition?

As you facilitate the discussion of *Transitions* be aware of the concepts outlined under Facilitation above. Create safety and trust, be an effective listener, and shepherd your employees through any obstacles to communication.

C. Overcoming Obstacles

1) What if your employees did not read the assignment or came unprepared? This is your opportunity to:

- Educate on acceptable levels of preparation
- Make your expectations clear. Reading and discussion is part of their job
- Make sure they understand the Training Notebook is an essential teaching tool and reference manual

2) What if you get stuck on a question?

- Use *Wamerjam!* to stimulate the dialogue and break into old habits of communication
- You may find some individuals resisting or trivializing your discussion. Make note of it. Ask for cooperation and commitment. If the disruptions continue, this may be the first indication that this individual is not a good fit for your business.

3) What if individuals take and defend positions?

- Ask: What is being said is Fact and what is Opinion?
- Ask: Can you back up your opinion with facts, research, data?

TASK: Facilitate a discussion of *Transitions* with your employees

Communication

I placed *Communication* after *Making Transitions* because transitions are easier to talk about. Everyone can relate to and share difficult transitions without feeling threatened. Delving into the communication styles of your team may rouse emotions and you need some preliminary discussions to prepare yourself and your employees.

Communication is the most important "soft" skill you and your employees can develop and means improving relationships and removing barriers to the flow of information. Everyone in your business needs to know that it is their job to obtain and share the information they need in the quickest and easiest way possible. It also means altering intentions, assumptions, attitudes, hierarchies, behaviors, inefficient systems, and your space plan if it inhibits communication. No one should feel like they must wait to ask a question or that any question is off limits; but it takes practice to communicate with ease and effectiveness.

This is such an important issue to me as a consultant that I included a psychologist as an associate in my private practice to teach workshops, run groups, and provide individual and group counseling to clients if they need it. As entrepreneurs, we need all the help we can get to improve *ourselves,* so we are capable of managing employees and improving our businesses. If you feel you are beyond your skill in educating your team in communication or any other subject, hire the professional help you need. It will pay you back dividends far beyond the cash you spend.

Let's start with some basic concepts you need to study and practice as you prepare to facilitate your first discussion on communication. You will find a concise explanation of each in *Communicating for Results* by Cheryl Hamilton (Boston: Wadsworth: Cengage Learning, 2011): Chapters 3, 4, and 6; they include:

- Improving Interpersonal Relationships
- Effective Listening
- Overcoming Obstacles to Communication

<u>Improving Interpersonal Relationships</u>

You may think improving relationships is unnecessary, that employees should just do their jobs because they are paid, or that relationships seem good enough already, but good relationships are not a given and many issues can remain hidden without examination. Relationships need attention to become a competitive advantage. They enhance job satisfaction, morale and problem solving, and reduce the expense of employee turnover. They can either be a hidden drag on your business or a propulsive force, and if your competition is investing in relationships, how can you ignore it?

Hamilton outlines four issues essential for improving relationships: creating clear expectations, reciprocity, and mutual trust and respect.

Expectations must always be based on the needs of the business in its market and start with clear hiring guidelines, job descriptions and "surfacing" the expectations of job candidates and employees. Finding the truth of everyone's expectations requires open communication and trust. You cannot obtain information regarding expectations instantly or by just asking. It requires many interactions that add up to an employee's willingness to share. The more trust you create the more honesty you reap.

Reciprocity means you get what you give. It can spiral up or down. If you stay late to help a colleague finish their work, they may do the same. If you make negative comments or gossip, others may do the same. If you reciprocate the positive actions of a coworker, the relationship grows; if you don't, the relationship deteriorates. Just as you are trying to fulfill your vision by creating a business, each employee is trying to fulfill *their* vision of life and work. Knowing you have an interest in their wellbeing is important for morale and the sense that they will achieve something for themselves by helping you.

One client had a superior who referred to their very sophisticated costing models as "your little charts." The clients had spent many hours constructing the analysis and his work had illuminated serious flaws in costs and pricing that would have eventually wrecked the business; but the superior, who was the owner, could not see the value in the effort and so diminished his work. The client quit that day and other colleagues followed soon after. The owner maintained his belief system and communication style but lost his best employees.

You must set the standard by modeling your own behavior and by instructing your employees when they behave otherwise. You can be soft in your explanation, but they need to know that relationships are a key competitive factor for your business and for the continued health of everyone's paycheck.

Mutual Trust and Respect is a bond that pervades your organization. It is a belief based on the quality of interactions. It falls neatly into the concept of Intentions, Structures, and Behaviors covered in the next section. The intention to trust and respect models the behavior for others. It is a straightforward concept that everyone understands: is the other person acting for *your* benefit, without expectation of reward?

Communication styles also affect the quality of communication. Hamilton identifies four styles:

- Closed
- Blind
- Hidden
- Open

She also defines each Style according to two characteristics:

- How much individuals disclose
- How much individuals seek feedback

Each of these characteristics can fall on a continuum from "rarely" to "excessive." Most individuals have a combination of characteristics but feel most comfortable in one style. Refer to Figure 16 as I explain Communication Styles.

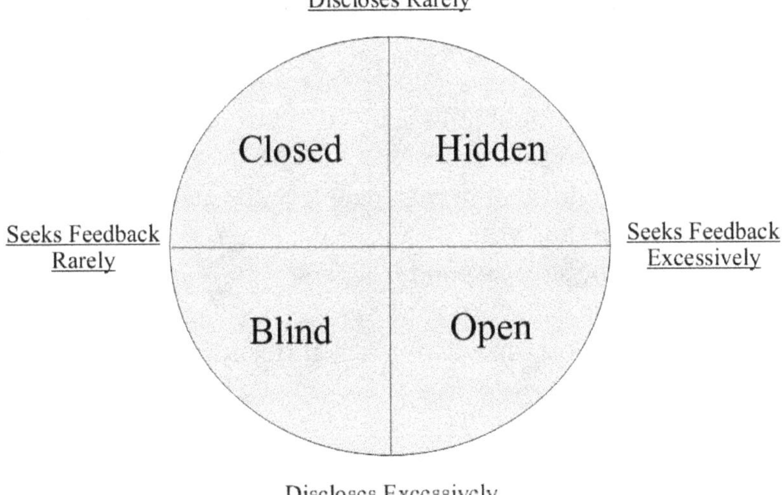

Figure 16: Communication Styles

Closed Style: Individuals with a closed Style disclose rarely and seek feedback rarely.

- They feel comfortable working alone and may be less effective serving customers or participating in group problem solving

- They find it difficult to communicate their expectations
- They may be seen as reserved and avoid conflict
- They seek security and their productivity may be low because of it. They may seem indifferent to others.
- They are "most successful working when little interpersonal interaction is required"

Blind Style: Individuals with a Blind Style disclose excessively but seek feedback rarely.

- They feel they have the best solutions and are always right
- They find it difficult to receive criticism
- They may be seen as critical and demanding
- They seek authority
- They appreciate quality and are most successful when their expertise is needed by untrained subordinates

Hidden Style: Individuals with a Hidden Style disclose rarely but seek excessive feedback.

- They feel comfortable in a social environment but disclose only on impersonal topics
- They find it difficult to trust people and perform in complex problem solving work
- They may be seen as good listeners
- They seek social acceptance
- They are most successful when teamwork is a social occasion

Open Style: Individuals with an Open Style disclose excessively and seek feedback excessively.

- They feel an interest in both the needs of people and the organization
- They find it difficult to work in environments with a lack of creativity
- They may be seen as trusting, friendly, and dependable
- They seek constructive criticism

- They are most successful when employee involvement in decision making is an organizational norm

This model is not a definitive approach to understanding communication. It is simply one perspective on the complexities imbedded in communication and an avenue to open a dialogue within your organization; but with this simple formulation you can probably see how communication styles might clash or create misunderstandings. That is why it is important for everyone in your organization to know the style of everyone else. If you have a misunderstanding, you can talk openly about style and not devolve into conflict.

Consider a superior with a closed Style giving feedback to a subordinate with an Open Style. The superior will give less feedback than the subordinate needs. Or imagine two colleagues with opposite needs for disclosure or feedback. Each interaction has the potential for less than satisfactory results. But with the knowledge of styles you can say, "I have a Blind Style, so stop me if I say too much," or, "I have a Hidden Style, I need a little more feedback."

If you know your own style, you can effectively relate to the styles of each of your employees, so take the "Style Survey – Short Form" in *Communicating for Results* Chapter 3. Later you will have your employees take this same survey and discuss the results.

But this is all theory and does not explain how to improve relationships. Again, you will accomplish this by facilitating group problem solving, but who is *your* guide? How do *you* practice? Who gives structure to *you* when you are at your worst? I suggest again some counseling with a qualified professional. Your need for support will not go away. You will continually be faced with understanding new problems and learning new skills and may need someone to talk to.

> TASK (for you): Lead a discussion of your Reading in *Communicating for Results*: Make sure you discuss each team member's Communication Style and how it relates to their work in your business. Make sure they can "pass" on disclosing uncomfortable information.

You may also want to take a full communications course at your local college. My short summary can't cover all the issues effectively.

Effective Listening

Effective listing is enhanced by a set of behaviors that may or may not be problematic for you and each of your employees. They are the same rules you will use for effective problem-solving dialogue covered later. Listening requires you to:

- Suspend your assumptions
- Use facts not assumptions
- Give your full attention to the speaker
- Understand your own habits
- Discover the speakers main points
- Not interrupt
- Not take and hold positions
- Not form a rebuttal while someone is speaking
- Not monopolize
- Not criticize, judge, or evaluate until a factual basis for dialogue is complete
- Not hold parallel conversations while someone is speaking
- Not react with emotion
- Not jump to conclusions

Effective listening is inhibited by barriers such as:

- Physical distance
- Sematic differences
- Personal differences
- Gender differences

This is a long list, and I won't cover each item in detail because you will read chapters in *Communicating for Results*. Just remember your group dialogues will fall into every dysfunction possible but it will gradually improve as you facilitate problem solving while pointing out communication barriers and assisting your employees with developing good listening habits. Educate your employees, and they can contribute to the awareness of these issues when they arise. The more everyone understands, the faster your groups will improve.

Overcoming Obstacles to Communication

Communication is also inhibited by:

- Anxiety
- Noise
- Layers of management
- Being a poor listener
- Rigid Assumptions

Anxiety arises from fear of consequences. The consequence could be the judgement of co-workers, the denigration of your views, or the possibility of losing your job. Being exposed and ridiculed will stop most people from sharing their views. The manager must remove this anxiety by valuing your views, even if they are not implemented.

Noise is irrelevant information that clouds your perceptions and slows your progress toward the truth. It could be false narratives, a clutter of conflicting opinions, or simply too much information, but they all disrupt clarity and consume time as you sort through the mess.

One of the most problematic issues for organizations that grow beyond the small business phase is that 20% of the content of a communication is lost with every layer of management it passes through. Information is altered, summarized or deleted as it works its way toward the lower levels of and organization until it becomes useless. Most employees of large organizations can't clearly provide the mission statement when asked.

You may think I'm overly concerned with this issue, but communication is the basic skill for effective problem solving just as swimming is the basic skill for surfing. Without attention to this basic skill, you place yourself and your organization at a disadvantage. Just being able to state issues clearly solves half of the problems you will encounter.

Poor listening has already been covered and assumptions will be covered in the next section.

Communication will be practiced and improved in three ways: in daily interactions, by discussing it openly in meetings, and by facilitating problem solving dialogues.

Diversity in the Workplace

- Cultural Variations
- Gender Identity
- Sexual Orientation
- Thinking Styles

If you restrict diversity, you will acquire all the same types of thinkers and not be able to solve unique or new problems. It takes many minds to contribute to solving complexity.

Outline for Your Discussion on Communication

A. Introduction: (Suggested)

I've asked you here today to discuss something I think will be important to the success of our business and the future of everyone in the company, and that is Communication. I think if we can do this better, everyone will be happier and more productive. I'm using a list of questions from a book I'm reading titled *SUCCEED!™ Your Essential Guide to Business Growth* and I'd like to facilitate a discussion to help us begin a better way of working together.

B. Discussion Questions:

- What is communication? What are its forms? Why is it important?
- Which forms are most effective? Advantages/disadvantages of each?
- What is your style?
- How can style effect communication?
- Think of a group activity you have attended. How effective was the listening?

- What are the obstacles to communication? Prompt: anxiety, noise, layers of management, being a poor listener, rigid assumptions. Discuss each.
- How can we overcome obstacles to effective communication
- How does diversity affect communication?

TASK (for you and your employees): Read *Communicating for Results*:
Chapter 3: Improving Interpersonal Relationships
Chapter 4: Effective Listening
Chapter 6: Overcoming Obstacles to Communication in Organizations
TASK (for you and your employees): Take the "Style Survey – Short Form" in Chapter 3

TASK (for you): Read *The Leader's Companion: Insights on Leadership Through the Ages*
Selection 55: Leadership Communication Skills

Basic Employee Training/Skill Sets

Each employee needs basic skills to contribute to your success. Ignorance is ineffective and can be seen in many societies that inhibit the acquisition of knowledge. Basic skills include:

- Spreadsheets
- Word Processing
- Internet
- Writing/Communication

Instruction can be found through your local EDC, SBDC, and

PRINCIPLE:
Leadership *is* your career.
WHY:
You must lead other people to solve complex problems.

community college. You can also hire private instructors to teach your employees in-house and improve all staff at the same time.

TASK: Train employees on Basic Skills

Delegation

You will be able to move forward more quickly if you can delegate some of the *SUCCEED!*™ activities to qualified employees. I have not suggested delegation until now because delegating too soon may result in you avoiding your own skill development. How this relates to Management Intentions and Leadership will be covered later in this chapter. Working more effectively with employees will be covered in **Chapter 3**.

Delegate some of the least difficult activities to employees now but be sure to maintain oversight and shepherd each task to completion. Include any training that might have been overlooked.

TASK: Train your employees, then Delegate some tasks

Intentions

Intentions

Peter Senge in his insightful book "The Fifth Discipline," outlined one of the most important concepts in business management: Intentions create Structures and Structures create Behaviors.

INTENTIONS ⟹ STRUCTURES ⟹ BEHAVIORS

Structures can be Cause and Effect Systems (psychological/behavioral systems that affect the way we make decisions) or Process Systems (physical systems for processing work: **Chapter 3**.) Refer to Figure 17 as I explain this principle for Cause-and-Effect Systems.

When anyone approaches a problem, they create an intention; sometimes conscious and sometimes less than conscious. This intention shapes their thoughts and actions. It is the same process whether you are creating a piece of art or making decisions in business. If you, as a manager, believe that you already know everything, your intention is to devalue new skills, training, and information. This creates an environment, a structure, that inhibits learning as you communicate your intention in your speech, problem solving, and interactions with employees. Without new learning, no one will question the inefficiencies in process systems, they may behave as if it doesn't matter. The result is that decision making will be based on old and probably invalid skills and information.

Your intention can be communicated subtly, as simple as saying, "I'm not interested in that new process you read about," "I already know that" or "Not now," when an employee tries to share something they believe is important. You have made it clear you do not value communication. It will only take a few interactions like this before they get the message that their opinion doesn't matter.

If you use anger as a manager, your intention is to devalue the person in front of you and use fear as a motivator. The result will be employees withholding information as they avoid interacting with you, high employee turnover as they seek a better working environment, and damaging equipment as they employ anger themselves through sabotage.

Management Intention	Structure (System)	Behavior
•We already know everything (We devalue new skills, training, and information)	•Hostile learning environment	•Employees accomplish only the minimum and create inefficient process systems •Poor decision making
•We yell at employees (We devalue people with our anger)	•Fear	•Employees withhold information •High employee turnover •Sabotage
•We suffer from untreated narcissistic behavior disorder (We make decisions based on ego)	•Discounting of facts •Blaming employees	•High employee turnover •Higher costs •Ineffective strategies
•We create competition between employees	•Distrust •Territories	•Employees do not cooperate with each other

Figure 17: Intentions, Structures, and Behaviors

Cause and effect can be separated by months or even years so that your intentions may seem unrelated to your employees' behaviors.

There are many examples, and we will cover them as we progress through each chapter but for now remember that this is a System that starts with Intentions and ends with Behaviors. The effective practical point of attack to solve a cause-and-effect system is always the manager's intentions. You *cannot* solve behavioral issues in a dysfunctional system that are caused by intentions further "up stream." When a new client begins pointing at their employee's behavior as their main issue, I look at the intentions of management including the Board of Directors if you have one. Sometimes you discover that an employee *is* the cause of a problem, but you cannot say this with certainty until you first solve intentions and structures.

I had a university as a client that had constructed terrible internet-based learning systems without feedback from professors: course shells did not function, were out of date, referred students to the wrong edition of the textbook, and provided wrong answers for assignments. The university administration at the national level believed they knew how to develop courses better than the faculty who taught the material, and so hired course designers to create consistency; but the administration never created quality control for each course or assigned it to a responsible party.

The *intension* of the administration was to create consistency in course content but without consulting the teaching staff or implementing oversight. The *structure* was dysfunctional course shells because they devalued communication with the professors who uncovered the course shell problems. The *behaviors* were administrators covering their incompetence by blaming professors for poor quality and firing anyone who voiced their opinions too strongly. Many of the teaching staff quit in frustration. All the students in one graduate program confided to me that they would have attended a different university if they were not getting a tuition break. The university ultimately ended up with the poorest quality staff and many angry students. None of the administrators lost their jobs and the problem was never solved.

Circles of Causality

Intentions can also create Circles of Causality. Senge1 calls this structure a "Balancing Process." The clue to finding one of these Circles in your business is to be aware of repeating patterns. I had one client who had lost all her employees several times; another who had failed at expanding his business five times. These cycles were caused by intentions that created a chain of events with the same result repeatedly. Each client began with an intention they thought would solve a problem or fulfill a need, but they always ended up back where they started after much effort and expense. Refer to Figure 18 as I explain this cause-and-effect system with an example.

I counseled a nonprofit organization serving underprivileged women that had experienced a recurring cash crisis for many years. The new Executive Director (ED) was worried because the cycle seemed to be occurring again within the first six months of her employment. We mapped the chain of cause-and-effect events and identified the practical point of attack to stop the cycle.

---

1 Peter M. Senge, *The Fifth Discipline: The Art and Practice of the Learning Organization*, (New York: Doubleday, 2006)

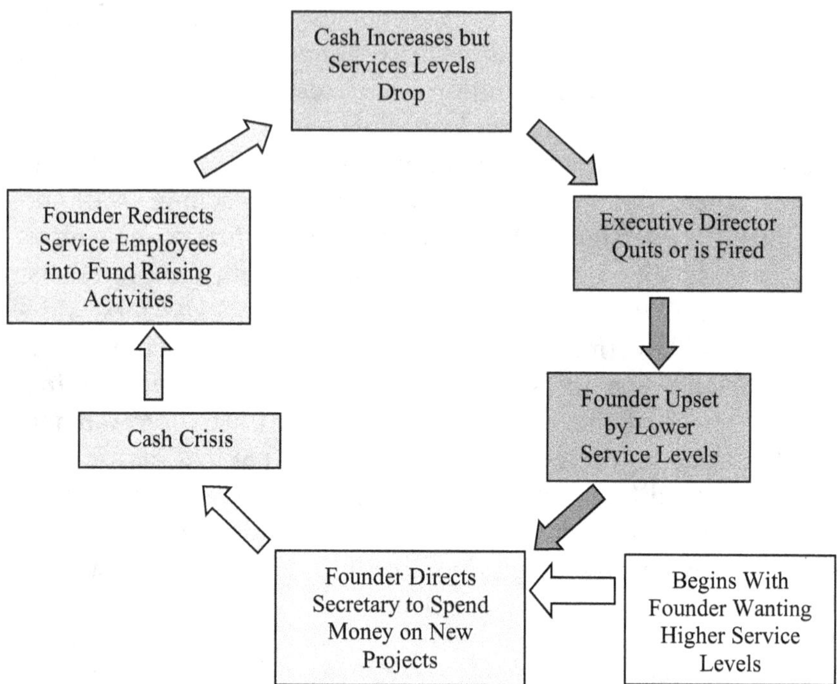

Figure 18: Circles of Causality

The organization's history showed the cycle resolving every 18 months and ending with the hire of a new ED. My client was the sixth Director. The Founder had started the organization with only himself and a secretary. After nearly 20 years they had a Board of Directors, an ED, and 11 service employees. The Founder was the main service delivery professional and expert and had great influence on the Board and all personnel, but no legal authority in the nonprofit structure (Managers and employees cannot legally sit on the Board of a nonprofit.) Each Director possessed skills in either fundraising or service but not in management or accounting.

The Circle began with the Founder wanting to create new services and attain higher service levels for existing programs. The secretary who was still with the organization had traditionally accomplished the bookkeeping and had responsibility for the checkbook. Though he had no authority to do so, the Founder would get an idea that excited him, direct the secretary to begin building infrastructure for the new service, and she would spend money without informing the

Executive Director. None of the previous EDs understood financial analysis and could not comprehend warnings emerging from the accounting system or why the cash disappeared. The secretary's loyalty to the Founder outweighed, in her mind, her responsibility to the Director. The Board approved activity after the fact.

After enough money had been spent, a cash crisis ensued with negative bank balances, non-sufficient funds charges, late payments, employee paychecks bouncing, and angry vendors cutting off service. The nonprofit was small and had no formal fund-raising staff so the Founder, now worried about the survivability of his creation, misdirected service employees into fund raising activities. As the service employees spent more time fundraising, cash increased but service levels dropped. The previous EDs were caught in the chaos and either quit or was fired. A new ED was hired as the Founder became upset with the lower service levels and started the cycle all over again. The cause and effect (wanting more service and getting less) were distance in time and seemed unrelated.

The Board had not provided adequate oversight, and each new ED was blindsided by the crisis. The long-term solution was to educate the Board about their duties and responsibilities and teach the ED accounting and financial analysis; but the practical point of attack was to take the checkbook away from the secretary.

When the ED locked up the checkbook and all the checks, the cycle stopped; but there was an explosion of negative emotion from the secretary, the Founder, and the Board. Though the ED and I explained the cycle, the need for financial control, and their legal responsibility, the Board was unwilling to back the ED and she quit like all the others who preceded her in the position. The cycle continues to this day.

You can see how the intention of the Founder to usurp authority and the intention of the Board to allow it, caused the Founder's and the secretary's behaviors to go unchecked. The result was a guaranteed Circle of Causality with the same result every time.

Note that, as I've said earlier, the long-term solution is always found "up-stream" in management intentions.

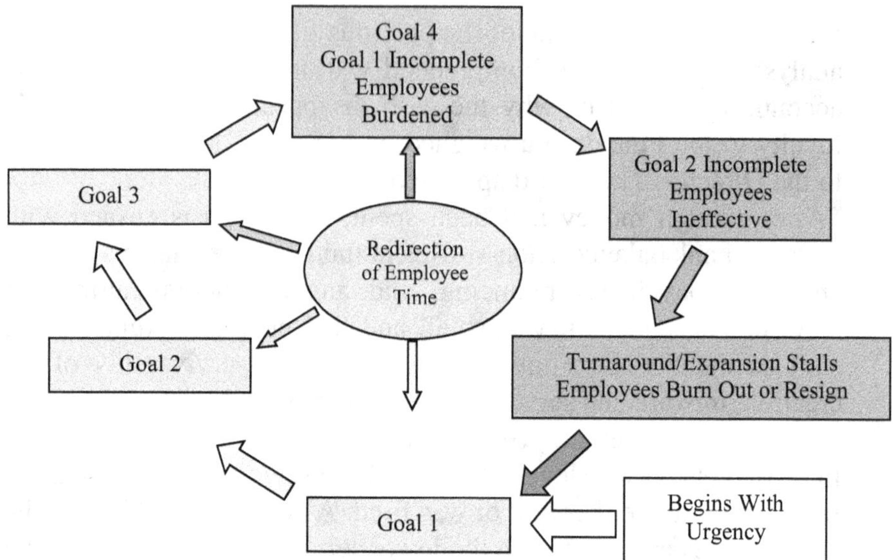

Figure 19: Circles of Causality 2

Another, and more basic version of a causality circle, is illustrated in Figure 19. Here the motivating force is the urgency of some manager toward a goal. Urgency, in this diagram, redirects employee time toward Goal 1 but before Goal 1 is complete, another urgency motivates the manager to direct time toward Goal 2. This continues around the circle until employees are burdened with too much work, ineffective in completing goals, and either burn out or resign. The turnaround or expansion stalls, and the manager finds they are back at the beginning of the circle with new employees, incomplete goals, and more urgency to accomplish critical activities.

Urgency is an intention and comes from:

- Fear
- Desire
- Time Constraints
- Mandates
- Deadlines
- Impetus to do Good
- Financial Stress and other Threats

Symptoms can be observed when:

- Urgencies/enthusiasms replace well considered goals/management
- More work is added with each new Urgency
- Important work is not completed
- Systems are left unfinished and not effective
- No prioritization of tasks
- No task template is available to place new activities in the most effective sequence
- Rushing to new activities without creating infrastructure first
- Employees are:
    - Constantly redirected
    - Stressed
    - Overworked
    - Increasingly ineffective
    - Stalled in their skill development
    - Taking an increasing number of mental health days
    - Quitting or burning out

Solutions are in the Succeed! outline and include:

- Finding the practical point of attack. The activity that, when completed, makes all other activities easier
- Prioritizing new Ideas/Goals (are your goals out of sync with the Succeed! process? Should they be prioritized lower on your list of critical activities?)
- Working on <u>One</u> Issue at a time (slow things down)
- Taking work/systems to completion before moving to the next activity
- Using a "Pull" System of time allocation (employees say when they are ready for additional work.)

Prioritizing Activities in the most effective sequence:

- Creates the Practical Point of Attack
- Illuminates Intentions
- Creates Information
- Creates Basic Infrastructure

- Enhances Problem Solving
- Creates Profits
- Reduces Risk
- Avoids wasted time when the wrong activity automatically pushes you back up the Sequence to find and complete Prerequisites?

Senge names and illustrates many more of these systems that have a serious and negative effect on your business. Identifying some of them now will prepare you to tackle them later. In Systems Redesign in **Chapter 3** you will solve them one at a time. For now, read Chapters 1-7 in the *Fifth Discipline* to begin your study of Systems.

TASK: Read "The Fifth Discipline" (Chapters 1-7)
TASK: Identify repeating patterns.

Assumptions

We all have deeply imbedded assumptions about life that blind us to facts, beliefs that foster poor decision making by creating conflict when we defend them without analysis. Instead of being neutral as we work out the details of a problem in a problem-solving dialogue, we take and defend positions that preserve our assumptions. We absorb many assumptions at an early age through our parents and our culture and can be completely unaware of them until we experience a dramatic reversal of our fortunes and have our erroneous thinking laid bare. No one is immune.

To manage a business well you need to uncover your assumptions and question their validity. The following is an exercise that gets to the heart of the issue.

Assumptions Exercise: Ask a close friend or marriage partner what they see as the most problematic assumption you hold about the world.

Rules:

- Suspend your assumptions and listen
- Be silent
- Do not respond automatically to yourself in your mind
- Do not explain, defend, or say how you will fix anything
- Ask questions only for clarification and depth
- Takes notes
- Thank your exercise partner for their insight and participation

This will be difficult but enlightening. You will be challenged by the other's perceptions and want to deny their point of view. You may try to buttress your opinions in your own mind and create a response. If you do, you will learn nothing new and only confirm your biases so – be silent and listen. Ask yourself if there is a factual basis for your assumptions.

If you are afraid of how you might respond emotionally, you may want to try this exercise with trusted others or perhaps work through your reactions and concerns with a counselor. You may need practice, but it *is* necessary to achieve a neutral frame of mind. You will have to facilitate this same exercise many times as you solve problems in your business with employees and other professionals. It is the same process in market research for uncovering why customers aren't buying your products and services. Practice with partners who care about you first and get comfortable with being uncomfortable.

Delving into intentions and assumptions is where organizational development concepts begin to apply in your study of management and the human side of change. For now, do the following:

- Observe intentions and assumptions operating in yourself and your employees
- Discover cause and effect systems
- Invest in your relationships: spouses, partners, children, family, and friends who can take the edge off your discomfort and be your support network on the days that seem most difficult. Cherish your relationships and they will assist you in your development.

We will employ the concept of intentions, assumptions, and systems throughout the remainder of this manual to maximize your management skill and effectiveness. You will practice these skills as you lead your employees through group problem solving in Systems Redesign (**Chapter 3**.) Each of the following subsections addresses a specific issue that will inform your intentions.

TASK: Participate in the Assumptions Exercise

The Entrepreneurial Problem

Many individuals who start businesses have an entrepreneurial spirit that motivates them to work hard and take chances, two characteristics important to success. They have a vision of what they want and create it with their own enthusiasm. But these same characteristics can create problems later if not informed by new skills. Enthusiasm and risk-taking can play itself out as lack of planning (causing a crisis) or blinding the entrepreneur to his/her own lack of insight into business. This may not be a problem if the business stays relatively small and uncomplicated but, in most cases, the successful entrepreneur creates a growing business with increasing complexity and needs to make the transition from entrepreneur to *manager* by gaining the necessary skill and going through the psychological process of transition as outlined by Bridges. If you want to continue to grow your business, your *intention* must be to learn everything you need to know to make this transition. The only other choice is to assign the management of the business to a qualified employee and take on a smaller functional role. For some entrepreneurs this means concentrating on the part of the business they are good at like marketing or product development, but not remaining "in charge" of daily activities. This does not mean you have given up control. You must always have oversight on major strategies and decisions, but the day-to-day administration of finances, personnel, and operations may be more effectively overseen by someone else. Many entrepreneurs do not have the choice to hire a manager because the market and/or the profit margin will not support it, and this leaves the owner with only one choice, to gain skill.

The tragedy is that some entrepreneurs do not want to develop the necessary expertise but will also not give up management responsibilities. Their *intention*, even if unstated or unconscious, is to believe the business does not need a qualified manager, because they cannot give up the idea of themselves as the creator and sustainer of the business.

Ask yourself who you are as an entrepreneur. Are you willing and capable of making the transition to manager or should you take a smaller role in the business you have created? As you progress through your development, keep asking yourself this question. The answer, and the course you take because of it, could mean success or failure.

Consider the story of the fisherman who fished without a hook, casting his line faithfully into the water time after time without any success. He does not need to cast his line more often — he needs a hook! Changing the *way* you think — changing your intention — is your hook.

Thinking Patterns

Everyone on this planet is wired differently. Some people think well in concepts (divergent thinkers), some in linear sequences (convergent thinkers). The difference in the way we think provides the human community with a valuable and diverse set of problem-solving skills. We all do better together because some of us will be efficient at solving types of problems. It is important to know which kind of thinking you favor so that you can manage your tendency to devalue the other.

Divergent Thinkers

Divergent thinkers are good at solving creative and long-term problems like marketing strategy, space planning, and the need for innovation because they focus on less detail. They instead perceive more of the whole picture and draw conclusions based on the intuitive links they make with a global information set. They tend, however, not to be as good at detailed, linear problem solving like tasks involved in accounting or creating cash flow projections. If you are a divergent thinker, you may have had trouble with math and spelling in elementary school and gotten punished by your teachers for drawing when they wanted you to listen to the lesson on dividing fractions.

Convergent Thinkers

Convergent thinkers are good at solving detailed, sequential problems like learning new software and coming up with the logical sequence for implementation of the marketing plan created by the divergent thinker. They may not see the whole problem, but they are able to place lots of detailed information into an understandable order. They tend, however, to be less visionary and creative and may not do well at understanding what motivates their customers or matching carpet and paint colors for the office renovation. If you are a convergent thinker, you probably liked math and science in school but had trouble developing a theme for your art projects.

Whichever kind of thinker you are, you will need to work on being more like the other kind and strive for a "middle brain" approach. You do this by problem solving in the areas that are hard for you. Repetition is what counts. You may never be an expert in the thinking style you are less comfortable with, but you will gain skill and know when to delegate certain tasks to employees who perform them better.

If you value one thinking pattern over the other, your intention is to eliminate a portion of the problem-solving capability of your organization by ignoring employees with the less preferred pattern.

Personality Types

Carl Young, the eminent psychologist identified two personality types: introvert and extravert. Everyone possesses both characteristics, but one typically predominates for any individual.

The introvert's interest is toward his/her own psychological processes (subjective.) The extravert's interest is in objects, the external environment (objective.) One gives energy and interest to themselves, the other gives energy and interest to the external object. One pattern is not better than the other; they are simply biological characteristics in the human landscape. There is undoubtedly some survival value to having both represented in our species, but no one can say why.

Figure 20 outlines some differences between the types.

Introvert	Extravert
Reserved	Open
Inscrutable	Sociable
Distant	Approachable
Few relationships	Multiple relationships
Decisions by subjective view	Decisions by objective conditions
Defends against demands from people	Positive relationship to people
Recharges by spending time alone	Recharges by spending time with others

Figure 20: Introvert versus Extravert

If you are an introvert, you may find it easy to sit alone and think for long periods of time. You feel a natural fit in planning, writing, and deliberating. At social events you might feel the need to escape or take a break from social interactions. If you are an extravert, you find it easy to work in groups. You feel a natural fit in sales, group process, and activities. One third of the world's population are introverts and two thirds are extraverts. The world is weighted toward extraverts but both types can be good leaders, and each can employ attributes of the other. An introvert can be good at public speaking and leading group problem solving. An extravert can be good at analysis.

You probably already know your type and have experienced the benefits and difficulties it entails. The most effective advice I can give you is to not do anything against your type. If you are an introvert, don't get a sales job. If you are an extravert, don't get a job where you work alone. Also be aware of your employee's types and use a communication style that works for them.

Commitment to Change

Both large and small businesses stumble over the issue of commitment to change. Many entrepreneurs know that their businesses will not survive without changing but personally have no intention of changing themselves. There are three reasons why someone might think this way:

1) They are afraid to change because they think it will be too difficult
2) They are not capable of accomplishing change in themselves
3) They believe the way they are doing things is the right way and that they don't need to change

This type of manager will implement change but not support the new systems and policies, sabotaging the change by example. He/she will require others to change and blame them for poor results when nothing happens. In companies that hire a turnaround expert to come in and save the business, you will often find the company in *another* turnaround a few years later because the managers reverted to their old habits after the expert left. They were not committed to change.

You as the manager of your business must be committed to changing your skill level, changing the way you manage people, and changing the way you solve problems. Your most tenacious competition will invest in change and manage it well, so you need to create your own competitive advantage and prepare to lead your organization to success by:

- Having the intention to study management
- Understanding your assumptions and thinking patterns
- Addressing your wellness issues
- Committing to change

Again, change can accrue quickly, but the psychological transition caused by change takes time and can be arduous.

PRINCIPLE:
Focus on Intentions NOT behaviors.
WHY:
It is the most efficient place to start when solving a problem because Intentions create Structures and Structures create Behaviors. Employees should not be blamed for behaviors caused by management Intentions.

Changing in the Here and Now

You are already an entrepreneur running your business, managing your staff, products, and supply networks. You may sometimes feel overwhelmed and discouraged. You may be fatigued and experiencing stress as you guide day-to-day operations to meet your current responsibilities and career goals. As an entrepreneur, you have already invested in your own independence, "be your own boss" and may want to rekindle the excitement you had experienced when you first created your business. In continuing your pursuit of financial gain, you may currently wonder if you are accomplishing all that is needed to prosper. Some business owners may question their feelings of being stuck or overwhelmed at this point in the process. The following sections will address many of the issues we experience in life that are distracting, depressing, or worrisome. Becoming more familiar with challenges that deplete your energy and mental clarity, will help to remove obstacles in developing the life you want.

When Personal Issues Distract and Divide

All of us know that living mindfully and accepting difficult situations in life is not as easy as it sounds. There are many common concerns that ebb and flow in our working interactions and relationships.

In the following list are a few of the losses, frustrations, and personal setbacks that confront us in our daily lives, normative stressors that obscure our focus and effectiveness. This lack of focus may result in an emerging self-doubt, reducing your confidence, impeding your vision, and altering what seemed to be going well prior to the disturbance. They include:

- Illness
- Relationship Difficulties
- Parent Child Difficulties
- Financial Reversals
- Unexpected Changes in your Business
- Debt

- Staff Problems
- An Untimely Move
- Illness or Death of a Beloved person or Family Member
- Loss of Faith in Your Ability to Cope Effectively in Managing Problems
- Anniversary or Difficult Arc of Life Stages that Deal with Disruption and Losses

Entrepreneurs face a multifaceted world of work and professional relationships resulting in a need to be self-aware, pay attention to emergent feelings, and consider what they mean to you. Being mindful of your own emotional responses helps you maintain a quieter mind during complex interactions and work tasks; you become less reactive and less prone to negative behavioral interactions and poor decision making. Your emotional states are valuable "data" because they help you understand who you are, when you need to practice boundary setting, and more clearly, deal with the reality of situations that stretch your limits. Simple calming strategies that function to slow destabilization when feeling threatened include:

- Focusing on your natural breath
- Slowly counting backwards from 100
- Use of emotional adjectives to name your feelings and learn, e.g. frustrated, angry, confused, excited etc.
- Rating the level of your feeling 0 to 10 (0 is the lowest level, 10 the highest).

These interventions can become, with practice, useful methods for understanding how and when you are close to losing self-control and risking unfavorable outcomes when you act out your emotional state of mind. Mindfulness interventions can be performed privately, taking a few minutes to change the negative outcome of your arousal. When you begin to understand your own emotional triggers, you can re-direct negative energy to pause, regain stability, and choose a useful strategy when dealing with upsetting problems.

Your mastery in choosing a best response, when emotions run high, helps you to build a comprehensive self-knowledge and mental stability.

Anniversary and Life-Stage Issues

When you experience work stress and anniversary or life-stage issues emerge, remember to quiet your mind. This allows you to make better decisions when painful situations feel overwhelming. When difficult issues arise, mindful practices can slow reactive tendencies to feel helpless, abandoned, angry, and anxious. If you understand how you are feeling, you acknowledge that you are suffering and need to decide how best to respond. Mindful practice places us in the here and now. It is helpful to recognize that we all have both good and bad times and suffering emotions and thoughts are normal when facing life's hardships. Painful life-stage events, sobering anniversary dates, periods of emotional stress arise, disrupting our usual schedule and statis-quo in daily living. You can manage your behavior when bad times occur and remind yourself to quiet your mind. Recognize your need for periods of rest and give yourself the time you need to process the depth of your emotions and confusion, especially when you are grieving.

Life *is* change but feelings, however strong, also change. We can be spinning anxiously because something disturbing has happened but instead of the usual reactive display such as yelling at a staff member, you can consider different behaviors knowing that you are working for positive outcomes. You can choose more effective ways of solving problems when disruptions occur. Simplifying the strategies used to rebalance your work and private life will help you get through intense periods of change.

Removing Obstacles to Growth

It's important to understand your feelings and thoughts throughout periods of emotional/behavioral instability. The practice of developing self-awareness enhances opportunities to strengthen your access to the many options for solving problems that you may not have considered. If you decide that you are stuck in old, inefficient ways of responding, it may be useful to seek outside help. There are many wellness/behavioral and mental health issues that prevent us from developing reliable solutions. Counseling and psychotherapy are helpful in talking through your feelings of being stuck and in pain. Finding a skillful, confidential, professional with whom you can share your concerns is a positive step towards personal empowerment.

Wellness and Behavioral Issues[2]

The variations in the way we think as described above are normal but there are more serious issues that can affect the success of your business. Some individuals are born with certain biological proclivities such as, dyslexia, attentional problems, learning issues, addictive issues, mood disorders, anxiety, and the many mental health and behavior concerns for which you may seek help to develop a better understanding of barriers to your growth. The following section focuses on some of these concerns.

Dyslexia

Individuals with dyslexia may experience problems with letters and can be slow to read at the elementary level. Some students read numbers and letters backward causing them terrible grief as school age children that inhibits their learning, sometimes for life. This has nothing to do with a child's intelligence and many talents. They are like everyone else except in this one respect, although they may carry a dislike of school and fear that "something is wrong with them." It's unfortunate that schools sometimes single out students who have a different learning style, or who are referred to special education. "No Child Left Behind" sounds like a promising idea but the children, who do not fit in with a teacher's curriculum plan, may come to believe the teasing and name calling they suffer from peers and family members is because they have different needs.

As an entrepreneur, if you experienced learning issues in school, you may have difficulty completing your monthly accounting, balancing your check book, and understanding your financial statements. It may be difficult, but it is not impossible. You need to find a patient, knowledgeable person to help you through these activities as many times as it takes for you to become competent.

2 Diagnostic and Statistical Manual of Mental Disorders DMS-5-TR, American Psychiatric Association, Fifth Ed. 2022.

You may never be great at them, but you can compensate by getting help in strategic areas.

Problem with Numbers and Math

Individuals with numbers deficit have trouble with basic math. They may not be able to accomplish simple addition and subtraction in their head, make mistakes balancing their checking account even when they are concentrating on it, and seem to forget basic math principles even when shown the process many times.

Attention Deficit Hyperactivity Disorder (ADHD)

Individuals with Attention Deficit Hyperactivity Disorder (ADHD) have trouble focusing on a single subject for very long, seem very busy but accomplish very little, and are impulsive in their decision making. If you have ADHD, you are quick to start on new projects but have trouble completing the work. Your interests can be wide ranging but not always deep because concentrated study feels arduous.

When Achieving Wellbeing is Elusive

Beyond the challenges mentioned above, there are conditions and behaviors that can severely affect the success of a business. Sometimes we learn unproductive behaviors from our life experience and sometimes we are vulnerable to developing symptoms during specific arc-of-life periods when symptoms often begin to develop. When severe enough, and symptomatology meets criteria for mild, moderate, or severe diagnosis, significant obstacles in maintaining stability over time are most likely. If you are suffering from a mental health syndrome, your business decisions and behavior are adversely affected. Getting effective assistance to manage your stability will help your business run more smoothly. Recognizing that you are not doing well is the first step. Taking action to get therapeutic support is the second step. See a qualified Psychologist with a Ph.D. or an ED.D. who possesses diagnostic skills. Master's level therapists will not always have the ability to diagnose nor to prescribe the proper medications if appropriate.

Many people are reluctant to invest in counseling because they think they can solve their wellness issue on their own. This could not be further from the truth. The reason it *is* a wellness issue, is because *you cannot solve it on your own!* I stress this because a wellness issue becomes a way of thinking, and you are inside the thought process. You cannot think your way out of a thinking pattern because it won't let you! One session of counseling per week would cost you a little more than you spend on lunch for that same week, but the benefits of successful treatment are lifelong. Make taking care of your own wellness a priority and everything else you need to do in your business will become easier.

Some of the more common issues are described below. Have your living partner read this section and ask them if they see any of these behaviors in you. If living alone, ask a good friend. You may not be able to see symptoms/adverse behavior in yourself because you may have been thinking this way for so long that IT IS YOU! And you may see nothing wrong with just being yourself — however unproductive it has become.

Mood Disorders

Depression is one of the most common disorders and one of the most insidious. It is characterized by lethargy, excessive sleeping, lack of motivation, irritability, and a general inability to get much done. You may blame yourself for being "lazy," "stupid,", or "no good," but you are none of these. You are depressed. You may have a hard time admitting you are depressed because you do not know what it feels like to have a normal level of motivation. Depression traps you inside your own thinking process and you literally cannot understand why your life does not work.

Depression can be situational (some events create a depressive response), episodic (falling into a depression at various intervals), or clinical (deep and long term). If your partner is saying you look depressed or tired a lot, take their word for it and consider getting help now.

Bipolar Disorders are a serious major mood disorder, which is characterized by destabilizing mood swings. To be diagnosed as having bipolar mood disorder requires support from a well-qualified psychologist or psychiatrist.

In business, someone in the manic phase may make grandiose plans, impulsively move forward without adequate planning, and spend lots of money on questionable projects; all with the firm belief that they are on top of the world and cannot possibly lose. The real details of the business may seem boring or inconsequential.

Someone in the depressive phase will be unable to motivate themselves to perform even the most basic functions in the business and will generally feel hopeless about their prospects and the damage they have caused during the mood swings

One client whom I believe suffered from mood swings cycled between rapid expansion and bankruptcy every three months. It was terribly frustrating to watch as he would impulsively hire six new employees, start another marketing scheme, and invest in expensive equipment; and then three months later begin to fall short on his bills, lay people off, and spiral into depression not once but three to four time per year.

Narcissistic Personality Disorder is characterized by a diminished ego sheltered by an inflated protective bubble. A narcissist talks with confidence but is frightened at the core. To feel better, they draw all attention away from others and make themselves the center of attention. They tend to blame others for reversals because it is too threatening to see their own culpability.

Border Line is a very severe personality disorder. In relationships the person who has this disorder moves from idealization to rapid devaluation. They will be manipulative, demanding, and dishonest but they will feel like the world and everyone around them owes them something. When all those other people don't deliver, the borderline is enraged by the supposed betrayal. This is black and white thinking in the extreme and the disorder is difficult to treat because they eventually may devalue their treatment team.

Anger should need little explanation, but it is surprising how many people do not know what a normal amount of anger looks like. Everyone gets upset occasionally in traffic, at their job, with their partner, and the government but with pathologically angry people, it is a style they employ to solve problems. Instead of teaching their employees, they yell at them. Instead of asking their kids at least ten times not to leave their toys on the stairs, they may hit them at the least provocation. They insult customers and destroy relationships with their anger and need help.

Alcoholism is probably one of the most visible disorders but is not always easily uncovered even by family members. Late-stage alcoholics go on drinking binges that can last three weeks and stop only when they are too sick to go on. Alcoholism in its early stages can be as moderate as having a six-pack of beers each day after work. Many alcoholics hide this behavior or minimize it by saying "it's only a couple of beers" but it's not, it's a symptom of what is coming. What is different about an alcoholic is that they drink regularly and can't stop. It only begins to look severe when they drink a *lot* every day. The result is poor decision making, unhappy employees, and customers reluctant to frequent their business.

After reading the previous section you may have conclude that you really are alright and that you do not have a serious wellness issue that is undermining your business, but you may now be concerned about your business partner as their poor decision making and impulsive behavior take on new meaning.

There are only four things that can happen if your business partner has a serious deficit or disorder:

1) You will talk about it, and they will get help
2) You will buy them out of the business
3) They will buy you out of the business
4) No one will talk about it and the business will continue to suffer (along with you and your family)

Employees can be equally problematic. This does not mean firing people who learn slowly or have normal amounts of frustration or inattention. But you *are* trying to create a successful team. Be careful who you work with. Some wellness issues like depression can be treated, some like border line personality disorder are more difficult.

Getting Help

If you need help, hire the right professional for the job. You need either a Psychologist or Psychiatrist with diagnostic skill. Each of these professionals has a doctoral degree with diagnostic training. A master's level therapist may not have this skill.

Whether you are experiencing a wellness issue or not, you may want to invest in therapy because you are progressing through a major transition, and you might need help at times with this difficult process.

TASK: Get help from a qualified Mental Health Professional to understand your wellness issues

Conflict Resolution

You will undoubtedly experience conflict as you implement change. It is natural for you and your employees to resist the arduous process of altering your thinking and the way your organization functions, and you will need to begin a dialogue at every level to obtain results. Address group issues in your staff meetings and individual issues in confidential private sessions. Much of your conflict will lessen as you address systems redesign in **Chapter 3** but even if you have done a good job of changing your intentions, you may find some employees continue with disruptive behaviors such as name calling, bullying, and undermining supervisors but do not be too quick to punish individuals. You need to create better systems before you can truly isolate the cause of behaviors and move to terminate people.

You can address behavior with a simple model. In the short term take your problematic employee aside and do the following.

- Identify the Issue
- State how it makes you feel
- Request a change in behavior
- Say what you will do if the behavior does not change

They may argue or explain. Give them a fair hearing and take responsibility if the conflict arises from your own intentions but do not allow destructive behaviors to continue. They will impact the morale of your good employees and cause inefficiencies.

Practical Point of Attack

Create a table at the bottom of the **Build Resources/Capabilities** section of the *SUCCEED!*™ Outline titled "Practical Point of Attack: Tasks for This Section." If you read all of *SUCCEED!*™ first as I suggested in the Introduction, you probably made some notes indicated which tasks you have already completed (the solid parts of your Swiss cheese.) What are left are the activities you need to address. A sample Task Table is shown in Figure 21 below.

Place all the unfinished activities for **Build** under Tasks in the left column and list all the Details you must complete to achieve each Task in the right column. Make sure the Tasks are listed in the same order as they appear in the Problem-Solving Sequence. The first activity in the Task Table is your Practical Point of Attack.

Task	Details
Project Costing System	Download Spreadsheet Learn spreadsheet operation Create New Bids
Cashflow Projection	Download spreadsheet Enter Inflows and Outflows for one year Test Scenarios
Planning	Create Planning Notebook and Word Document
Higher Profit Margins Products	Complete Profit Analysis for each Product/Service or Profit Center

Figure 21: Sample Task Table

It immediately becomes clear where to start (the practical point of attack) and where your "hot button" issue belongs in the sequence (usually later in the diagram.)

Focus your actual work on only one Task, the next practical point of attack. If you are the sole employee in your business and you try to take on more than one Task at a time, your work will go to diffusion, and you will complete nothing. If you can delegate some activities to qualified employees, you may be able to work on more than one, but make sure you have oversight over all activities that are underway.

When you encounter new threats, information, or problems, place them in the Task Table according to the sequence in the *SUCCEED!*™ Outline so they are recognized but do not distract you from your current problem-solving. For example, if you need a Project Costing System, it should be placed above Planning in this Task Table. If you discover major systems that need to be implemented, they should be placed below Planning. The Task Table should keep you from redirecting your efforts when you feel threatened. As you prioritize each new piece of information within the Problem-Solving Sequence you will remain focused on the most important activities.

Remember you must take each task to completion for it to become institutionalized and have a lasting effect.

Interim Financing

You may at any point in your business development find a need for interim financing, but you are not ready for a substantial loan. Resist the temptation to go to the bank at this point unless it is absolutely the only alternative. You will probably choose the wrong amount, apply it to the wrong activities, and go back for more when you discover how much you really need in long-term financing. Going back to the bank destroys your credibility, so look for some other source of interim financing until your long-term planning is finished. The only reason you might go to the bank at this point would be for a line of credit. If you have been banking at the same bank for a while you might easily add as much as a $10,000 line of credit to your regular checking account, just for the asking but this can be problematic. You will be tempted to use this line of credit for all your cash needs, quickly deplete it, and have it turn into an unintended term loan at a high interest rate.

The following sources of interim financing are the traditional sources for entrepreneurs: family, friends, neighbors, home equity, cash value of your life insurance, a payout from your IRA, local investment networks, and loans or credits from parent companies or distributors. But be frugal; if you have completed your baseline cash flow, you only know how much you need to get through the next few months, *not* what it will take to get your business back to profitability or through expansion. Also don't forget to plan with the

IRS and your State agencies if you owe back taxes.

If you must take out a loan, do the best you can with your current knowledge of your business and the future. See **Appendix H**: Writing a Winning Loan Proposal for creating the loan document.

Debt Consolidation

Begin to look at debt consolidation. This means taking all the outstanding debt you have and consolidating it into one new loan with a lower monthly payment. This is accomplished by lengthening the term of the loan, that is, the number of years given to pay it off. You may be paying a higher interest rate than you had on the old loans, but the extra time lowers the overall payment. Look for the best combination of interest rate and term and look at all sources of debt consolidation: friends, neighbors, relatives, banks, debt consolidation companies, consumer counseling agencies, but not credit cards. Many credit card companies send out offers for balance transfers at special introductory rates that could reduce your interest rate from 18% to as low as 5.9% for up to nine months. This is not a wise long-term strategy and gives you only short-term relief.

If you are not current on credit card and other debt payments, your credit rating may not be high enough to qualify for these offers and that is probably good. They are a trap. The terms of these transfer offers set you up for failure. Some may offer only a few months at the lower rate; then jump to 21%! And remember, one of the hidden terms in many of these offers is moving you immediately to a higher interest rate if you miss even one payment.

You may need to ask your creditors for forbearance. For a bank loan this means either making no payment for a given period or paying just the interest due. If you make no payment, interest will accrue and become additional principal rolled over into the loan balance. For creditors who are holding debts other than loans, like vendors holding accounts payable, you should contact them as soon as possible and let them know you are making arrangements to pay them, but that you first need to complete enough tasks in the *SUCCEED!*™ Outline to develop your cash.

Factoring

Factoring is selling your accounts receivable. You accomplish this through a factoring company or possibly a bank, but I do not recommend it unless you are desperately in need of cash and have exhausted all other sources. A factoring company will discount the value of your accounts receivable. That means giving you less for them than they are worth. If you had $100 in accounts receivable the factoring company might give you $80 and make $20 on the deal when they collect from your customer. Consider the extreme interest rate this implies: 20/80 = 25%! You could be giving away all your profits.

A bank might work a slightly different version of this by giving you a loan that is backed by your accounts receivable or a confirmed purchase order. The interest rate will undoubtedly be lower than the factoring company, but you typically *must* pay off the full amount of the loan as soon as the payment from your customer comes in.

Factoring companies can be found on the internet or in the phone book.

Bankruptcy Protection

One solution for solving your cash crisis and getting control of your finances might be bankruptcy protection if you are still behind on your cash and your debts are growing. This does not mean closing the business. Even in a Chapter 7 bankruptcy filing (liquidation) you may be able to keep some of your business assets and continue to operate if you are a sole proprietor. If you file a Chapter 11 Bankruptcy, you can place your creditors on hold and work out a plan with the courts to get the business back on its feet before you start paying off the heavy debt burden. But bankruptcy should be your last choice. Many creditors will want to work with you as you pay down your debt and both parties would be more profitable not incurring legal fees from a bankruptcy filing.

If you are forced to choose bankruptcy, be smart about it. See a bankruptcy attorney and get complete information about the filing options in your state. Typically, you can choose to file either under State or Federal regulations. There may be an advantage in the amount of assets that are exempted depending on how you file. Plan your bankruptcy for six to nine months in advance of your filing date. The strategy is three-fold: 1) Stay current on your credit cards up to sixty days before you file, 2) Transfer as many of your obligations out of secured debt and into unsecured debt (credit cards), paying off non-dischargeable debt first like taxes and school loans, and 3) Make sure the equity you have in the assets you want to keep is at the right level.

Any transfers of debt or assets needs to be accomplished about six months before you file (check this time period with your lawyer), otherwise the bankruptcy court will assume you made the transfers to avoid payment and will throw this debt back into the proceedings in its original form. Try to pay off secured debts and non-dischargeable debts with credit cards. If you can, stay current on the payment of your credit cards. It may seem odd, but you may get an increase in your line of credit because you have maxed out your cards but are still making regular payments. The credit card companies, in an odd twist of logic, assume you are a good credit risk because you make regular timely payments but need a higher credit limit because you have used up the one you have. Separately from this issue, cash advances you take on credit cards need to stop sixty days before you file, otherwise they could be thrown back into the proceedings.

You can automatically keep some assets like personal possessions, automobiles (up to a certain dollar limit), and assets used to run your business but beyond these assets there is a total dollar limit on what you can keep. For a single person this exemption is approximately $16,000, for a married couple about $32,000. This means if you own a house, you can't have more than $16,000 in equity in it if you are single ($32,000 equity in the house if married). Going over the limit means the court can sell the house. If you have more equity than the limit, you might try to reduce it by getting a home equity loan to pay off some of your non-dischargeable debts. You will have to justify the value of your house, and therefore its equity, to the court. Some courts will accept the value assessed by the county; others may want an appraisal. Be sure to ask your lawyer how your local court operates and know the value of your house before you file. If you don't own a house you might want to apply this exemption to other assets such as cars, cash, and stocks and bonds that may help you reconstitute your resources.

Remember that Congress can change bankruptcy laws at will. Up until a few years ago student loans could be discharged in a bankruptcy, currently they cannot. Other rules may require some kind of repayment plan. Check with your lawyer about the latest developments and plan.

All of Us

Claire faced three problems, all related to a lack of skill in accounting. Although she had a bookkeeper who accurately accounted for transactions, neither Claire nor her bookkeeper understood financial analysis. Their intention was not to value this skill because it was not interesting and seemed daunting to learn. They did not understand that:

- Expenditures for equipment and software were shown on the Statement of Cash Flows not the Income Statement, inflating their conception of available cash
- Loan payments were not split into Interest and Principal, showing the loan being paid off rapidly as both portions were applied to the loan balance
- The business manager had embezzled $40,000 by charging personal expenses on the company credit card and raising her hourly pay rate from $20 to $30 per hour

With a quick financial analysis on-site with Claire and her bookkeeper I uncovered the discrepancies and asked her to complete the Embezzlement Check List. She called me two hours later and had caught the embezzler. The other accounting issues were taken care of with instruction.

Embezzlers are criminals. Call the police when you catch one.

Moving Forward

I hope you can see how important the activities within **Build** are as prerequisites for solving more complex problems, and the time you must invest to complete each task thoroughly. I want to stress again to take your time. Do not rush ahead. Complete each task and place your finished work in your Development Plan so that it becomes an integrated resource for your business.

When you get relief from some of your longstanding issues do not become overly confident. Only the preliminaries have been completed. Now is the time to dig in and solve more basic issues, while maintaining the changes you have already implemented. I encourage you to keep going. The results will be satisfying and exceptional and elevate you to a new level of competency.

Your effectiveness as a manager is determined in part by the issues covered in this chapter but is also influenced by your problem-solving abilities. In **Chapter 3** you will begin with problem solving and prepare to work effectively by training and leading a well-organized staff. You will begin a thorough restructuring of the way you work with people and redesigning the systems that bring efficiency.

CHAPTER 3: Maximize Cash Flow/Productivity

Leadership
Problem Solving
Efficiency
Strategic Compensation
Productivity Measures and Incentive Pay
Practical Point of Attack

ALL of Us

The Clarkston family was worried. They had just received their first order from a major chain store to manufacture 28,000 units of their best-selling product. The order had been prepaid but they had never produced so many units with such a short deadline. They estimated it would take three weeks with their current systems to finish the order, well beyond the deadline. Their assembly process was complex and slow, but they felt they had no time to change it and would lose their first big customer if they could not perform as contracted. They were in a do or die situation but could not see a clear solution.

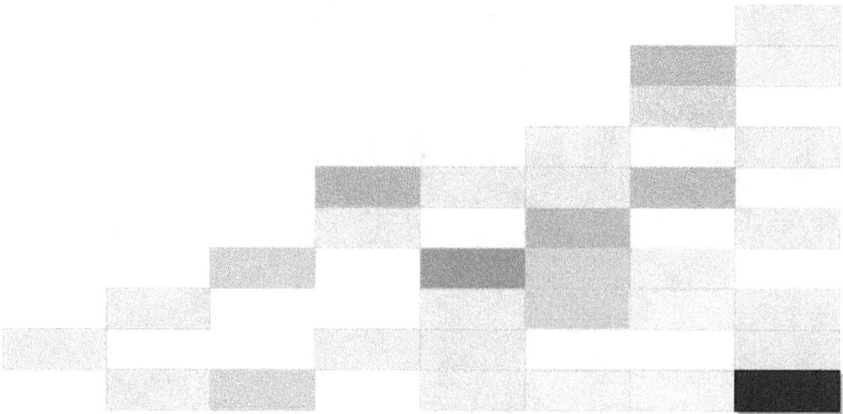

Maximize Cash Flow/Productivity

<u>Leadership Lesson 2</u>

Balance/Expertise/Honesty/Integrity/Availability

<u>Problem Solving</u>

Vetting Existing Employees
Problem Solving/Learning Organizations
The Systems Dialogue
Group Problem Solving
Facilitation of Systems Redesign
Conflict Resolution

<u>Efficiency</u>

Types of Systems
Systems Redesign
Capacity: Space Planning

<u>Strategic Compensation</u>

Skill Blocks
Market Pay Line
Internal Consistency
Personnel Policy Manual

<u>Productivity Measures and Incentive Pay</u>

Beyond the 20% Profit Margin
Productivity Measures
Benchmarks and Goals
Incentives

<u>Practical Point of Attack: Tasks for This Section</u>

Figure 22: Maximize Cash Flow/Productivity

Maximize Cash Flow/Productivity is the second Box in the Problem-Solving Sequence and will prepare your organization to survive and prosper in our rapidly changing business environment. Wherever you are now and whatever your intentions are for the future, you need to build an organization that can solve problems and create efficiency. **Maximize** is a prerequisite for crisis management, profit improvement, recession recovery, expansion, or organizational change. Complete these activities faithfully and thoroughly and you will create an organization ready to achieve your goals.

Maximize can be completed in parallel with the third Box **Evaluate Your Market** (Chapter 4) because evaluating your market may take a long time and you can build efficiency as you accomplish your research but remember not to take on too many tasks at once and get diffused. Stay focused on one task and take it to completion, or you may become overwhelmed and distracted and accomplish nothing.

Maximize activities focus on:

- Leadership
- Problem Solving Organizations
- Efficiency
- Productivity Measures

Completing them will:

- Create effective problem solving teams
- Prepare you to lead your organization to success
- Maximize your efficiency
- Create a 20% Profit Margin or greater

Leadership Lesson 2

You have applied some concepts of Leadership through Leadership Lesson 1 and by facilitating discussions, but I'd like to delve a little deeper and outline some characteristics of leadership that will help you succeed in systems redesign.

Balance

You give continuous structure to your business by overseeing systems, conflicts, strategies, and morale; and sometimes it feels like a heavy burden staying in balance to facilitate productive activity. Understanding and acting toward the issues in **Chapter 2** related to your intentions, assumptions and wellness is a start. Getting help from a supportive other when you get stuck is effective and affirming. Beyond that you need to develop guiding principles and find a way to relieve yourself of stress. Regular vacation breaks are great but what informs your choices and relationships daily and in each communication?

Some employ religion, philosophy, or wellness strategies to enhance relationships and create internal balance. Walking, running, reading, art, music and family activities can quiet the mind. I play an instrument and understand how it works for me. You need to find something that works for you.

Whatever practice you employ, it needs to create an internal balance and give you a respite from the daily edginess of life. You can get caught up in the pursuit of success and neglect sustaining activities and relationships.

Where do you go psychologically when you:

- Feel the world is destructive
- Argue with others
- Desire something you cannot have
- Suffer from fear, grasping, or social duty

The answer must be a way of thinking that calms you and gives perspective.

TASK (for you): Read *The Leader's Companion: Insights on Leadership Through the Ages*
Selection 15: Tao Te Ching
Selection 16: Satyagraha

Expertise

To lead you need to be expert in your craft, the craft of Business, and you need to continually improve your expertise.

Musicians practice all the time. It takes about 10,000 hours to become skilled in an instrument, but most musicians continue to practice and learn throughout their lives because they know there is always more to understand about their field and invest time in a continuous deepening of their knowledge.

The skill you develop is the single most important factor in determining your success, and building skills in the right areas and in the right sequence is the whole point of this manual. We began by building your capabilities in managing information and understanding your finances, and continued with management issues that might affect your decision-making. In subsequent sections, we will cover building proficiencies related to personnel, operational processes, marketing, finance, and long-term planning.

You can gain additional mastery by taking weekend workshops and semester long courses in various business topics but the main thing you need is to practice *solving problems*. The process of learning the skills you need through problem solving is the key to embedding new knowledge in your business. This means not giving up on an issue until you have solved it and not caving in when the skill you need to develop seems difficult. If you get frustrated, take a stress break, but don't give up. This will lead you to becoming an expert in your business and result in your growing ability to instruct employees in their own skill development.

Honesty

An essential step toward becoming a leader is creating honesty, both with your employees and within yourself. This does not mean telling your employees everything about yourself and your business, but it does mean admitting when you're wrong, knowing when you don't have enough skill to solve a problem, and making decisions based on real information, not wishful thinking. You might decide to try a new marketing idea and find that it brought in very few customers and didn't pay for the effort, or you might assign an employee some new responsibilities and find that they failed at the task. Honesty in these cases means finding out the REAL reason your plans didn't work as expected. The first step is to admit, without blaming anyone, that the idea didn't work, then get everyone involved who were part of the project and determine why.

You might find out that the marketing idea was simply timed badly, or that the employee who failed needed more training. You might also find out you just had a bad idea and that your employees were just too afraid to tell you. If you are not honest with your employees, they will certainly not be honest with you. If you make a mistake, admit it and make solving the problem the most important thing. Then, when your employees fail, they'll be willing to tell you because you set the standard: being open and honest about the outcome.

This does not mean holding onto employees that have no interest in improving their performance, but it does mean letting people learn from their mistakes.

Integrity

Do your employees trust you enough to tell you the truth? Do they illuminate problems because they do not fear your reaction. Do you have a style that encourages openness? Are you fair under all circumstances, even when people are mad at you?

Integrity means having a firm adherence to a moral code so that your employees can confidently say, "Tell the boss. He/she will never burn you for telling the truth." You don't have to be superhuman, but you do have to be balanced and self-aware.

Availability

Availability means you are present to answer questions, but it also means making sure your employees *want* to ask you questions because you treat them well and encourage them to communicate with you.

Are you physically present at your business, enough so that critical decisions can be made when they come up? Have you left someone in-charge, but not given them the training or authority they need to do a good job? In a small business the owner may be the only one who knows the business well enough to keep it organized. Also think about how you respond to employees when they approach you. Your style will determine how much your employees talk to you. If you are always too busy, do not take them seriously, make them feel like they are wasting your time, or that you have no interest in them, you will get less and less information about your business *from* them.

Other Characteristics

Drive

Do you have the drive to learn, work diligently, be independent, get help when you need it, and solve problems? If not, business could be overwhelming for you. It is not a failing to lack drive in business. You might find resonance in other fields, but business is not a passive enterprise. Very little can be accomplished without constant attention to managing details.

Motivation

Do you *enjoy* being in business? Do you feel satisfied and entertained by solving complex problems and teaching your employees. If not, what is your motivation for running your business and is it enough?

Confidence

You may begin your entrepreneurial journey with high or low confidence, but real confidence comes from skill, knowledge, and results. Make these your goals

Problem Solving

Vetting Existing Employees

Behavioral Dimensions

From your experience leading discussions with your employees, you are gaining insight into their personal makeup, and you will need to decide if everyone can make the transition as your business improves. I would rather bring everyone along and educate them as I go, but it is not always possible.

Robert E. Kelly, in his article *In Praise of Followers* identified two underlying behavioral dimensions for employees: critical thinking and activity. Refer to Figure 23 below as we investigate employees.

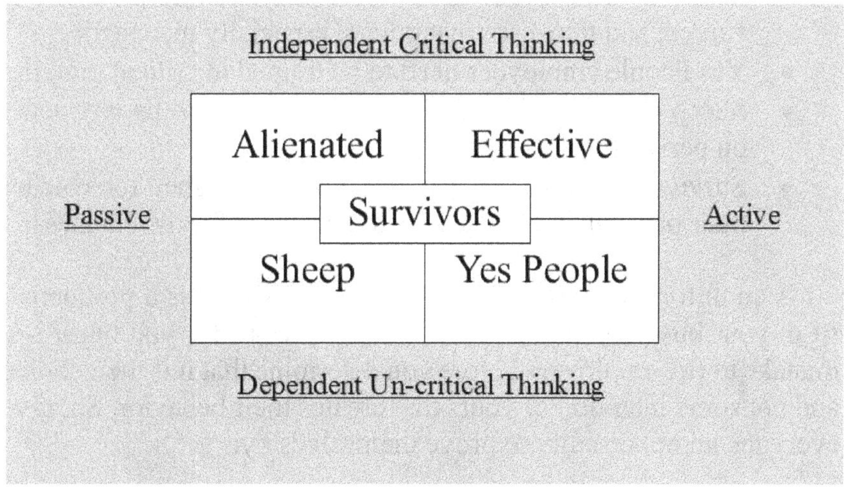

Figure 23: Followership Patterns (Robert E. Kelly)

The vertical axis categorizes employees as exhibiting either independent critical thinking or dependent un-critical thinking. Independent critical thinkers can define and solve problems on their own. You can depend on them to have useful ideas. Dependent un-critical thinkers cannot solve problems without guidance.

The horizontal axis categorizes employees as exhibiting either active or passive behaviors. Active individuals participate in problem solving, passive ones don't.

The diagram can be divided into four quadrants and named.

- Active, critical thinkers are Effective
- Passive, critical thinkers are Alienated
- Active, un-critical thinkers are Yes People
- Passive, un-critical thinkers are Sheep

The middle box represents Survivors who will move into any other box as needed to remain employed. Your task is to understand each employee's makeup and shepherd as many into the Effective quadrant as you can. What do each of these patterns need?

- Effective employees need only training
- Alienated employees need to see that their contribution is valued, and they can trust others, especially managers
- Yes People employees need to be trained in critical thinking
- Sheep employees need all of the above and to be instructed on personal responsibility
- Survivors need to see they will not be punished for voicing their opinion and being an effective asset for the business

It is an unfortunate truth that not every individual is a productive fit in your business. Some of them already work for you but it is a mistake to fire employees before you determine that it is their choice and not some intention of yours that creates their behavior. So, give everyone an opportunity to prove themselves by:

- Training
- Matching skills to tasks
- Implementing Productivity Measures (later in this Chapter)
- Pushing decision making down the hierarchy
- Matching responsibility and authority
- Providing clearly define goals and job descriptions
- Creating an organizational chart with reporting relationships
- Creating a forum for problem identification and resolution that requires employee inputs and creates benefits.

Hold regular staff meetings once a week with problem solving always the first agenda item as you follow the *SUCCEED!*™ Outline and make the business more efficient. This will be covered in more detail later.

The Kolbe Corporation offers employee assessment tools online.

TASK (for you): Vet each of your employees according to the R. Kelly Diagram

TASK (for you): Read *The Leader's Companion: Insights on Leadership Through the Ages*
Selection 31: In Praise of Followers
Selection 49: What It Means to think Critically
Selection 35: Challenging the Barriers to Opportunity

Wellness Issues

Employees suffering from a wellness issue are possibly the toughest problem to solve. Behavior that seems odd, unproductive, immature, or confrontive may be the symptoms of deeper issues. You may give them the benefit of your empathy and understanding. You may believe they just have a quirky personality, but consistency in behaviors that diminish their effectiveness may be a behavioral issue. The question is whether the behavior undermines the success of your business.

You are always vetting people for your success team, whether you are hiring or giving a performance review. If unproductive behavior persists in one of your employees, you can ask for change as outlined below. In a private one-on-one conversation:

1) Identify the behavior
2) Tell them how it is affecting your business
3) Tell them specifically what you need from them
4) Tell them they have a grace period, but the behavior needs to change

For most employees this is enough to motivate improvement. For employees with challenges, it may not. If the behavior does not change you have some alternatives. You can create a plan to assist them, reassign them to a less demanding job, demote them, or terminate their employment. I prefer helping individuals if I can, but your business can only provide so much assistance and remain profitable. We cannot understand or help with all behavioral issues, but we can ask for the performance the job requires and let the employee determine if they can rise to the challenge.

You can probably see now that to hire and motivate people to become good employees you must become one yourself, and you may need help to get your own skill, motivation, and self-esteem to the level where you are an effective manager. Again, do not worry about how long it takes. It is involving yourself in the *process* of becoming that person that eventually gets you to a higher level of management skill. Be satisfied with small gains in skill and knowledge and do not be fooled by business fads or books with "quick solutions." Nothing in business has a quick fix. If you want advice, call your EDC or SBDC counselor. They are certified and, in most states, must have minimum competencies. Invest in *your* long-term skill development not a fad.

Problem Solving/Learning Organizations

Because the business world has become so complex, all managers, even in small business, must create a problem solving/learning organization. This means having a team that can interact efficiently and effectively to solve complex problems. The team members don't all have to be your employees, but you must have a complement of talents, and a template for bringing people together to identify and solve problems.

As the business advisor for my county EDC, I was on many teams in many businesses adding my expertise to theirs to help them build problem solving capabilities. Refer to Figure 24 as I explain problem solving/learning organizations.

Most Organizations

Most organizations have the characteristics listed on the left side of the diagram:

Most Organizations	Problem Solving Organizations
Closed Communication	Open Communication
Use Blame	Use Dialogue
Focus on Behaviors	Focus on Systems
Individual Ambition	Teamwork
Career oriented	Mission Oriented

Figure 24: Problem Solving Organizations

Communication is typically closed because managers degrade open communication by minimizing employee contributions through shaming, blaming, and sometimes anger. Employees withhold useful information out of fear or spite and diminish the organization's ability to solve problems. Managers focus on employee behaviors instead of management intentions and the systems that create those behaviors. These organizations reward individual ambition instead of teamwork and make employees career oriented. Reintroducing teamwork takes culture change.

A quote from Dr. W. Edward Deming, the father of Total Quality Management (TQM from the 1960s) says it more succinctly:

"Our prevailing system of management has destroyed our people. People are born with intrinsic motivation, self-respect, dignity, curiosity to learn, joy in learning. The forces of destruction begin with toddlers — a prize for the best Halloween costume, grades in school, gold stars — and on up through the university. On the job, people, teams and divisions are ranked, rewarded for the top, punished for the bottom. Management by Objectives, quotas, incentive pay, business plans, put together separately, division by division, causes further loss, unknown and unknowable."

The prevailing system of management has certain characteristics. Not all are bad. They include:

- Management by Measurement
  - Focusing on short-term metrics
  - Devaluing intangibles (you can only measure about 3% of what matters)

- Compliance based Cultures
  - Getting ahead by pleasing the boss
  - Management by fear

- Management of Outcomes
  - *Management* sets targets
  - People are held accountable for meeting management targets (regardless of whether they are possible within existing systems and processes)

- Right Answer vs. Wrong Answer
  - Technical problem solving is emphasized
  - Diverging (systemic) problems are discounted

- Uniformity
  - Diversity is a problem to be solved
  - Conflict is suppressed in favor of superficial agreement

- Predictability and Controllability
  - To manage is to control
  - The "holy trinity of management" is planning, organizing, controlling

- Excessive Competitiveness and Distrust
  - Competition between people is essential to achieve desired performance
  - Without competition among people, there is no innovation

- Loss of the Whole
    - Fragmentation (of business segments, divisions, departments)
    - Local innovations do not spread beyond the local work group

It is the same system imbedded and socialized in our School Systems

- Teacher = Boss (they set the goals)
- Student = Employee (respond to the goals)
- Pleasing the boss does not fix the system
- Many individuals have felt that their interests and learning style do not fit the Prevailing System

Deming's Objective was the transformation of the Prevailing System, taking the system from a short-term performance focus to profound knowledge including:

- Understanding systems
- Theory of Knowledge (importance of mental models)
- Psychology (understanding motivation, vision, and genuine aspiration)

<u>Problem Solving/Learning Organizations</u>

The right side of Figure 24 is nearly the opposite of most organizations. Here, management models and encourages open communication, dialogue, systems thinking, and teamwork. It is mission oriented, and individuals are defined by the success of their teams.

As defined by Peter Senge in his book "The Fifth Discipline," learning organizations extend Deming's idea of "Profound Knowledge" and make it fundamental to the "Five Disciplines" of the Learning Organization. They can be found at the core of Senge's book and can be mapped into them. You will be reading all "The Fifth Discipline" as a preliminary to creating efficiency in your business, so I will explain the concepts only briefly. They include:

- Systems Thinking
- Personal Mastery
- Mental Models
- Building Shared Vision
- Team Learning

Systems Thinking illustrates how each part of a system has an influence on the rest. This can mean the functional areas of business such as marketing, finance, and operations but also includes causality relationships. Managers tend to focus on snapshots of isolated parts and make decisions in isolation without regard to the effect in other areas. Systems thinking illuminates all the parts and their interactions.

Personal Mastery represents a practical level of proficiency where you consistently realize results that matter most deeply to you, continually clarifying and deepening your *personal* vision. This is life as art, focusing your energies and developing patience as you become a more integrated person. You begin to see reality objectively in a non-reactive mindset. Most people do not find this encouraged in their organizations and live for their weekends.

Mental Models are deeply ingrained assumptions, generalizations, and images that influence how we understand the world and how we act. They are very often unconscious. In business, mental models can inhibit good decision making. Adaptation to a dynamic business environment depends on "institutional learning," changing the shared mental model. Changing mental models means holding them up for scrutiny and investing in open dialogue.

Building Shared Vision means holding a shared image of the future we seek to create. An organization needs a relevant mission, values, and goals to prosper, a mission relevant to the environment and the members of the organization, a common identity. Managers need to translate individual visions into a shared vision through a set of policies and guidelines and foster commitment rather than compliance.

Team Learning means developing extraordinary capacities for coordinated action. Here, teams are the fundamental leaning unit where individual members grow more rapidly than they could have alone. It starts with dialogue, suspending assumptions, and recognizing patterns of team interaction such as defensiveness. Team learning is a developmental path supported by skills and competencies in the five disciplines. You never fully arrive, rather, you are in a continual state of practice. Simply emulating a model is insufficient. It is a personal practice of discovery.

The "Five Disciplines" represent theories and methods for developing three core-learning capabilities:

- Fostering aspiration
- Developing reflective dialogue
- Understanding complexity

TASK (for you): Read *The Leader's Companion: Insights on Leadership Through the Ages*
Selection 38: Defining Organizational Culture
Selection 39: Strong Cultures: A New "Olde Rule" for Business Success

TASK (for you and your employees): Read "The Fifth Discipline" Chapters 1-7

The Systems Dialogue

Investing in a systems dialogue means when things go wrong, you talk about intentions and systems not the behaviors of your employees. Employees will feel involved, understand intentions behind changes, and commit to the solutions. In the previous chapter we discussed how intentions create systems, and systems create behaviors, so you need a place to practice this important skill. Practice is accomplished through group problem solving in systems redesign.

Group Problem Solving

Whenever I mention group problem-solving, I can see the cash register in my client's mind begin to calculate: How many hours, how much time, what will it cost me for all my employees to sit around a table for an hour; but the world changes too quickly for any one person to be effective in solving complex problems. Rapid change is a feature of our economic life, and the only effective countermeasure is to create problem solving teams. An example will help.

I had a client in the trades who was worried about his profit margin but could not make any progress. He wanted to incentivize sales through compensation but did not know how to motivate his employees. I convinced him to address the issue with group problem solving.

We began by inviting his three tradesmen to meet every Monday morning to discuss their work and how compensation might be used to reflect skill levels and incentivize skill development and productivity. We asked *them* because only they had the answers concerning what would motivate them. I gave the owner a goal of a 20% profit margin.

At each meeting we discussed how to make their work more efficient and created policies that would improve results without any additional incentives like never leaving the garage without a full set of tools and parts. We created a basic pay ladder based on skill and then turned to incentives. We discussed what was fair to measure and integrated incentives into the cashflow projecting, detailing minimum levels of productivity to remain employed and threshold for increased pay.

It took six months and a $15,000 consulting fee to complete the work. We tested it for one month and showed the employees what they could have done, then implemented the system. In the next month sales went from $55,000 to $95,000 and the profit margin rose from 5% to 20% as predicted. These were the same three employees but with an incentivized structure they helped create.

I will present a detailed example of incentive plans later under Strategic Compensation, but your next activity is Systems Redesign, and this is your opportunity to initiate Learning Organization principles.

TASK (for you): Read *Communicating for Results*
Chapter 9: Small Group Communication and Problem Solving

TASK (for you): Read *The Leader's Companion: Insights on Leadership Through the Ages*
Selection 46: Developmental Sequence in Small Groups

PRINCIPLE:
When solving problems talk about systems, not behaviors.
WHY:
Free of blame, your employees will apply themselves to the real issues and adopt a more effective point of view using productive language.

Efficiency

Most of the cost savings in your business, and your standard of living, come from efficiency improvements. In fact, the entire standard of living in the world is based on efficiency. Nations that can do things faster and better at a lower cost create excess value they can spend on other activities. That excess value could be extra time for your vacation, more products produced per week, more customers served in a single day, and much more.

The problem for entrepreneurs is that we do not think about *in*efficiencies until they are out of control, but we create them almost every time we make a decision. This happens because we create products and services without thinking through the processes needed to design, construct, market, support, and ship them.

Think about the service business that decides to sell tickets to local sporting events but does not consider how the tickets will be printed, spooled for easy disbursement, and credited for refunds. The first time each of these processes occur, someone is going to create a way to accomplish it, and it will *not* be efficient. The printing may be on the wrong thickness of paper causing handling problems, the way they are spooled may require two hands, instead of one, to rip off a single ticket, and refunds may require a phone call to the boss to figure out if it is valid and how the customer will be paid.

The processes and policies behind selling the tickets needed to be thought out before any had been produced. This is true for *everything* that flows through a business. If *you* do not design the flow, someone else will, and at the wrong time and in too big a hurry to get it right. Then you will have yourself and too many employees running an inefficient process you may never have time to reconsider.

Types of Systems

A system controls flow. People, paper, materials, and information flow through every business. It may be your customers or employees, invoices or checks, products or raw materials, computer files or Faxes and especially intensions, but something flows. It is up to you to identify all the items that flow through your business and consciously make them more efficient. You do this by making it a priority and then taking on one system at a time. If you have employees, the best time to do this is at a weekly staff meeting. If you are running your business alone, the best time is first thing in the morning, even if it is only for half an hour.

You have probably heard other entrepreneurs say that they spend so much time working *in* the business they have no time to work *on* the business. Systems redesign is working *on* the business and if you do not accomplish this important work, you will never free up your time and maximize your cash flow. Your entire focus will remain *in* the business.

Product/Process Redesign

Product/process redesign is not rocket science, it is common sense, and you should not be afraid of it. It is easier and more fun than the accounting you have been working on and has visible results. You can watch the process in motion and make changes to its moving parts. Process systems are usually stepwise transformations that add value with each step like assembling a product.

Causality Redesign

Unlike a process system that you can watch operating before you, causality systems have unintended results distant in time. Causality redesign is concerned with identifying and changing intentions. In the next section we will take each of these types of systems and redesign them.

Facilitation of Systems Redesign

You have, hopefully, facilitated many discussions by this point in your business development, and systems redesign is no different, but it is easier in some ways because it has a very clear stepwise structure. Remember you are creating a Practice Field for dialogue. The ground rules include:

- Having all team members (system employees) present
- Using dialogue versus discussion (see "The Fifth Discipline")

- Suspending assumptions
- Encouraging the raising of difficult issues

The activities of previous chapters have been constructed to prepare you for this moment.

TASK: Read "The Fifth Discipline" (Chapters 8-11)

TASK: Read Appendix F, LEAN Principles

Systems Redesign: Process Systems

The failure of many business plans, and businesses in general, lies in the fact that they have outlined all the concepts for success but not translated those concepts into effective, usable systems. For example, in the construction business everyone understands that they may eventually have to file a construction lien against a customer who refuses to pay them. That is the concept. But how many owners of these businesses have the paperwork on-hand, know how to file the lien, and understand the important time limits set by the courts? Not many, until they lose a substantial amount of money dragging themselves slowly through the process for the first time only to miss the filing deadline by one day. A well-organized system would have allowed them to file the lien on the first day the customer refused to pay.

When small business owners fail to create systems, they leave efficiency in the hands of whoever has to complete a particular task for the first time. It may be a clerk asked to take inventory without an inventory system, or a salesperson faced with their first big customer without a sales system, or the owner asked to grant credit without a credit policy and collections system.

What I want you to do is redesign systems in your business. As you work through each system, you will gain skill and your business will gain efficiency, and with skill and efficiency comes additional increments of profit.

Some processes you might consider for your first redesign include:

- Telephone answering
- Scheduling
- Customer relationship management
- Production

To complete the process of redesigning a system you must:

1) Form the Redesign Team
2) Understand how the systems works now.
3) Draw your process map
4) Draw your value stream map
5) Draw your spaghetti diagram and current space plan
6) Redesign the process with new space plan
7) Document the system
8) Avoid implementation problems
9) Maintain oversight

I will use a Case Study in systems redesign: a business manufacturing kits to illustrate the process but before we begin, make sure you read **Appendix F: LEAN Principles** to get you oriented to the process and terminology of efficiency.

Step 1: Form the Redesign Team

The redesign team must consist of everyone who is involved with or affected by the current process: whomever "touches" the process. In a small business this will be you and *all* your employees or you and the one employee responsible for the process, like the bookkeeper for accounting.

In your first staff meeting get everyone who works in the business together teach them LEAN thinking. Then, identify *all* the important processes. Prioritize them according to how costly or time consuming they are, then start at the top of the list and begin forming your teams. Take on only one process at a time for each team. This might take several hours just for this step, so allocate the time.

Step 2: Understand How the System Works Now

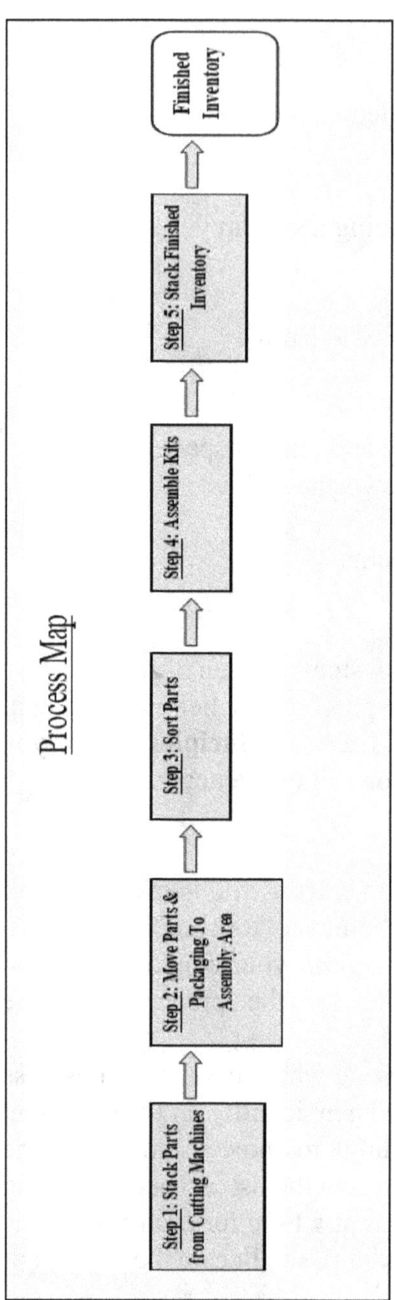

Figure 25: Process Map

To understand how the system works you need to list the steps in the current sequence, and the tasks within those steps. Gather your team and begin on a whiteboard or with sticky notes on a wall. This is an iterative process, meaning you must talk through the process many times to get it right.

Step 3: Draw Your Process Map

With this basic information you can draw your process map. I use Publisher or Excel and project the map onto a screen so everyone can participate. Refer to Figure 25 as I explain the production process for the sample company.

The process begins with moving parts from the cutting machines and stacking them in a holding area. The parts are then moved along with packaging to the assembly areas where they are then sorted in stacks, so the assemblers have easy access to each part. Kits are assembled by two assemblers and stored at their stations. Finally, finished packages are moved into inventory.

This process seems reasonable and efficient but needs data to understand each step.

Step 4: Draw Your Value Stream Map

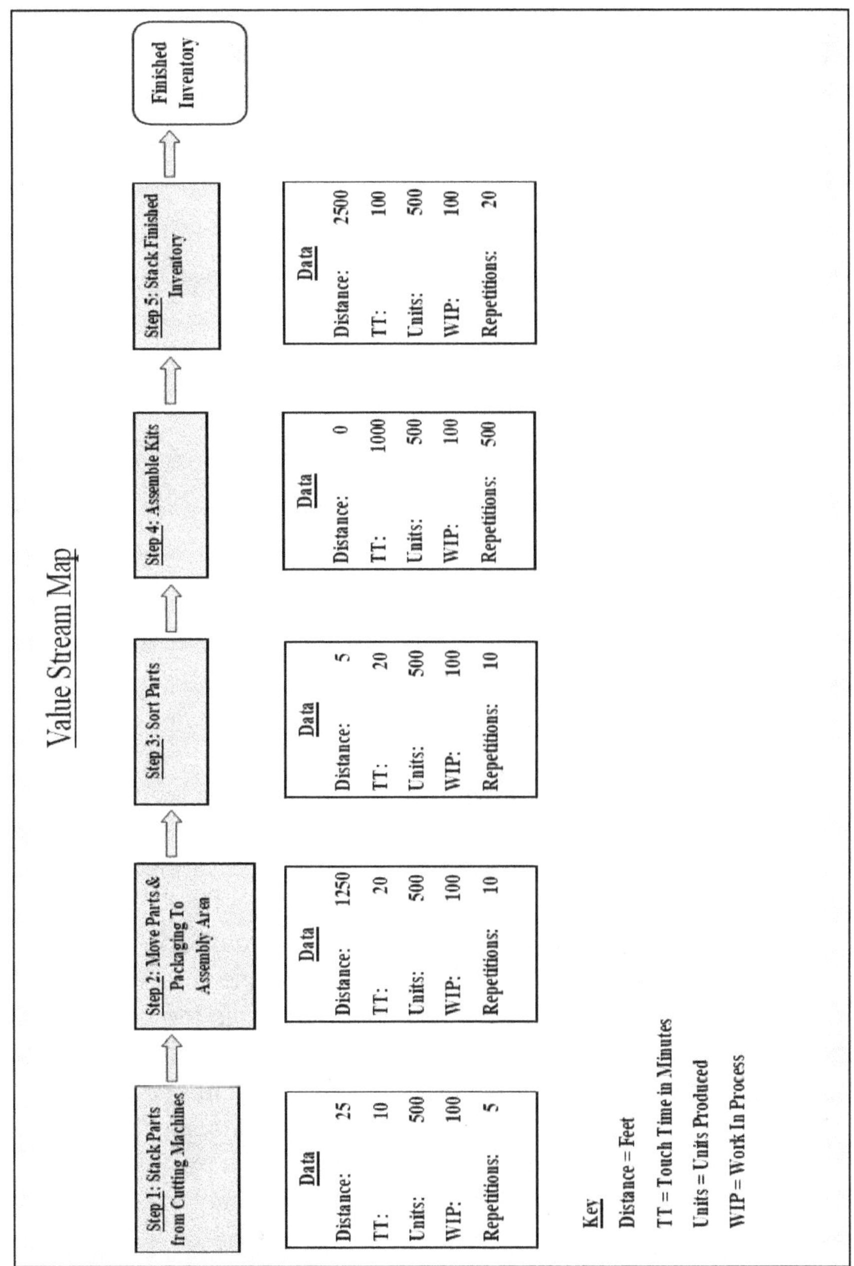

Figure 26: Value Stream Map

The purpose of the value stream map is to measure the process and identify where value is being lost. You can measure many variables but try to pick the ones that are meaningful. Examples include:

- Distance traveled
- Touch time (TT)
- Units produced
- Work in process (WIP)
- Repetitions
- Number of people
- Space used
- Rejects produced

In our example we will use the metrics below for production of 500 units:

- Total distance traveled for product components
- Total touch time (time manipulating the product by people)
- Total units in production
- Total work in process (a snapshot of product not yet in finished inventory)
- Repetitions (the number of times an action is repeated)

We list the metrics under each step and begin to look for waste. Refer to Figure 26 as the data collected is explained. Distance in feet traveled seems to vary widely and present some large numbers. Touch times seem reasonable for assembly but seem excessive for stacking finished inventory. Units in production is the goal of 500 but work in process looks high. Repetitions are hard to evaluate without connecting them to some other metric. The Value Stream Map seems to have costs accruing in distance, time, and repetitions but no clear cause. We can find causes for this data by observing the process and drawing a spaghetti diagram with space plan.

Step 5: Draw Your Spaghetti Diagram and Current Space Plan

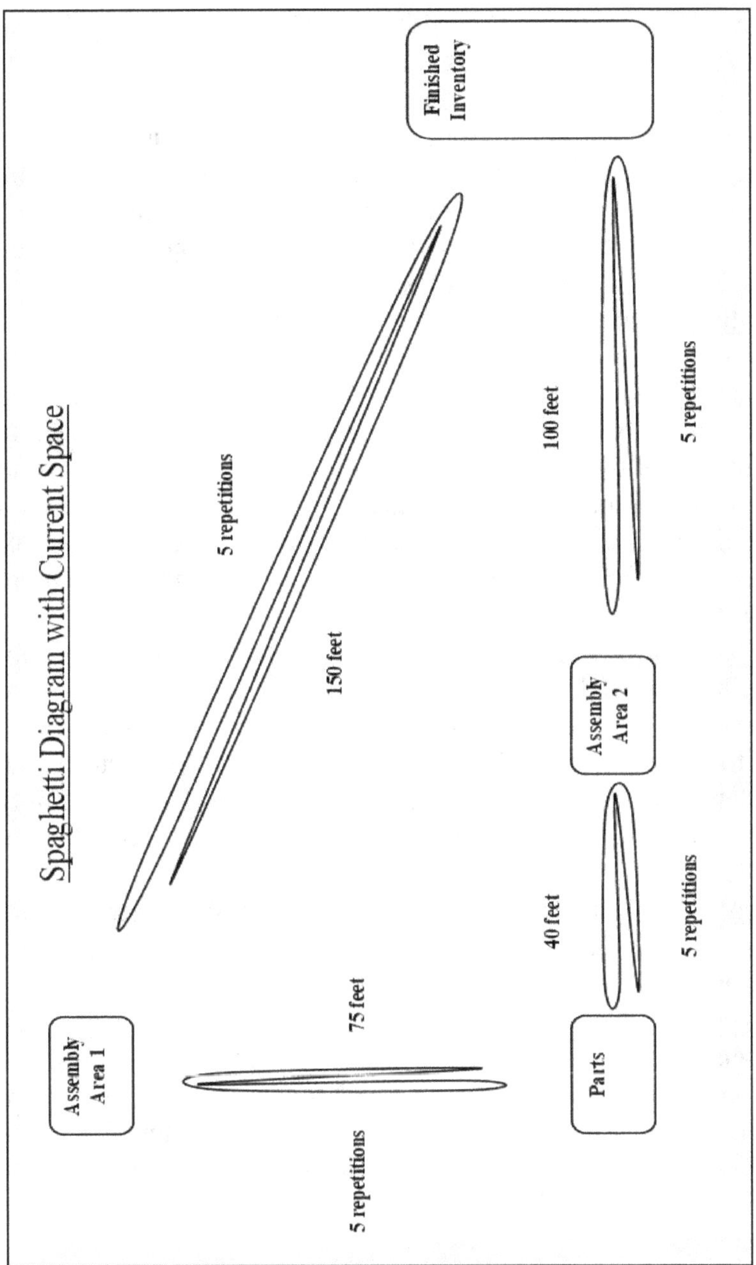

Figure 27: Spaghetti Diagram with Current Space Plan

The spaghetti diagram with current space plan reveals multiple wastes. Refer to Figure 27 as the spaghetti diagram is explained. The squiggly lines represent repetitions. Distances traveled and repetitions for that travel are identified.

Waiting: Components for assembly were hard to manage. This occurred in a 10,000 square foot warehouse and the distances were overlarge. I've simplified the space plan, but clutter and industrial shelving for other inventory impeded travel between parts, assembly areas, and finished inventory. Because finished inventory stacked up in assembly areas, work in process remained high.

Non-utilized talent: The division of assembly areas caused a doubling of distances in travel and the ad hoc assembly areas with insufficiently organized storage for parts caused the assemblers multiple instances of travel to get resupplied. Parts were sorted in different places by the assemblers, causing a complex activity to interrupt their assembly work, instead of sorting in one place by a dedicated employee who could feed them parts. The placement of assembly areas far from the finished inventory storage caused more travel and further interrupted assembly.

Transportation: Assembly work had no personnel support for moving kits, so each assembler had to transport finished goods to inventory multiple times, further interrupting their work. This caused the assembly of each kit to take 2 minutes to complete, a total of 1,000 minutes for 500 units. Distances to move parts to assembly areas equaled 75 feet time 5 repetitions plus 40 feet time 5 for a total of 575 feet traveled and caused more delays.

Motion: The motion identifies people moving from one place to another. The two assembly areas were far apart and resulted from the two assemblers preferring quiet spaces they could call their own. The owners granted them their preference but they each set up ad hoc assembly stations on desks without oversight.

You may think I am inventing this example to make a point, but it was a real company and the problems evolved incrementally as the business grew because the owner left systems development to individuals without a global perspective on the process or training in systems redesign.

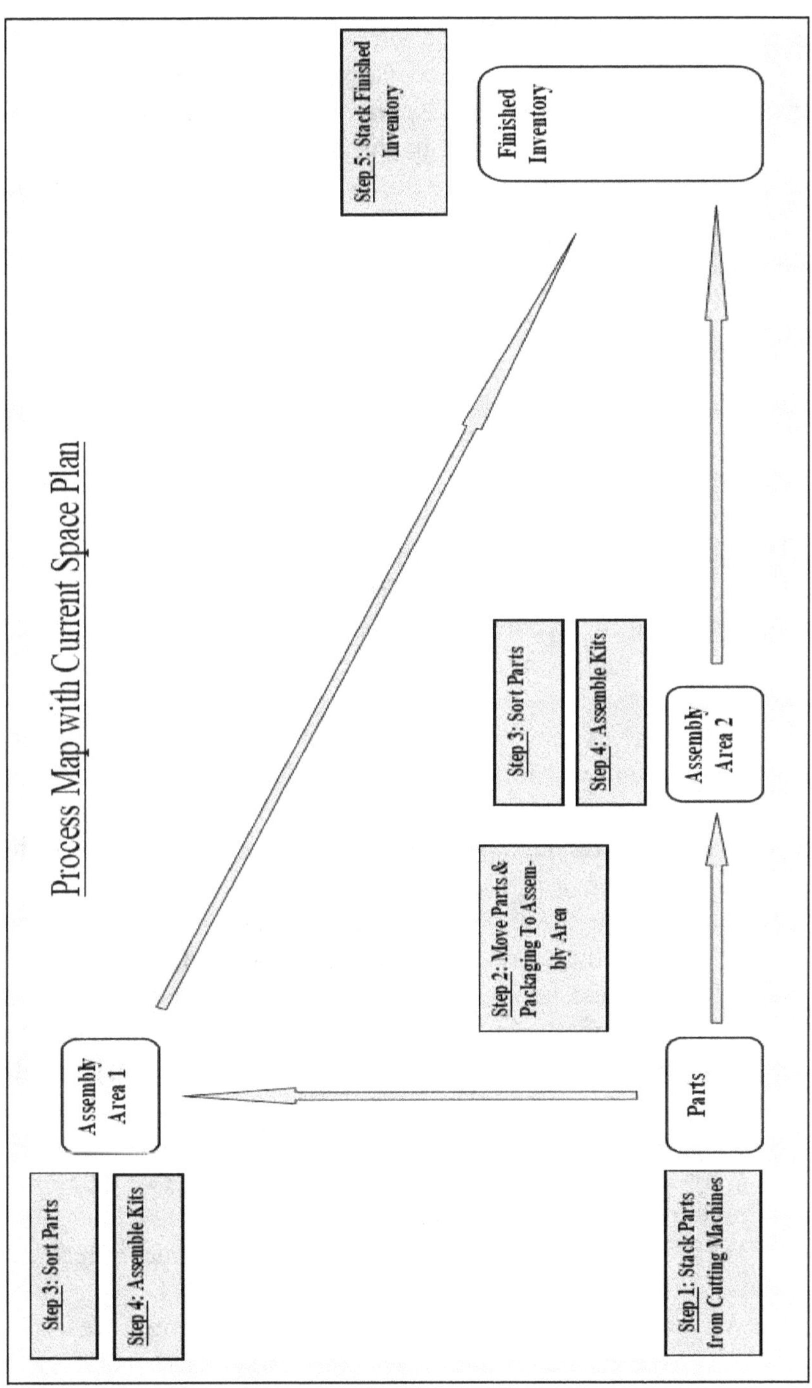

Figure 28: Process Map with Current Space Plan

The data begins to make sense when you combine the spaghetti diagram with the value stream map and space plan. The process map with current space plan (Figure 28) provides additional information. You can see the steps outlined in the dark boxes and the arrows leading to each step, but they are not as linear as they appear in the Process Map. Step 1 is the same but Steps 2 and 3 are duplicated due to the separation of assembly areas.

Step 6: Question Assumptions: What *Should* the System Do?

In your next meeting with the redesign team some basic questions should be answered:

1) Is the process connected to the Mission Statement?
2) Is the process efficient?
3) What intentions informed the old system?
4) What intentions will inform the redesign?
5) Have you minimized your chosen metrics. In this example: distance, touch time, WIP, and repetitions?

We assume part of the owner's mission was to maximize profit, but the old intentions focused on the volume of sales without addressing pricing and efficiency. The root cause of this is a lack of skill in marketing, finance, and operations and a lack of interest in learning new skills.

Part of the root cause is that the entrepreneur does not perceive the need for skill until there is a crisis; part is due to being overly busy due to inefficiencies; but the most troublesome cause is that the owner does not validate new knowledge. You can trace the source of any problem by asking "why" five times and giving yourself answers.

1) Why is the system inefficient? Because distance and repetitions cause excessive costs.
2) Why did we not perceive excessive costs sooner? Because we were overly busy.
3) Why were we overly busy? Because we were afraid we could not cover our new warehouse costs and focused on sales.
4) Why did we focus on sales? We did not understand systems and the importance of efficiency.

5) Why did we not understand systems? We thought we already knew everything we needed to know and did not validate the acquisition of new skills and knowledge.

With this new information you can consciously change your intention to: we value new skills and knowledge and will continuously train ourselves and our employees to solve new problems.

Other sources of inefficiency included: too many process steps in stacking, sorting, and moving parts; disorganized parts storage in assembly areas; and too many activities for assemblers.

Investigate all the assumptions that caused *your* systems to be inefficient.

Step 7: Redesign the Process with New Space Plan

This is where you can apply the LEAN principles of eliminating waste in defects, over-production, waiting, non-utilized talent, transportation, inventory, motion, and processing; and gain the benefits of applying Sigma 6 principles when you sort, safe, straighten, scrub, standardize, and sustain.

The redesign process follows the sequence below:

- Use Sigma 6 to order the clutter and clean up the workspace
- Place the process steps in the right order
- Place tasks in the most efficient sequence in each step
- Apply LEAN Principles (Appendix F)
    - Reduce distances and processing time
    - Standardize
    - Simplify (Least motion, fewest moving parts, fewest steps
    - Quality control at each process step
- Create an efficient space plan
- Use technologies to automate for efficiency
- Create jobs that fit the process
- Cross-train employees
- Set minimum levels of productivity
- Create incentives for higher productivity

Figure 29 shows the new process map with new space plan. The first and easiest solution was to move the work and storage areas closer together. With this accomplished, it was clear that parts needed to be sorted and stored in one step. Purpose built assembly stations and parts racks were built so parts could be loaded directly within reach of assemblers. Assemblers placed 500 finished kits on a purpose-built dolly within their reach that would be moved only once into the finished inventory.

Assemblers no longer had to leave their stations and had only one task: to assemble kits, reducing their assembly time from two minutes to one minute. You can also see it is easy to add multiple assembly areas to feed the finished inventory rack and that the entire process has changed from five steps to three.

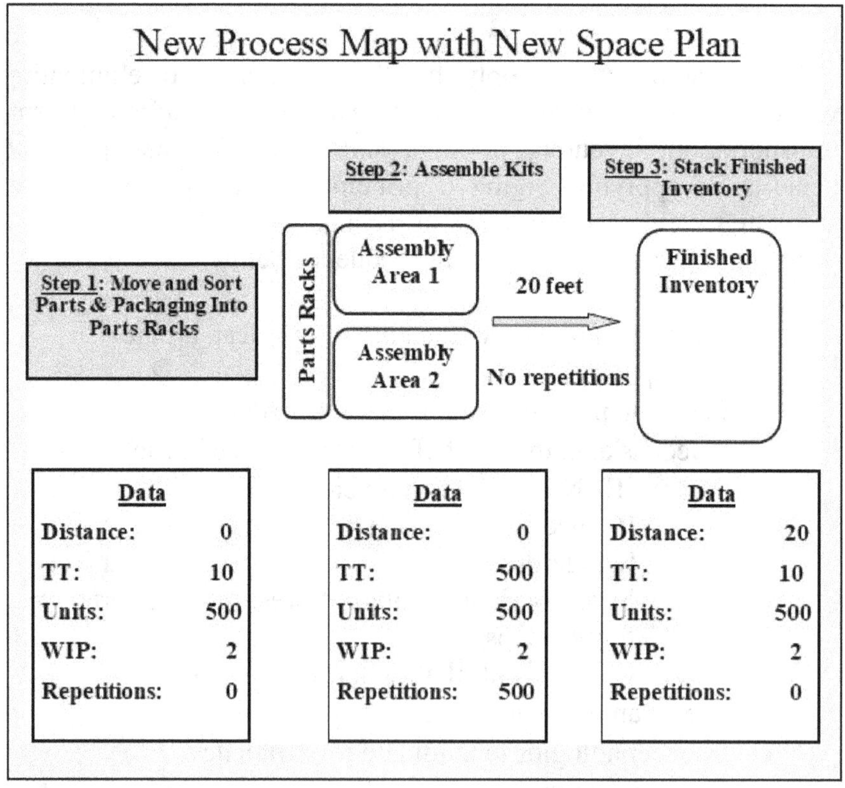

Figure 29: New Process Map with New Space Plan

Figure 30 shows the metrics for the old and new systems.

Metric	Old System	New System
Total Distance	3650	20
Touch Time	1150	520
Units Produced	500	500
WIP	100	2
Repetitions		
• Move Parts	20	0
• Move Inventory	20	0

Figure 30: System Metrics

This represented a radical reduction in all metrics and amounted to more than a 400% increase in productivity without even calculating the cost savings in labor. With the systems finished you need to broaden your dialogue beyond the system boundary, that is, outside the department, outside the business, with anyone who connects with the beginning or the end of the process to make sure you create a system that connects with other efficient systems.

Step 8: Document the System

Now you have an efficient system, but you cannot maintain that efficiency without documenting the following:

- Policies
- Procedures
- Control Forms
- Technologies

Policies state what you will and won't do in your business. Procedures outline the detail for the tasks in each process step and for completing each task in the most efficient way. Documentation means writing it all down in mini operations manuals and placing it in your planning notebook.

The goal is to create many of these manuals to assist you and your employees in completing work in the most effective way possible. Each system (mini manual) should start at the top of a page and have the following organization:

- Page1:
  - Title of the System
  - Policies
  - Procedures
- Page 2: Process or Value Stream Map
- Page 3: Step Form (step by step tasks and procedures)
- Page 4: Control Forms (forms, contracts, etc.)
- Page 5: Technologies

The pages for our sample system appear below.

Page 1: Title Page and Policies

Kit Production System Manual

Policies:

1) All warehouse employees must:
   a. Be trained on the Kit Production System
   b. Read the Kit Production System Manual
   c. Attend the Daily Production Huddle before production begins.
2) Systems Oversight Meetings will be held monthly.
3) No change can be made in the system without signoff by all employees.

Procedures:

1) Follow the Process Diagram and Step Forms
2) See next page for Process Diagram

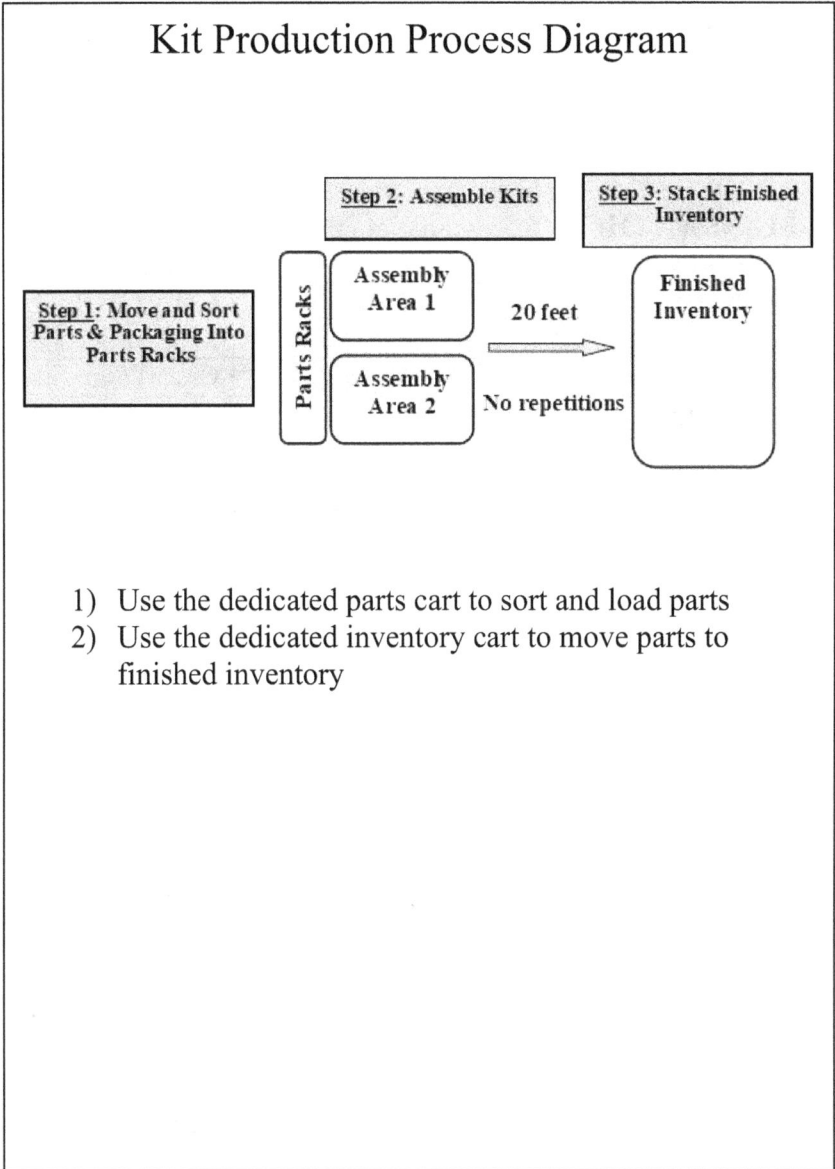

Page 2: Process Diagram

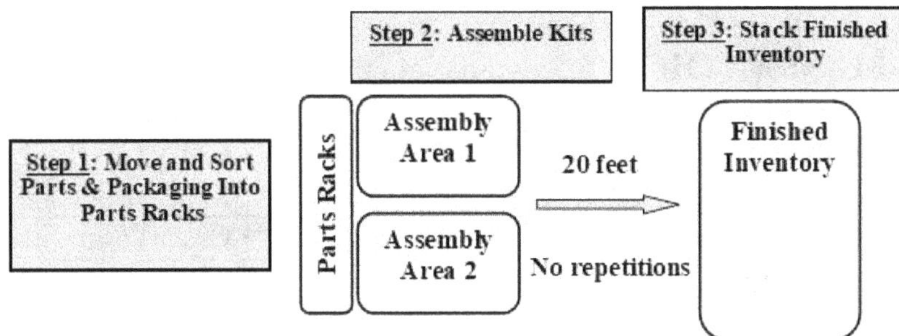

1) Use the dedicated parts cart to sort and load parts
2) Use the dedicated inventory cart to move parts to finished inventory

Page 3: Step Form

Step 1: Move and Sort Parts & Packaging Into Parts Racks

PARENT SYSTEM: Kit Production Process
PURPOSE: Move parts to assembly area
BEGINS WITH: Load parts into parts cart
ENDS WITH: Return parts cart to cutting room

TASKS:	**WHO IS RESPONSIBLE:**	**CONTROL FORM:**
Load parts cart	Warehouse 1	Order Form
Move parts to assembly	Warehouse 1	
Load parts racks	Warehouse 1	
Track defects	Warehouse 1	Defects Form
Return parts cart to cutting room	Warehouse 1	
CUSTOMER RELATIONS ACTIVITIES:	None	

REPORT OUTPUTS:	**WHO IS RESPONSIBLE:**	**REPORTS SENT TO:**
Defects	Warehouse 1	Production Manager
MEASUREMENT:		
Time with stopwatch	Warehouse 1	Production Manager

Page 4: Control Forms

Production Order Form

Kit #	Quantity	Due Date	Instructions

Defects Form

Kit #	Part#	Quantity	Defect

Pre-production Meeting Form

Team Leader:
Attendees:

Item	Result
Updates	
Problems	
Current Orders	
Staff Needs	
Goals	

Visual Aids

Team Leader:
Team:
Location:

Item	Detail
Metrics	
Time	
Workflow	
Updates	
Improvement Actions	
Customer Feedback	

Visual Aids are typically whiteboards placed in a location where team members can see it and make changes as needed.

Page 5: Technologies

You will have to decide what technologies you will use to make the system efficient. If you use computer files provide the path to access the tech.

Path: Google Drive > Production Docs > Production system
ID: Myself
Pass: 1234!

Screen shots are useful for instruction.

Step 9: Avoid Implementation Problems

You have already trained your employees in basic skill sets but you need to continue that training with pre-production meetings to reinforce the skills and create oversight and prevent old habits from reemerging.

Use visual aids in the production space like whiteboards to organize activities and update important information.

Step 10: Maintain Oversight/Continuous Improvement

In addition to pre-production meetings, you need to create feedback and review meetings that create oversight and institutionalize the process. You can designate a portion of your weekly staff meetings to systems redesign and follow the PDSA continuous improvement diagram in Figure 31.

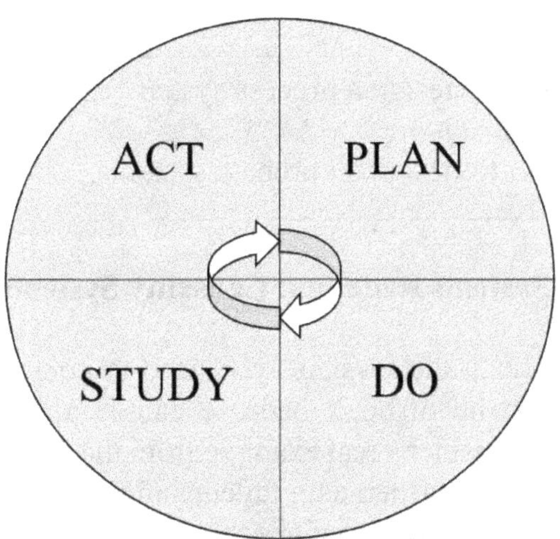

Figure 31: LEAN Continuous Improvement

The diagram is a circle because you are in a never-ending pursuit of efficiency as you:

- PLAN: Set objectives and develop a plan
- DO: Execute the plan and gather data
- STUDY: Analyze data and determine results
- ACT: Adjust the system and standardize

You will automatically spread your knowledge to other systems and other areas of your business. This may seem overly elaborate for a small business, but it saves time and money, especially when there is employee turnover, and you must teach the system to a new individual. Without the system documentation and oversight, your new employee will create their *own* system.

With each system you complete, you will create efficiency and increase your capacity. This capacity can be applied to creating more products, services and sales which create a higher profit margin.

PRINCIPLE:
Systems require frequent oversight.
WHY:
Without oversight, current employees will revert to old inefficient habits. New employees will create their own inefficient systems.

TASK: Redesign a process system using group problem solving
TASK: Redesign all process systems

Systems Redesign: Causality Systems

To redesign a causality system, you need to connect results with causes. This can be difficult because causes and results can be distant in time. Consider a real example from the last century in New York State when an earthen dam failed, and many lives were lost. You can use the "5 Whys" to make the connections.

1) Why did the dam fail? Because the structure was altered.
2) Why was the structure altered? Because the top was cut down to make a road.
3) Why was the road constructed on the dam? Wealthy landowners wanted easy access to their property without paying for a bridge.

4) Why wasn’t a bridge constructed? Because a bridge was expensive and dam inspectors were bribed to approve the dam alteration.
5) How could inspectors be bribed? Because a lack of public policy, oversight, and felony laws were not in place.

You can see this process of asking questions leads us back to the intentions that enabled the disaster to occur. Once you have identified the cause, you can create a process system to control it with policies, procedures, and even penalties. Draw a causality diagram like Figure 32.

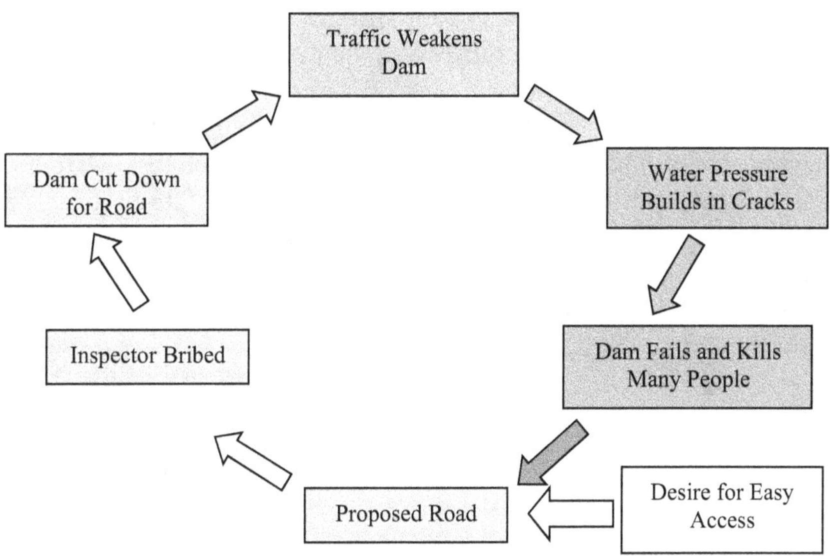

Figure 32: Causality Diagram

Capacity: Space Planning and Reducing Square Footage

Do not just fill the space you have. Make the most efficient space plan you can and then find the right amount of space in the right location. Also don't wait to make the decision to lower your square footage. It is one of the major costs you incur every month and reducing it will put cash back in your pocket. But choose wisely. Try to rent out some of your space before you make a final decision on moving. See a more comprehensive discussion of location in **Chapter 4**.

Organization Chart and Job Tasks

As you create systems and incorporate personnel into their design you can begin to draw your organizational chart and list all the tasks for each position. The object is to find additional inefficiencies in the way job tasks have been assigned, or more likely, have evolved by chance. This is important even if there are only two people in your business because it makes you conscious of how little time you have spent thinking about it.

In one case, this simple method saved a small software company $50,000 for one hour's worth of drawing. This company was facing expansion due to a high demand for their consulting and programming services. All their programmers were at 100% capacity with code writing duties and the management was ready to hire another programmer, at $60,000 per year, to take on the additional work. When we drew the organizational chart, listed each person's tasks, and how much time they spent on each task we found that the four programmers were spending 40% of their time on clerical work! The obvious solution was to hire a part time clerical person at $10,000 per year and free up the programmers for code writing — a savings of $50,000.

Strategic Compensation

Just as in a market for products and services you compete for your employees in the labor market. So, some questions need to be asked:

- Have you created a business that can afford the best employees?
- Is your offering superior to other employers?
- Have you analyzed compensation?
- Is there housing in your county where employees can live?

If you have completed the tasks outlined so far, you will be ready to address these issues in strategic compensation. According to Joseph J. Martocchio there are seven steps to creating a pay structure.[3]

- Decide on the number of steps in the skill ladder
- Determine a market pay line for each skill
- Define pay ranges for each skill level
- Testing
- Create internal consistency
- Create personnel policy manual
- Create productivity measures and incentive pay

We will use a trades contractor as our example.

Your Skill Ladder

The first task in strategic compensation is to determine the number of steps in your skill ladder. Think of this as a way of defining increasing levels of skill but also as a way for your employees to advance in your business, a path they can follow for their own success. You can have as many steps as you want but they should spell out in detail the skill, certifications, time, and training the employee needs to attain each step. You will publish this in your personnel policy manual so your employees can work with

---

3 Joseph J. Martocchio, *Strategic Compensation*, (Boston: Pearson, 2015)

confidence toward their own advancement if they follow your plan.

Eventually this will include job descriptions, duties, and performance evaluation to match each position. I use a spreadsheet as in Figure 33 to model the ladder because I can easily place steps

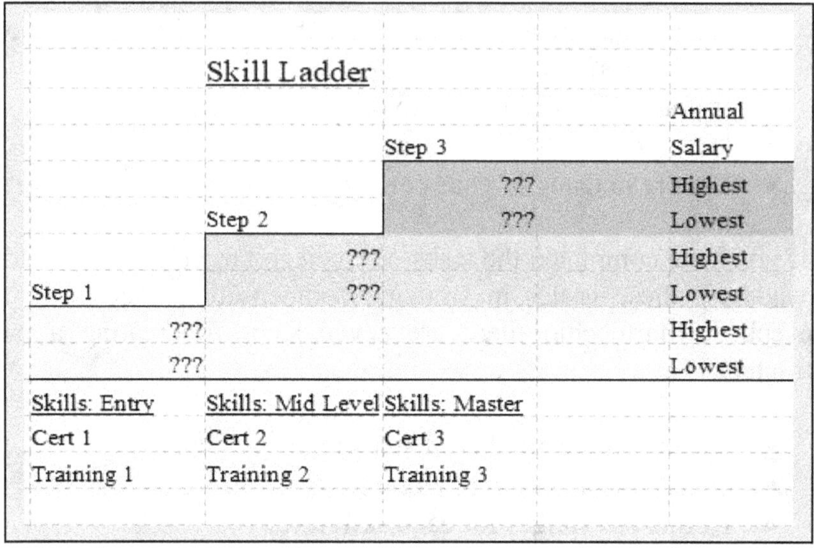

Figure 33: Skill Ladder Without Salary

in ascending cells and manipulate the math. This is only a rough approximation, not the finished system, but it gives you a place to store data and begin to list certifications and training you believe represent the requirements of each step.

Start with your employees and list their specific skills and skill levels. In our example the business owner has identified three levels: entry, mid-level, and master. The employees already have pay differentials but the method of determining pay has been informal and based on what the owner believes they deserve, not on research.

TASK: Create a Skill Ladder in Excel

Market Pay Line

The next task is to identify the market pay line for this job in your business. Some data may already exist in your industry or be identified by your state employment agencies. In the State of Washington where I live, they are the Employment Security Department and Labor and Industries. Both collect data on employment trends. Find the median pay for your location at each skill level. Plot the market pay line for each skill level as in Figure 34 and place your pay for each skill level in the graph. For our sample business you can see the entry level is higher than the

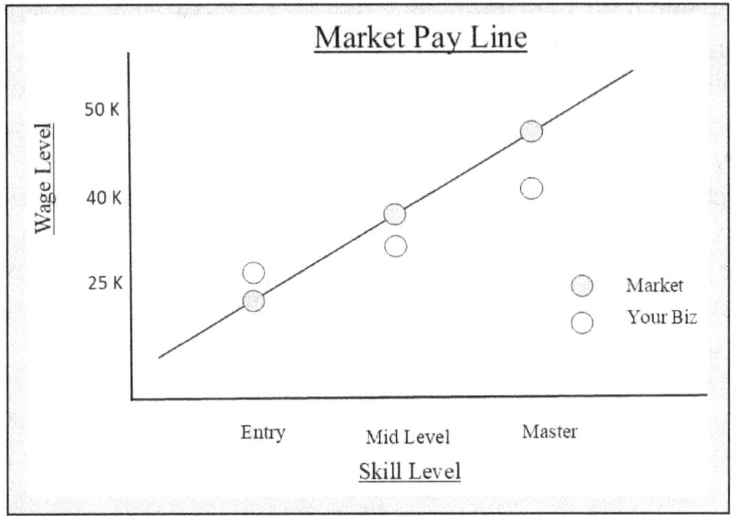

Figure 34: Market Pay Line

market, but mid and master levels are lower. To keep the best employees, you need to be above the market pay line in every category. You will be able to afford this premium by running an excellent business with pricing, efficiency, and volume better than your competition and motivate good employees not to look elsewhere for better pay.

TASK: Research and Create a Market Pay Line in Excel

Skill Blocks and Pay Ranges

Your next task is to create skill blocks and pay ranges. Your industry may already have skill block norms like apprentice, journeyman, and master. You need to create a graph like Figure 35 that represents skill on the horizontal axis and pay ranges on the vertical axis. The blocks must not overlap. You get to decide how broad the range is from lowest pay in the category to highest, but it must make sense for the market, the employee's career path, and a living wage. Ask other businesses in your area with similar skill requirements. This is your competition for labor and it's worth knowing how they think but they may be wrong. Check rents, mortgages, and housing prices in your area. An employee's rent should be 25% to 30% of their take-home pay. If you believe you cannot create a 20% profit margin *and* pay your employees what they are worth, you have more work to complete.

Determine where your proposed pay ranges fall on the market pay line. Adjust the ranges so each range is mostly above the market pay line. With this information you can complete the pay ladder on your compensation spreadsheet as outlined in Figure 36. Your concept of adequate pay may change many times before you settle on a workable system so don't be in a hurry.

You might think this is too much work for the lowest level employees but remember the most capable individuals, even at the

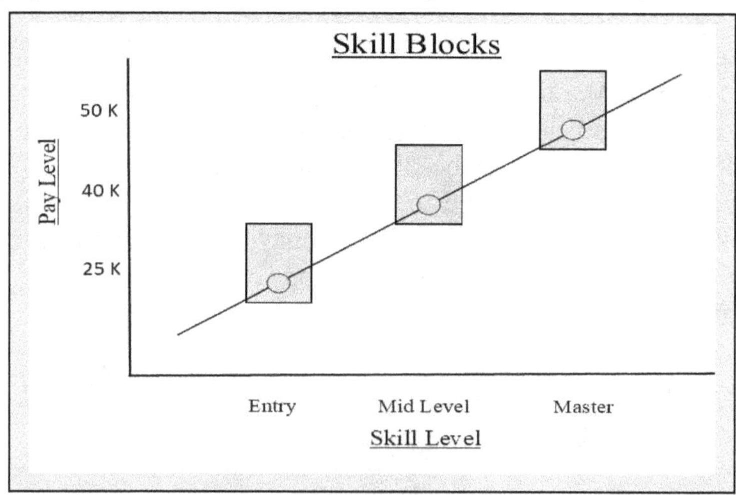

Figure 35: Skill Blocks and Pay Ranges

entry level, quit first, and you don't want to be left only with the ones who can't help you prosper.

You must now begin defining each skill level in detail with job descriptions, duties, required certifications, years of experience, training, and any other characteristic you believe a competent employee must possess. You may find some of your employees lack important skills or have lapsed certifications. You can address the simplest issues as you find them, but the real process begins with your first systems redesign meeting for compensation that includes your employees. They should be comfortable with systems redesign and be able to contribute to the data collection. They will also have

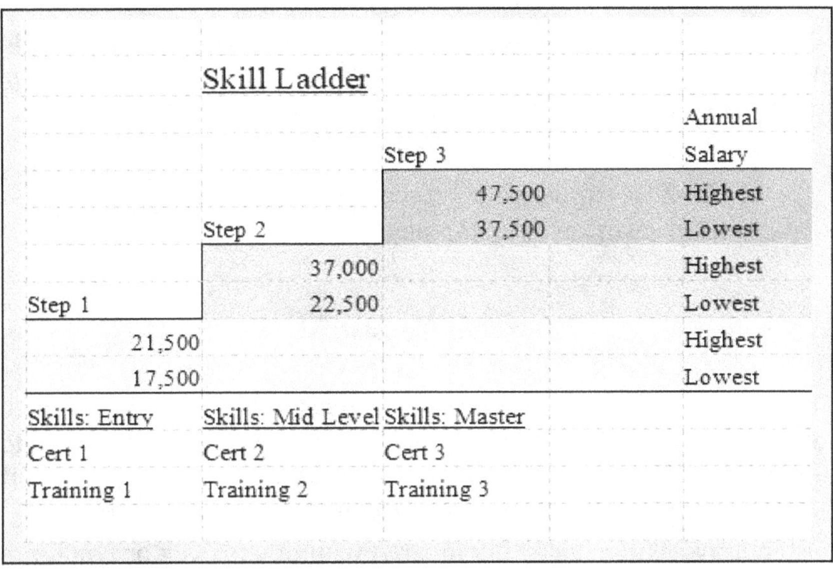

Figure 36: Skill Ladder with Salaries

opinions about a livable wage and benefits. Be clear that you are not committing to specific pay ranges yet but are in the process of defining how your business will incorporate competitive pay as a strategy.

Your model of compensation will change many times and each variable must be manipulated to obtain the result where employees are satisfied, everyone is effective, and you have a high profit margin.

TASK: Create Skill Blocks and Pay Ranges
TASK: Place Salaries in the Skill Ladder

Testing

You begin testing your compensation assumptions by adjusting your project costing system and your cashflow projection. In the project costing system, adjust your overhead and direct labor costs. In the cashflow, adjust your payroll. You may find initially that you have a lower profit margin but if you have been diligent about creating efficiency you still have pay levels, pricing, volume, and incentive pay to move your profit margin higher. Run multiple scenarios by changing each of these variables to find the right mix.

TASK: Adjust your Project Costing System and cashflow projections to find the best profit

Internal Consistency

Internal consistency means determining the relative value of each job among *all* jobs. Responsibilities, complexity, training, and experience all play a part in determining what any individual needs to be paid to keep them in your business. They also need to see that their relative skill is valued compared with others. Key or lynch-pin skills may receive higher pay even over highly educated individuals. The new owners of one business thought that they were being clever when they fired the oldest engineer, thinking they would save money by hiring younger graduates. They forgot that the company's products were based on the patents that the older engineer owned in full. He simply raised the royalty rates and clawed back his entire salary in retirement. Valuing employees under all circumstances is a good policy.

Personnel Policy Manual

Now is the moment to create your personnel policy manual and begin to document your policies but you do not have to write one yourself. There are several software programs on the market that have complete policy manuals for download. Typically, they have two or three alternative policies for each subject area. You choose the one that suits you, do a little editing, and delete the rest. Going through one of these software packages top to bottom makes you aware of all the issues you need to consider in providing a good working environment while at the same time organizing the behavior of your employees, but it saves you the trouble of creating it from nothing.

You can add your items for career paths, productivity, and incentive pay but don't put the termination policy in print. If you write it down in your manual, you are required to follow it. An employee who has been terminated can file a wrongful termination lawsuit or labor relations board complaint and claim you did not follow your own policy.

TASK: Create your Personnel Policy Manual

Compensation of Sales Personnel

Sales is a special case in compensation. Individuals making their career in sales need to be motivated to perform at the level the business requires, not excessive but still challenging. Not everyone is wired to be a successful salesperson. Introverts are typically not as good as extraverts. Your sale force must be self-motivated people who respond well to incentives so a compensation scheme for them must have two components: base pay and sales commission.

No business can afford to pay a salesperson for very long without producing sales, so you must create a system with declining compensation until they self-terminate. Refer to Figure 37 as I explain. First determine what pay level good salesperson should have. Research the market pay line for these positions. In our graph I have set this at $50,000.

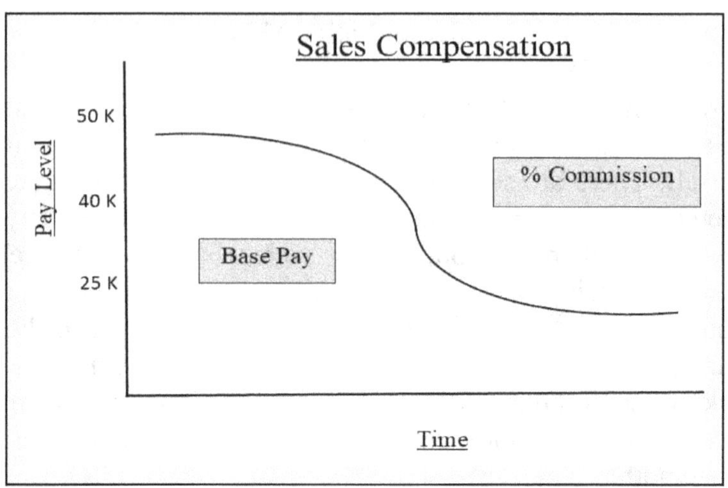

Figure 37: Sales Compensation Graph

You divide the new employee's compensation into base pay and commission. Initially the base pay portion is larger than the commission because the new hire needs time to understand the products and the market. The base pay is set at less than the full $50,000 so they have an incentive to be productive.

Over time the base pay is reduced so that the employee must make up most of their compensation in commissions. The base pay is your investment in the individual and there is no way to avoid it but it must end if they cannot make sales. How much time you give them is based on your understanding of the market, whether you have a sales training system and sales manual in place, whether you have already developed your customer base, and what you believe you could accomplish in the same position. The commission percentage is tested in your project costing system and cashflows, so it is integrated into the strategy for the whole business and creates a 20% profit margin.

Commissions may also change over time. The ease of making a sale in each category of sales may either overcompensate an employee's efforts or motivate them to sell only in one area. You should reassess the compensation percentages regularly to motivate sales in critical categories.

TASK: Create your Sales Compensation Graph

Setting Policy and Maintaining Changes

As in all areas of your business, you must maintain compensation policies with oversight, feedback, and systems redesign meetings. Make compensation discussions a part of your staff meetings at least once a year and you will maintain your competitive advantage in your industry.

Productivity Measures and Incentive Pay

Beyond the 20% Profit Margin

You may have reached a 20% profit margin through your project costing system, cashflow projections, and systems redesign but more profit is available to you through incentive pay. People are motivated by self-interest, and we all calculate the best value for the time we spend working, and we all respond to various incentives. Some individuals want time, some money, and others a lifestyle.

Your job is to find out what motivates your employees to higher levels of productivity and create a system that rewards that effort but also creates new profits for yourself.

Creating challenging goals is the first step. No one should be bored at work or have time on their hands. Most professional managers are constantly busy with productive activities: management, marketing, educating their employees, operating the accounting system, and solving any problem that may arise. Many work longer than 40 hours per week.

Productivity Measures

Business productivity is defined as: how many units, dollars, or profit you create over a given period. The most important measures of your productivity are your Profit Margin and Return on Equity (ROE.)

$$\text{Profit Margin} = \frac{\text{Net Income}}{\text{Sales}}$$

$$\text{ROE} = \frac{\text{Net Income}}{\text{Equity}}$$

Both measures show you how your business is performing overall and how changes to your pricing, efficiency, and volume result in more profit.

Employee productivity is defined as: how many units, dollars, or profit an employee produces over a given period. The measures are almost always compared to a standard. See examples below comparing employee outputs to various standards:

Dollars Per Service Hour:	$175/$250	=	70%
Dollars Per Day:	$1050/$1350	=	77%
Units Produced Per Day:	475/500	=	95%

As an entrepreneur you can control pricing, costs, and efficiency in systems, but you must create productivity measures and incentives that can be implemented by your employees to control productivity. As you begin your design of incentive pay remember the following.

<u>The Productivity Measure Must be:</u>

- Within the control of the employee
- Measurable
- Compared to a standard
- Easy to understand

<u>Steps in the Productivity Process include:</u>

1) Understanding the Current System
2) Proposing and Testing Measures
3) Setting Standards for Productivity
4) Creating Thresholds for Incentives and Continued Employment

Let's use a service firm I counseled as an example of creating productivity measures and incentive pay.

1) Understanding the Current System

The owner had not followed the *SUCCEED!*™ diagram and performed all the activities to create good pricing and efficiency in systems and had only achieved a 5% profit margin, but efficiency in labor is still high on the diagram and was an appropriate counseling focus. He began the incentive pay process by collecting data for several months on service hours, sales, travel times, mileage, and the number of daily trips to the supply warehouse for parts. He placed GPS devices on all the trucks and monitored location and travel throughout the day in real time. With this basic data he invited his three technicians into a systems redesign process for compensation.

He had already created skill blocks, pay ladders, and advancement policies and printed an employee policy manual. The first task for the incentive process was discovering what motivated each technician. They all had three key desires: pay, benefits, and vacation time. The next task was to propose and test productivity measures.

2) Proposing and Testing Measures

In monthly systems meetings the owner and his techs discussed what could be measured and whether those measures were fair. This took five months of proposing and testing various items and entering the continuous improvement paradigm: plan, do, study, act. The owner proposed that the techs should be responsible for performance on large bid jobs, but the techs said the bid was not within their control and that measure was dropped.

They all believed that monthly employee hours, and monthly sales dollars for service calls were the important items to measure, and then compared to $250, the average rate for an hour of service in the businesses flat rate book.

In developing the measure, the manager needed to test it and get feedback from employees on its fairness and accuracy. The spreadsheet, Figure 38, outlines successive versions of the measure that was tested.

The initial measure in Scenario 1 would be calculated as follows: If Technician #1 billed an average of $200 per hour in sales for the month, his productivity would be: \$200/\$250 = 80%. In this Scenario Tech 3 is the most productive, but the other techs proposed that not all hours should be counted because vacation hours did not represent income earning work. In addition, they all occasionally used subcontractors to complete jobs but thought that subcontractor fees should be subtracted from the total sale to better represent the work each tech completed.

Stand.								250/hr.	
Tech	**Sales**	**Sub Fees**	**Real Sales**	**Hours**	**Vaca Hrs**	**Mgt Hrs**	**Real Hrs**	**Sales Per Hr**	**Prod**
Scenario 1									
1	25,000			125				200	80%
2	30,000			140				214	85%
3	35,000			160				219	87%
Scenario 2									
1	25,000	2,000	23,000	125	8		117	196	78%
2	30,000	5,000	25,000	140	0		140	178	71%
3	35,000	10,000	25,000	160	10		150	166	66%
Scenario 3									
1	25,000	2,000	23,000	125	8	2	115	200	80%
2	30,000	5,000	25,000	140	0	2	138	181	72%
3	35,000	10,000	25,000	160	10	4	146	171	68%

Figure 38: Employee Productivity

In Scenario 2 you can see that real sales divided by real hours result in very different sales per hour. Here Tech 3 is now the least productive because he has been inflating his sales with subcontractor fees, but also working more hours than any other tech. When management hours in Scenario 3 were also removed Tech 3's productivity improved but he was also booking twice the management hours of the others.

These results also matched the personalities of each employee. Tech 1 was steady and predictable. Tech 2 was an apprentice learning new skills but a responsible individual. Tech 3 was the highest paid employee and thought he was the most experienced and valuable technician and constantly let everyone know. He did not like the results of the productivity measure because it pointed out the flaws in his level of organization. GPS showed he took three times as many trips to the parts warehouse as the other techs.

3) Setting Standards for Productivity

The owner first set a policy to have all the trucks fully loaded with parts each morning to reduce trips to the parts warehouse and set a minimum level of productivity for continued employment. The owner set a profit margin goal of 10% in his cashflows and gave the techs two months to improve their performance.

Thresholds for continued employment:

- 76% productivity, 131 hours at $190 per hour
- Minimum $25,000 in sales per month

Employees had control of efficiency (scheduling, trips to the parts warehouse, and dollars per hour) and could reach 76% through a modest effort.

4) Creating Thresholds for Incentives

The first step in creating incentives is to set challenging but attainable goals. It does not matter if you are creating computers or chocolate chip cookies. In most businesses there is far too much unproductive time spent outside of the core activities and people possess an incredible ability to fit their work into reduced time frames if they are motivated.

Test various goals in your cashflow projection to obtain the highest profit margin. Create two income lines for each employee: regular sales and bonus sales. Then create two payroll lines: regular pay and bonus pay. You can write formulas in the bonus pay line to automatically give employees bonus pay when the bonus income line increases. Adjust all these lines to obtain at least a 20% profit margin and set a threshold. Remember you must add additional costs for bonuses if your employees reach these goals. After several cash flow scenarios, the business manager determined thresholds to receive a bonus:

- 86% productivity, 140 hours at $215 per hour
- Minimum $30,100 per month
- Bonus: half the new profits

The system was tested for a month to make sure the techs understood the goals and the owner gave feedback to employees on what bonus they would receive. When implemented the next month, sales rose from $75,000 to $140,000 per month. The Profit Margin rose from 5% to 29% and settled back down to a consistent 20%. The owner had the same three employees, but they responded positively to incentives and the productivity measures they had created in cooperation with him.

Later, when a recession hit and work volume dropped, the entrepreneur was able to make an appropriate choice and layoff the least productive technician, Tech 3, thereby rewarding the others for their better performance and maintaining the highest profit margin possible but productivity can only hint at a *lack* of productivity. When Tech 3 was fired, the owner found that he had been running his own business on the weekend with the company truck and poured sugar in the gas tank, ruining a $3,000 engine. The owner's comment to me, "Believe the numbers. They don't lie."

Some cautions are in order:

- When pricing changes, your productivity measure, continued employment threshold, and bonus threshold must change also, so recalculate.
- Other costs like subcontractor fees may need to be subtracted from sales to get an accurate measure.
- As you refine the productivity measure you will have to revisit your cash flow projections to make sure you are obtaining the profit margin results you want.

Benchmarks and Goals

Even though you have set monthly standards for productivity, employees need a straightforward measure to gauge their productivity on a daily and hourly basis, and weekly feedback to maintain performance. For our sample business the benchmark was sales dollars invoiced per day for a regular eight-hour shift. It was easy to understand and track and employees reported that they adjusted their goals if they found themselves short on any day.

TASK: Create productivity measures, benchmarks, and goals.

Other Incentives

You can also create other incentives that may motivate your employees such as prizes or awards. The esteem of coworkers can be important to some. You can also enhance results by choosing personalities and communication styles that fit the job. Don't expect introverts to make add-on product sales on a service call or extraverts to limit their conversations with customers.

TASK: Create Productivity Measures and Benchmarks

Practical Point of Attack

Remember you are completing Tasks in a Problem-Solving Sequence. Review Figure 1, **Chapter 1** to renew your awareness of the broader process. Assuming you have completed all the tasks in **Chapter 2**, your Practical Point of Attack for **Chapter 3** is the first task in Maximize Cashflow and Productivity that has not been taken to completion. It is likely that you have completed some of the activities in Chapter 3 simply by being in business, but have they been addressed in a thorough and thoughtful manner? Have you given them the attention required to bring them to a higher level?

All of Us

The Clarkston family had not invested in systems redesign, and they had placed their business under threat by burdening inefficient systems with new sales. With a few hours of space planning and application of LEAN principles, they achieve a 400% increase in efficiency and were able to complete the order in three days.

Moving Forward

If you have a relatively simple business with a ready local market, you may have completed all the tasks necessary to achieve success, but there is more profit available to you if you want to expand.

With pricing and efficiency in place and under control you are ready to add volume. In **Chapter 4** you will begin by learning basic marketing and move on to gain a more effective market focus through strategic planning,

---

PRINCIPLE:
Compensation is a profit center.
WHY:
Competing for the best employees makes your business more capable and profitable.

CHAPTER 4: Evaluate Your Market

Marketing Basics
Strategic Planning
Selling
Retail Sales
Practical Point of Attack

ALL of Us

The ballerina had a high level of skill. She had been a professional dancer at several major American ballet companies but had decided to change careers and continue her college education. She arrived late to the college town and all the jobs had been taken. The only skill she possessed was dance but there were already three dance schools in town, and she wondered how she could create a ballet school with so much competition.

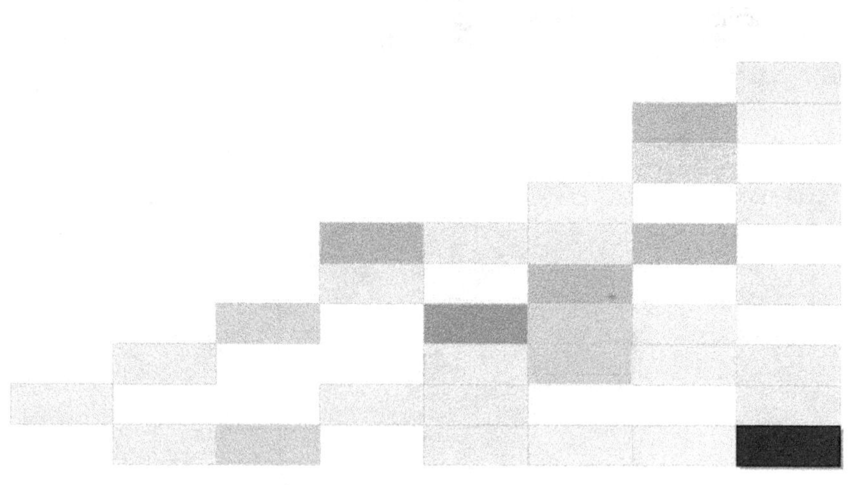

Evaluate Your Market

<u>Marketing Basics</u>

- The Marketing Process
- Target Markets
- Customer Profile
- Market Research
- Critical Motivators
- Market Strategy
- Leverage Points

<u>Strategic Planning</u>

- The Right Time for Strategic Planning
- Strategic Planning Diagram
- Process Steps
- Strategic Focus
- Creativity/Innovation

<u>Selling</u>

- Sales Planning
- The Sales Notebook
- The Selling Process

<u>Practical Point of Attack: Tasks for This Section</u>

Figure 39: Evaluate Your Market

Evaluate Your Market is the third Box in the problem-solving sequence and will prepare your organization to take advantage of the capacity you built in previous chapters. It can be completed in parallel to **Maximize Cashflow and Productivity** but should not be implemented until pricing and efficiency have been addressed. Remember to complete one task at a time and stay focused.

Evaluate activities focus on:

- Understanding marketing principles
- Understanding your customers
- Choosing the highest profit margin targets
- Creating a market strategy and increased sales

Completing them will:

- Organize your marketing approach
- Create your unique selling proposition
- Prepare your organization to exploit volume
- Maximize the effect of marketing communications

Marketing Basics

Marketing is the subject most business planning guides start with because the first thing you want to know, if you are not already in business, is whether there is a market for your products or services. Investing time and money in changing your marketing should not be attempted until after you have solved the prerequisites and gained efficiency in your business processes through the methods outlined in **Chapters 1, 2,** and **3**. Marketing is where the long-term planning begins toward refocusing your business. But without first getting the business under control, you would simply compound and amplify the existing problems in pricing and systems by putting more ineffective marketing activity on top of them.

We will begin with basic marketing principles and build a marketing strategy through all phases of the marketing process by using the ballerina from *All of Us* as our example.

The Marketing Process

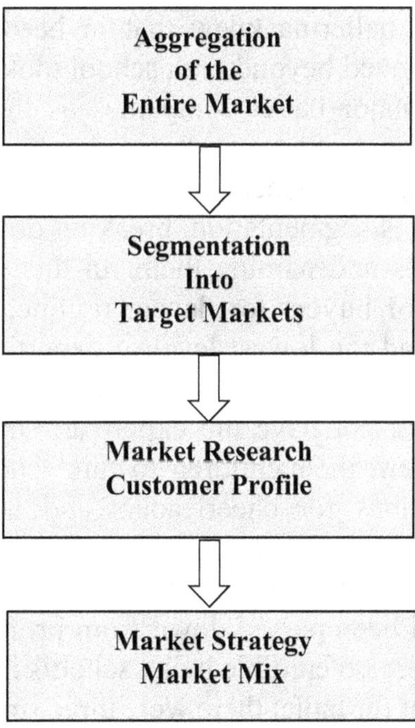

Figure 40: The Marketing Process

The marketing process, Figure 40, begins by imagining all the people who may purchase your product or service, breaking that group into small segments, profiling the customers in those segments, and developing a market strategy focused on the most profitable groups.

Aggregation/Segmentation

Targets are a convenient way of categorizing your customers into groups with similar characteristics. This helps you understand their interests and needs and target communications directly to those needs. Refer to Figure 41 as I explain the aggregation/segmentation process for our sample business: ballet instruction.

The process begins with aggregating the whole market into the broadest category that could still be considered your market. The aggregate market is all after school activities for kids. This includes music, dance, soccer, swimming, baseball, track, and other sports. In dance, the steady paying customers are 5 to 19 years old girls. You might think that there is a market for adult students but that is not the case. The ballerina knew that in her own development, students who continued beyond high school took class at schools in large cities near major ballet companies as they worked toward becoming professionals. She was starting her business in a mid-size college town where no advanced opportunities existed.

The next activity is segmentation, breaking down your customers into smaller groups and naming them. In this college town there were three types of buyers for dance: routine, baton, and ballet. Routine schools had the lowest level of expertise and taught their students dance routines but not technique. They purported to teach ballet, but they did not have the expertise. Only unsophisticated buyers of dance sent their children to this school. Baton schools taught baton routines for cheerleaders and might not even be considered dance, but they had the same customer base. Ballet schools teach highly developed dance techniques that have evolved over centuries and been passed down from professional dancers to students. There were no credible ballet schools in town.

Within the market for ballet there were three smaller segments: the daughters of merchants, farmers, and professors. There were daughters of married college students, but they were a small segment. This will become important later as each segment requires a different type of marketing.

Outside the Box (the aggregate): people who purchase after school activities for kids.

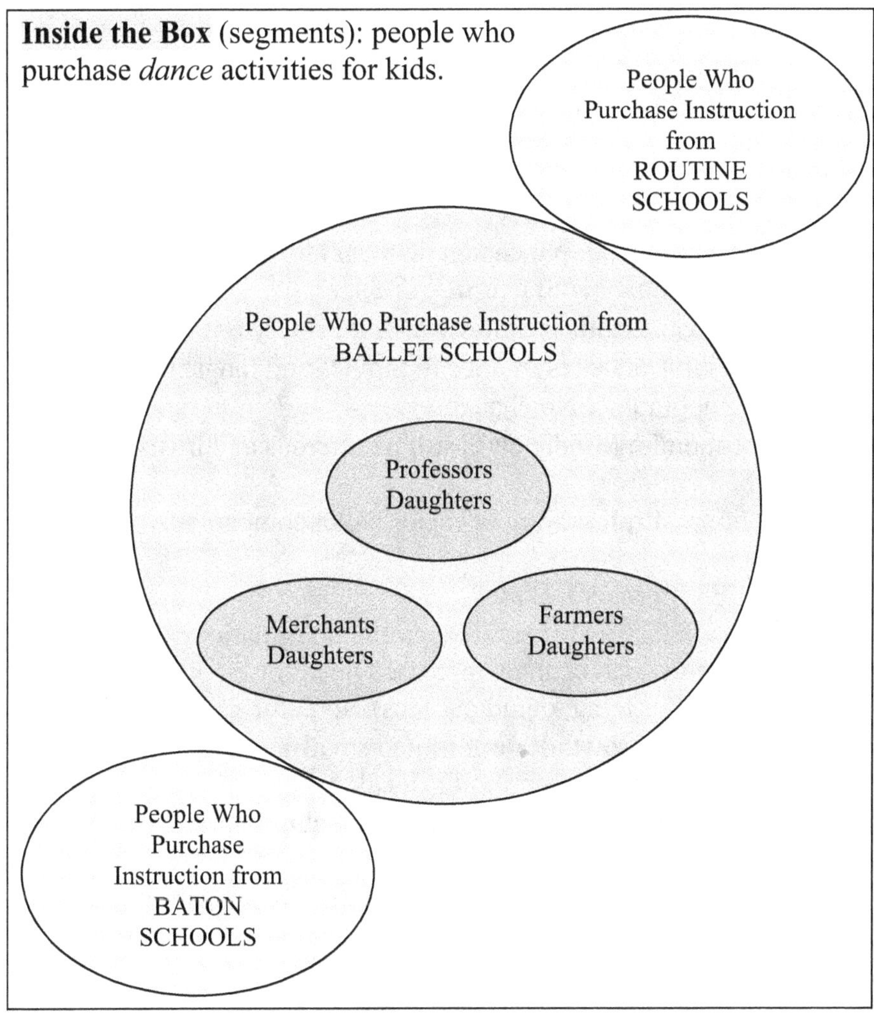

Figure 41: Aggregation/Segmentation for Ballet

TASK: Aggregate and Segment your market into target markets.

Environmental Analysis

You already know a lot about your business environment and might be able to fill in information about the industry environment without research. The ballerina understood the following:

Macro Environment: Ballet

- Technological: No change in technologies in a hundred years (shoe manufacturing, dress, etc.)
- Political/Legal: sensitivity to child safety issues
- Social: Dance resurgence in movies and magazines (1980s)
- Demographic: No change
- Economic: Middle class still prosperous and investing in their children
- Global: Proliferation of major ballet companies

Industry Environment: Ballet

- Key Industry Drivers (Government regulations, technological change, increased need for quality, cost control, pricing, demographics) None for ballet.
- Industry Growth Rate: Limited small-town market, no growth. The competition is local.
- Suppliers: few suppliers of dance equipment before internet.
- Competitors (products, services, research capabilities, interests): Poor competition. See competitive analysis below.
- Customers (what they want): girls want art in dance.

Additional research is usually required to completely understand your market and your customers.

TASK: Complete your Environmental Analysis

Market Research

Market research is nothing more than asking questions. Market surveys are all specific to the needs of the business, but some general guidelines apply. Questions typically fall into several categories including:

1) Qualifying Questions: Should they be in or out of the survey?

- Will they or do they use the product/service?
- Are they located in the right geographic area?

2) Process Questions: How do they search for information and make decisions?

- What is the stepwise process the customer uses to find the product/service?
- What information sources are used?
- How does the buying system work? (For a business)
- Who does the buying? Who influences the buying?
- What are the critical motivators? (psychological speedbumps)

3) Credibility Questions: How do they qualify the provider of the product or service?

- What criteria do they use to judge credibility?

4) Product/Service Feature Questions:

- What do they want?
- What are they willing to pay for?
- What does the competition offer and does the customer validate the offering?

5) Pricing Questions: How much are they willing to pay before they stop buying?

6) Demographic Questions: What information about the customer is useful in identifying other lucrative customers like them?

- For businesses: location, number of employees, sales volume, professional associations, referral source and more.
- For individuals: age, gender, location, occupation, income, car they drive, purchasing patterns, memberships, where they shop and more.

Survey questions must be phrased in a way that obtains the information you need without misdirecting the customer. Follow the sample questionnaire below to understand bad and good ways to phrase questions.

Sample Questionnaire: Ballet

Qualifying Questions:

- BAD: Do you like ballet? (Too general and obtains no useful information.)
- GOOD: Will you begin or continue ballet lessons this year? Do you live within five miles of the proposed location?

Process Questions:

- BAD: Have you ever shopped downtown? (Not specific to ballet)
- GOOD: Which ballet related magazines do you read? How often? If you moved to a new town, how would you find the best ballet school? What don't you like about buying ballet lessons? (covered in detail later)

Credibility Questions:

- BAD: Were our staff helpful and knowledgeable? (Dual issue question, no specific information)
- GOOD: As far as choosing a ballet school, which issues establishing credibility in your mind? Please rank the following from most important to least important (1 most important, 6 least important)

Instructors have been professional dancers.

Knowledge base of instructors.
The school décor.
Live accompanist.

Product/Service Feature Questions:

- BAD: Do you like ballet class? (No actionable information will be generated)
- GOOD: Which of the following are important features for a ballet school?
  Variety of dance styles taught.
  Suspended wood floors.
  Students dressed by level.
  Additional classes: stage makeup, auditioning, etc.

Pricing Questions:

- BAD: What would you like to pay for a ballet lesson? (Generates only a low dollar figure)
- GOOD:
  What is the maximum you would pay for a daily ballet lesson?
  □ $5 □ $10 □ $15 □ $20 □ $25 □ $30 □ $35 □ $40

  At what price level would a daily ballet class begin to sound suspiciously cheap?
  □ $5 □ $10 □ $15 □ $20 □ $25 □ $30 □ $35 □ $40

Demographic Questions:

- BAD: Do you own a computer? (May not be related to ballet buying)
- GOOD: Do you have a subscription to Ballet Magazine? Name the top three internet sites that you visit on a weekly basis? What search terms would you use on the internet that would identify you as a ballet buyer?
- What is your annual household income? (Always ask the income question last and tell them not to answer if the information feels sensitive.)

Formatting, Tabulation, and Other Issues

Tabulate on a spreadsheet, Yes/No check boxes on right if possible.
Validate assumptions in the Market Mix
Bias
How to Phrase Questions
- Single Issue
- Specific
- Prompts
- Check Boxes
- Forced Yes/No
- Will it generate actionable information?

How to Implement
- Mail (typically less than 10% are returned)
- Phone (must be fairly short)
- Focus Group
- In-person interview

Research Information
- www.trlib.org (for data questions "Reference U.S.A.")
- Survey Monkey

TASK: Create and implement your Market Survey

Critical Motivators

Beyond the basics, you must identify what really works in the marketplace: communicating the critical motivator. You can identify your target market, accurately profile your customers, and still misdirect your marketing if you have not identified what really motivates your customer.

The critical motivator is the key element that makes the customer buy from *you* and not someone else. If asked, most businesses owners and their customers would say price and service are the critical motivators, but prices are relatively the same due to competition and so is service. A critical motivator is something deeper in the customer's thinking that is rarely satisfied by design. Some business managers trip over these critical motivators or address them intuitively but few do it consciously. Some examples might help.

A few years ago, in the State of Washington, one of the main sources of client referrals for psychologists was the Department of Social and Health Services (DSHS). The referrals were made by case workers who had to match up their clients with an appropriate therapist. It is difficult to start a new private practice under these circumstances but a new psychologist in the state sent thank you notes to the case workers after each referral and after a case was closed and had a full client load within six months.

The critical motivator was *appreciation*. Case workers at DSHS are beat up every day by clients, administrators, doctors, and therapists who want them to do more than they can possibly do and at low pay. To be thanked for doing their job motivated them to have more interactions with this psychologist. She enjoyed them and treated them like real people.

If you had asked the case workers and psychologists what the critical motivator was for referrals, they would have said that the psychologist had a contract with DSHS, or that she did good work, but the real motivator was the pleasure the case workers experienced in interactions.

One way of getting to the critical motivator is to ask customers what really bothers them about buying the products or services you offer. Ballet students, girls 5-19, would have said they disliked walking into a studio that did not feel like the real thing, meaning they compared every studio to the images in ballet magazines, from, performances, and videos from classes at major ballet companies. Parents would have said they disliked poor quality such as unprofessional dress of the instructors, fingerprints on mirrors, dust balls floating in the corners of the room, and the dance experience of the owner. In other words: quality.

There may be more than one critical motivator but there are usually no more than a few that are the key to your customers' motivation.

Customer Profile

The next step in the marketing process is to profile your target customer. You have gathered data on age, gender, location, price, buying patterns, critical motivators, influencers, and household income, and should be able to create your customer profile. For this case, there are two customers, the ballet student and their parents and they each have a different profile. You may find as you develop your profiles that you only have a marginal understanding of your customers and will need to conduct additional research. The ballerina understood the profiles intuitively from her long experience as a student, professional dancer, and teacher. See the profiles for ballet customers below.

Customer Profile: Ballet Student

Age:	5-19
Gender:	95 % Female
Location:	Cities & Towns
Price Level:	Don't care
Buying Pattern:	Follow the parents
Critical Motivator:	Feels like the real thing
Who Influences the Purchase:	Parents, media, girls in dance
Income:	Middle Class

Customer Profile: Ballet Parent

Age:	30-50
Gender:	Male & Female
Location:	Cities & Towns
Price Level:	Middle class
Buying Pattern:	Go and see, verify quality
Critical Motivator:	Quality
Who Influences the Purchase:	Other parents
Income:	Middle Class

TASK: Complete you Customer Profile

Strengths and Weaknesses

Through implementation of all the tasks so far in *SUCCEED!*™ you have added strengths and eliminated weaknesses and should be prepared to add volume through marketing. If you have skipped over activities, they are lingering weaknesses that may create a crisis later. In a crisis, you want to focus your energies on solving the crisis, not basic systems, skills, and policies that should have been in place. The nightmare that entrepreneurs create for themselves comes from having to solve both basic and crisis issues at the same time and working past midnight to get it done.

Relevant Business Opportunities

Your relevant business opportunities are the ones that are: within your expertise, financially feasible, profitable, and provide what the market wants. You will need to create a list of the skills and product/service features that you identified through your market research that you can compare to the competition.

Competitive Analysis

Your competitive analysis begins by identifying the critical features of your market offering, the ones that are most important to your customer.

The features that the ballerina thought important included:

- Instructor expertise
- Suspended wood floors
- Complete class offerings to instruct at various levels of accomplishment
- A dress hierarchy with colors of leotards and tights to indicate each level
- Location within the town
- Artistic studio appearance
- Cleanliness

These items fit somewhere in the categories of the Market Mix: product, price, place, and promotion.

Product/Service Features include selection, quality, availability, hours, warranties, expertise, technical ability, after-sales service, reputation, special orders, reliability, and credit policy. You can also bundle products and services to add value.

Place includes the quality of their image, location, availability of transportation, parking, physical space esthetics, customer flow, cleanliness, age of fixtures, customer service, behavior, and personalities.

Price includes price level (too high or too low,) discounts, specials, sales, and product combinations.

Promotion includes media selection, the message, packaging, and the unique selling proposition.

<u>The Competition's Market Mix</u>

The ballerina went to each of her competitions' studios and observed class, being aware of their strengths and weaknesses.

Product: One school had professional instructors, but the others did not have the technical training to teach ballet. Actual harm was being done to the children by asking them to perform dance choreography without proper strengthening first.

Price: Pricing was equal between schools, but pricing has been left out of this analysis because it is rarely relevant, and you should not create a price war by undercutting your competition. Compete rather on expertise, quality, and experience and you may be able to charge a premium.

Place: Three competitors had cement floors, dirty rooms, poor lighting, limited space, basement locations, old carpet, limited classes, limited technical abilities, no uniformity in dress. One competitor had professional instructors but was in another town 8 miles away and instructed in a gym. The ballerina may have concluded a larger town might be a more lucrative opportunity, but she did not have a choice and a larger town would also mean more competition.

Promotion: Newspaper advertising. Window displays.

Market Matrix

The market matrix, Figure 42, compares the critical features of the competition with the ballerina. Dark cells indicate that the business possesses the feature.

Competition Name	Instructor Expertise	Suspended Wood Floors	Complete Class Offerings	Dress Hierarchy	Location	Artistic Studio Appearance	Clean
Dance School 1							
Dance School 2							
Dance School 3							
The Ballerina							

Figure 42: Market Matrix

You can see the competition is variable in its coverage of the critical features. The ballerina had the ability to cover all of them at a superior level and she constructed every feature to compete. We will cover the details of her strategy below under Market Mix.

Key Strengths

Completing your market matrix, any additional research on customers, and what the competition is offering should illuminate your key strengths and point you toward additional skill development or product/service offerings that will give you a competitive advantage. If our ballerina had lacked a competitive advantage in any area, she would have had to address it before opening, or risk reduced sales.

TASK: Complete you Market Matrix

Unique Selling Proposition

Your *Unique Selling Proposition* differentiates your business from the competition to gain this competitive advantage. All communications with your customers must make a proposition: *buy our product/service, and you will receive a specified benefit.* The proposition must be unique. Something competitors cannot claim or have not chosen to emphasize in their promotions. The proposition must be so compelling that it motivates individuals to act. The proposition must be multifaceted and cover the entire Market Mix.

Leverage Points

There may be other leverage points that enhance your competitive offering. Some examples may help.

- Controlling key distribution nodes
- Exposing the competition's weaknesses
- Brand Preference: market dominance
- Profit Centers: best combination of high profit centers
- Cost Curve: low-cost producer
- People: strategic compensation
- Vertical Integration: owning your inputs and outputs
- Sole source supplier: dominance in expertise or results

Distinctive Competencies/Strategic Focus

You should now have a Strategic Focus, a refined target market in which you have an advantage in your distinctive competencies. If you do not have an advantage, there is no reason for your customers to choose you over your competition and you may want to consider the changes you need to invest in to win. Being equal to the competition means you will only split the market share in your location, and that level of sales may not give you the living you want.

Developing an appropriate strategy as a preliminary to the market mix is important. You will find yourself in one of four market positions, each with a relevant strategy.

Market Position: Premium Product with High Relative Market Share (RMS)
Strategy: Maintain Prices/Innovate around the critical motivator.

Market Position: Premium Product with Low RMS
Strategy: Follow the leader in Pricing/Find a Niche/Innovate around the critical motivator.

Market Position: Value Product (middle income) with High RMS
Strategy: Cut Costs/Lower Pricing/Build Brand Equity

Market Position: Value Product with Low RMS
Strategy: Massive Development/Move product into another category or trump the market with a new product.

The ballerina chose the first alternative, premium product, because she believed she had superior skill and would quickly gain a high relative market share. She would maintain market prices and innovate around the critical motivators. You will have to decide which market position you inhabit and use the most effective strategy.

The strategic focus of your business will change over time because the people in your market change. You and your business will go through *more* than one crisis due to change, so you might as well get good at tracking it and responding to it. If you have created a Problem-Solving Organization that understands Strategic Planning, you will be able to focus on implementing solutions, without stumbling over prerequisites, and continue to prosper while others fail.

The Market Mix

With all your research and skill development complete, you can create your market mix, the strategy you will implement through product, place, price, and promotion.

Product/Service

1) Target: girls aged 5 to 19
2) Schedule: complete offering of classes from pre-ballet/creative movement through advanced professional levels
3) Dress: color coded for each level. Pre-ballet: pink leotards, pink tights, and pink ballet shoes. Intermediate level: burgundy, pink, and pink. Advanced level: Black, pink, and pink. No student could wear higher level colors without being physically ready and promoted by the ballerina.

Place

The ballerina found an old high school with suspended wood floors that rented rooms to small businesses. She rented two and knocked down the adjoining wall to create a large dance space. With her dance experience and artistic abilities, she renovated the space into a professional studio with sanded floors, a wall of mirrors, professional ballet bars, large photos of ballerinas, and a waiting area with a deep navy-blue carpet. Ferns and house plants added color. On one wall she hung the full-dress scheme for each level. Significant photos of the ballerina dancing with the San Francisco opera and ballet were hung in a special display. Another businesswoman opened a dance shop to supply students.

When parents and students came into the studio it *felt like the real thing.*

Price

Market rate with premium pricing to be implemented later.

Promotion (Communications Strategy)

You will have to choose the most effective media that you have identified in your research and not waste money on avenues that do not place your offering directly in front of your customers, then create a compelling message that promotes your unique selling proposition.

1) Media Selection:
Internet

- Website: SEO data, data format, domain names (buy from www.namecheap.com)
- Social media: Facebook, Instagram, and Google adds.

Print: Direct Mail Pre-internet ballet

- Format
- Frequency
- Content (Message)

Print: News Paper

- Format
- Frequency
- Content (Message)

Radio: None
Signage: Building and Room

2) The Message:
You may understand your unique selling proposition, but will you communicate it effectively?

Would you buy something from someone who seemed competent but unenthusiastic about their life, their job, and the products and services they sell? Not if you had another choice. Would you buy something from a winning, someone who liked seeing you when you came to them for service, someone who showed their success through their enthusiasm, someone who was prosperous and approachable? Of course, you would. You would enjoy the encounter, feel taken care of, and trust the quality of the product or service.

But how many small business owners truly believe they are effective and express that sense of winning in their advertising, in the look and feel of their retail locations, in their employees' attitudes, and in all the things they say about their business in their daily interactions with customers? Not enough. Business managers need to promote their own success by telling their customers they *are* successful in many ways. Self-promotion, the story of your own success, and a positive attitude are essential for making sales because everyone *does* love a winner, but it's surprising how this story of success gets lost over time as the small business manager falls into comfortable habits and well-worn routines.

If you have not found anything to be enthusiastic about you may be in the wrong line of work. Chapter Seven will cover the important issue of deciding to sell your business. This decision is difficult to make and should not be done lightly. You should also finish *SUCCEED!*™ before making such a big decision. But you might begin to consider at this point whether you are happy being a small business owner and what else you might do for a livelihood. Life offers us an almost infinite supply of fun and challenging work. You should begin to ask yourself if small business is fun and challenging for *you*?

Create promotional materials that:

- Promote what is unique about you. The Unique Selling Proposition for the ballerina was: *we have the expertise and the artistry to transform your daughters into serious students of dance.* In short, *the Real Thing.*
- Expose your competition's weaknesses from the market matrix including professionalism, innovation, expanded services, and premium pricing.
- Create compelling language that uses dynamic motivating words such as better, exiting, professional, clean, organized, safe, fun, reliable, like, love and delighted. Talk *to* the customer as if you are in a conversation with them and make your words come right out of the page. Test your new phrases and concepts with potential customers and choose the best. Create a verbal, 60 second commercial in your mind that you can say to anyone who asks about your business and be ready to recite the phrase in conversation. Use customer review.
- Create Integrated Marketing Materials so there is congruence between all the media you use.
- Use Success Stories about yourself and your students to enhance your credibility.

You might ask how unique you can be in a large world, but you *can* because most competition is local. You probably have only three serious competitors in your local area. If you have competitors from outside, then some of your uniqueness comes from *being* local and promoting your longevity in your community.

TASK: Create your complete Market Mix with all promotional materials

Re-marketing

Don't forget your existing customers as you create a new marketing plan. They are your next best sale, and you can easily create a mass email with your new promotional materials. If your competition is innovative, you will need to stay ahead of them by creating new products and services and communicating better.

The ballerina understood this and created new offerings every year: the Pocket Players (a theater group), and workshops in stage makeup, auditioning, hair, shoe care, and much more. The competition tried to mimic the offerings but could not keep up and ultimately failed.

PRINCIPLE:
Marketing is effective communication with a target market.
WHY:
You must stimulate customer interest in your products and service to create superior sales.

Strategic Planning

Strategic planning is the process of wedding your distinctive competencies to the most lucrative market opportunity and is therefore a marketing process.

The Right Time for Strategic Planning

All of your Strategic Planning has already been accomplished by completing the activities outlined in the *SUCCEED!*™ process, but you have avoided the confusion and lack of direction in strategic planning by implementing the most effective sequence for business development. You have maximized your profits and efficiency and prepared yourself to complete the remaining activities in the *SUCCEED!*™ Diagram. Refer to Figure 43, Strategic Planning.

You have completed:

- Chapter 2
    - Internal Analysis
    - Strengths and Weaknesses
- Chapter 3
    - Environmental Analysis
    - Relevant Business Opportunities
    - Competitive Analysis
    - Key Strengths
    - Distinctive Competencies
    - Strategic Focus

Consider, though, that the market changes constantly. Consumer tastes, the competition, regulations, and even the weather may affect your offering, and strategic planning will be an annual activity to track these changes. You have an advantage because you have built a strong business with continuous improvement in your systems. Your strategic planning will be easier each time even if you are in a crisis or market downturn.

We will cover contractions plans in future chapters but for now, your strategic planning is complete.

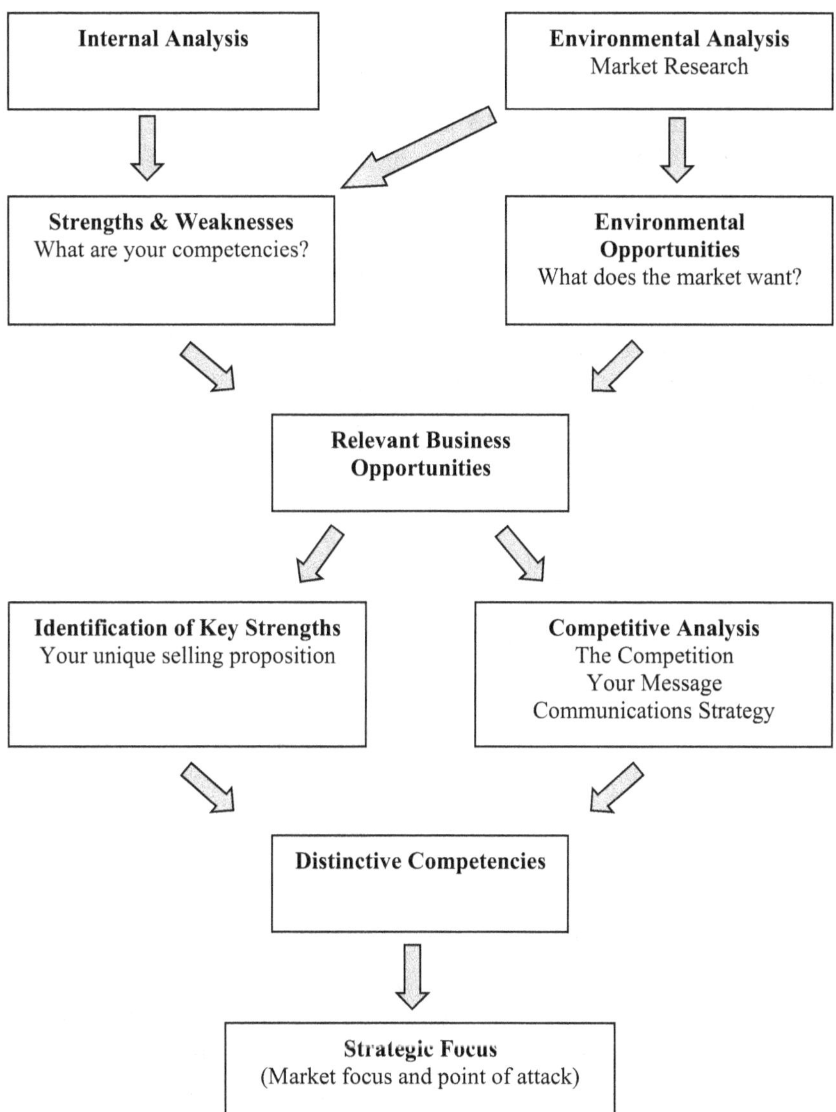
Strategic Planning Diagram
Internal Analysis
Environmental Analysis
Market Research
Strengths & Weaknesses
What are your competencies?
Environmental
Opportunities
What does the market want?
Relevant Business
Opportunities
Identification of Key Strengths
Your unique selling proposition
Competitive Analysis
The Competition
Your Message
Communications Strategy
Distinctive Competencies
Strategic Focus
(Market focus and point of attack)

Figure 43: Strategic Planning

Selling

Selling is solving a problem for someone else. It is not the "hard" selling of the 1950s where aggressive tactics and manipulation forced a buyer to make a rash decision, it is a counseling/consulting process in which you listen to your customer vent, ask questions to clarify their issues, and then describe a solution path that may include your products and services.

Sales Planning

Before you approach a potential customer, you must have a clear picture of your customer profile and develop supporting materials that will help you present your solutions.

- Product/Service Descriptions (specs)
- Website
- Portfolio (Sales Notebook with photos, samplers, testimonials)
- Letterhead, business cards
- Sales Training

TASK: Create your supporting sales materials

The Buyer

The buyer is rightfully suspicious. We are approached everyday by scammers and incompetent service providers and the buyer hides intentions due to lack of trust. They may be suspicious of your value and expertise and obscure their intent. They want unpaid consulting services and will try to get useful information without payment, but they also want relief from long-term problems and resonance with a person who can understand their feelings.

They want guidance and instruction but may not know how to ask for help and may feel embarrassed at their failure. When a client experiences a crisis or downturn, they may be more willing to explore new options and listen to you as their advisor.

You

You must display characteristics that give the buyer a sense of who you are and whether they can trust you. You do not have to fake anything. If you have a good product or service, you will have a natural tendency to be convincing. You need to be:

- Confident in your skills
- A problem solver not a salesman
- Ready to refer the customer to the best solution provider

The Selling Process

The selling process has well-defined steps and is the same one I use to counsel business clients, whether in the public or private sectors. The steps include:

- Intentions
- Venting
- Clarifying Questions
- Solution Path
- The Proposal

Intentions:
Tell your customer you are there to identify problems and create solutions, whether you are the provider of those solutions or not. I tell my clients I want to obsolete myself so that, at some point, they know what I know and can implement their own solutions. I also tell them I will eliminate myself from consideration if my solutions are not helpful and will refer them to another provider if that is better for them. This is why short-term wins are necessary.

I describe my process, so they know there is a finite process and not some endless sales call, including:

- Venting, where I ask the client to tell me everything they think I should know about their business.
- Clarifying questions, where I delve in to better understand their problems.
- Solution path, where I provide a practical point of attack and give them the *SUCCEED!*™ Diagram. I explain the stepwise process of business improvement and provide examples of successful clients who have used my techniques before.

You will do the same but with your specific products and services.

Venting:

Venting gives you information from your client's perspective, creates trust, and provides a first diagnostic concerning the client's skill. Let them tell you the whole story and do not interrupt. They will describe their business history and the problem they are trying to solve, even if it is the wrong practical point of attack. If you let them speak, they will come to an end and will be satisfied that they were heard.

Be attentive and take notes. You are creating a connection that is formed mostly through body language and your empathy.

Clarifying Questions:

Asking clarifying questions is your opportunity to diagnose, analyze and create rapport. You are not just uncovering the technical difficulties clients face but also their suffering and can build trust through empathy. Questions show your expertise and can be an opportunity to uncover the impact of the problems they face and illuminate their fear and pain.

Develop your own set of questions and ask them in the same order in which you would implement solutions. Ask what their ultimate goals are. They will all say they want more profit, but some may really want more free time or to sell their business after bringing it back to health. You don't want to create a solution that solves a problem but does not move them toward their goal.

You will have to adapt to the buyer's personality and address their fears to approach a resonant dialogue. Figure 44 shows personality types. Give their personality type what they want to calm their fears but provide the solution that they need to fix their problems.

Personality Types	What They Want
Aggressive	Control
Analytical	Time
Social	Inclusion
Quiet	Accord

Figure 44: Buyer Personality Type[4]

If their story is long, rambling, and confusing, go back to basics and build information by asking elementary questions from your field of knowledge. I start with questions from the top of the *SUCCEED!*™ Diagram such as:

- Do you understand financial analysis?
- Do you have cashflow projections or a project costing system?
- Do you understand accounting?
- Do you have an accounting system?
- Do you have a planning document or notebook?

Your client's deficits will become clear, and you may uncover the cause of the problem you have been hired to solve.

Solution Path:

You need to give your client a well-defined solution path for them to be interested in hiring you. The solution path shows your competence and helps to reduce their level of stress. The solution must be integrated with the other business functions and address the prerequisites in the *SUCCEED!*™ Outline to be effective. You cannot simply sell them a machine without training, a space plan, and financing. You cannot sell them a service that is implemented at the wrong time or out of sequence. A one-off solution can do more

4 Sadler Sales Training System.

harm than good. If you can also implement your solution with a short-term win in profits or efficiency, you will gain the trust and respect you deserve.

The Proposal:

With the solution path identified you must offer your customer the opportunity to work with you. The offer begins with a question: "Would you like to schedule another appointment so we can work on this issue?"

They may be convinced immediately but it is more likely they will ask about time and costs and be daunted by the expense. The tech services firm from **Chapter 3** spent six months and $15,000 to understand and implement incentive pay. The result was long in coming but highly profitable. In this part of the sales process and later as you begin to implement the solution, your customer may want to exit the solution process and gain no result. You will need to shepherd them through their objections by illustrating the consequences of inaction and the benefits of the solution. They will say they do not have: the time, the dollars, the expertise, or the personnel to accomplish the solution. You must tell them success stories to confirm how the solution can be accomplished but, ultimately, it is up to them to decide if they have the desire to invest their time and dollars. Reiterate the Practical Point of Attack and the solution process and make the sale.

Now that you understand the *SUCCEED!*™ problem solving sequence, you may understand that the solutions you are selling to your customer may be in the wrong sequence. If you tell them they need to delay the purchase to accomplish another activity first, you will gain their trust.

After the Sale

The time immediately after the sale is important to keep your customer interested. Communication is the key. Reinforce the solution path by sending them useful information, spreadsheets, and an additional thought you had about the process to keep yourself relevant and reduce their fear. If you are competent, the first appointment should be a revelation to your customer as you begin to address their problems, teach them new skills, and obtain a short-term win.

Practical Point of Attack

As in previous chapters, the practical point of attack for **Chapter 4** is the first task that has not been taken to completion. Again, it is likely that you have completed some of the activities in **Chapter 4** simply by being in business, but have they been addressed in a thorough and thoughtful manner? Have you given them the attention required to bring them to a higher level of skill and understanding?

All of Us

You know from reading this chapter that the ballerina competed effectively, even in the face of multiple local dance schools, because she provided a superior service. She had confidence in her skills and that confidence and expertise carried her to market dominance. Focus on your skills and it will be the basis of your success.

Moving Forward

With your business running effectively, and possessing a deeper knowledge of pricing, efficiency, and volume, you can alter your personal and business goals. Chapter 5 will help you redefine your mission and values and develop strategies to achieve them.

PRINCIPLE:
Selling is psychological.
WHY:
You must build trust to get your customer to close the sale.

CHAPTER 5: Set New Goals

Mission/Values
Leadership Lesson 3
Expansion Strategies
Status Quo
Contraction Strategies

<u>ALL of Us</u>

The Clean Corporation had a profitable history and great community relations. They were the major retail business in a thriving city. The managers were proud that they took care of their employees and celebrated their successes. With an excellent team, financial stability, and market opportunity they began an expansion with certainty in their success. Six months later they were short of cash, heavily in debt, and were considering laying off employees for the first time. The managers felt embarrassed and concerned that they had ruined their business, but they could not understand the causes.

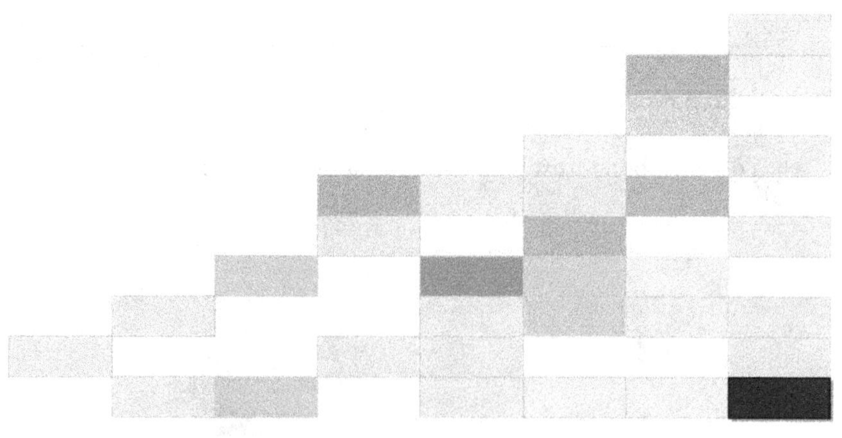

Set New Goals

<u>Mission/Values</u>
- The Mission Statement
- The Value Statement

<u>Leadership Lesson 3</u>
- Transformational Leadership

<u>Expansion Strategies</u>
- Profit Centers
- Horizontal and Vertical Integration
- Strategic Partnerships
- Tools and Analysis
  - Differential Analysis
  - Break Even for Expansions
  - Staging Each Strategy

<u>Status Quo</u>
- Threats

<u>Contraction Strategies</u>
- Skills
- Equipment
- Employees
- Square Footage

Figure 45: Set New Goals

You should now be managing a profitable and efficient business in your current market, but you may understand that the market and your goals have changed. You may want or need to expand to survive; you may be satisfied with your work and want to remain as you are; or you may find yourself in a recession or under a stairstep of expenses and need to contract. You have a strategic focus but now need to create a strategy to realize your goals.

Set New Goals activities focus on:

- Mission and Values
- Leadership
- Expansion Strategies
- Status Quo
- Contraction Strategies

Completing them will:

- Refine your strategic focus
- Give you new management skills
- Size your business for the new market
- Prepare you for a recession

Mission/Values

At this point you should have an efficient well-run business, so the next question is: What do you want and what is possible? You have already thought about your personal goals and gone forward with some intention, but have your goals changed in the process? What do you really want?

You can:

- Expand
- Maintain the Status Quo
- Downsize

Your mission statement will point your entire effort at some result. Be sure you want it.

The Mission Statement

The Mission Statement is not a lofty goal, it is a practical statement that aims at the market and focuses the efforts of everyone in your business. Every employee should be able to understand whether their activities contribute to or degrade the mission. It needs to be concise and memorable, or it will become useless. Display it prominently and state it regularly in your staff meetings and interactions. Like marketing, you are trying to rent space in your employee's minds so they incorporate it in all their decisions or can question activities that seem contradictory. It should include the following concepts:

- Quality
- Competitive Position
- Market Focus
- Size/Reach

Examples:

We will become the preferred brand of skincare products on the west coast, servicing the needs of women who desire organic remedies.

We are the premium provider of ballet instruction for girls five through nineteen in Whitman County.

We provide value products to underserved and economically disadvantaged consumers in Chicago.

Hone your mission statement until it rings true and test it on your employees, customers, and family. This can be accomplished in staff meetings or systems redesign and imbedded in the very way you conduct business.

The Value Statement

Values must promote fulfillment of not only the mission but of the owner's and every team member's resonance. They must be values *you* believe in. Paying lip service to values and then undermining them with behaviors that support the opposite, will slowly destroy your business. Everyone has probably had a job that ran so counter to their values that they quit in disgust. Create values that you and your employees feel great about and are proud to promote.

Examples:

We believe in quality products that maintain a clean environment and support our community through charitable contributions.

We treat our employees, customers, and community with respect.

We accept personal responsibility for our mistakes and seek solutions as a team.

TASK: Create your Mission and Value Statements

PRINCIPLE:
Mission and value statements must be short and to the point.
WHY:
They cannot focus the entire efforts of your business on the most lucrative target unless employees can remember them.

Leadership Lesson 3

By investing in your skill development and leading problem-solving teams, you have gained leadership skill that has increased your profits and made you and your business more capable in a dynamic business environment, but there remains another level beyond competence encompassed in Transformational Leadership.

As stated by James Burns, *transactional* leadership is an "exchange of value" but "the bargainers have no enduring purpose."[5] Employees are simply punching the time clock, and employers are simply buying their time. Transforming or *transformational* leadership occurs when you "engage with others in such a way that leader and follower raise one another to higher levels of motivation and morality."

As stated by Nadler and Tushman, the transformational leader develops characteristics including envisioning, energizing, and enabling, that motivate and inspire organizations to higher levels of achievement and sustained activity.[6]

Envisioning includes:

- Articulating a compelling Vision
- Setting high expectations
- Modeling consistent behaviors

Energizing includes:

- Demonstrating personal excitement
- Expressing personal confidence
- Seeking, finding, and using success

Enabling includes:

- Expressing personal support
- Empathizing
- Expressing confidence in people

---

5 "Transactional and Transforming Leadership," James McGregor Burns, *Leadership*, 1978.

6 "Beyond the Charismatic Leader: Leadership and Organizational Change," David A. Nadler and Michael L. Tushman, *California Management Review 32* (Winter 1990): p 77-97

Envisioning

All three components of transformational leaders are meant to "change an individual's values, needs, or aspirations." Envisioning is meant to generate excitement and articulate a desired future state. The vision needs to be "challenging, meaningful, and worthy of pursuit," and become a way for employees to feel successful.

Energizing

Energizing generates the motivation to act. It requires the leader to have personal contact with employees and express "confidence in their own ability to succeed."

Enabling

Enabling "helps people act or perform in the face of challenging goals." The leader must "demonstrate empathy, and have the ability to listen, understand, and share the feelings of those in the organization." You are providing a role model and a standard that acts as a "source of sustaining energy."

How you become a transformational leader depends on *your* personal resonance. Do you wholeheartedly believe in the mission for your business and your life? Do you have the communication skills to project your belief outward to your employees and the world? It does not take an extravert to accomplish this. Even an enthusiastic introvert can be compelling. Remember to ask yourself if there is resonance between your personal vision and your employees' personal visons? Have you communicated your vision and intensions in all your interactions, and do you practice it in staff meetings and systems redesign?

In the next section I will show you how to expand your business without creating a crisis.

TASK: Read *The Leader's Companion: Insights on Leadership Through the Ages*
Selection 19: Transactional and Transforming Leadership
Selection 20: The Transformation of Transforming Leadership
Selection 21: Beyond the Transforming Leader: Leadership and Organizational Change

TASK: Lead your employees in a discussion about their personal visions and connect it to your mission and values

Expansion Strategies

You may have completed some of the following activities in combination with earlier task assignments, but you still need to consider and review them here in an effective order. Expansion strategies include:

- Profit Centers
- Vertical and Horizontal Integration
- Strategic Partnerships

Profit Centers

In **Chapter 1** you applied overhead to profit centers to analyze their profitability. The same must be done again so you can choose the best combination of profit centers to efficiently use your resources and achieve your strategic objective.

Some profit centers may be less profitable but remain a necessary component of your product/service offering when sold in combination with other products. Break your profit and loss statement into profit centers and apply overhead through a proxy such as the percentage of direct labor used in each.

TASK: Apply overhead to profit centers and chose the best combination.

Horizontal and Vertical Integration

Horizontal Integration

Horizontal Integration includes:

- Multiple locations/Relocation
- Acquiring the competition (buying their business)

A first logical step in an expansion is to replicate what you do in a second location. If you have completed all your *SUCCEED!*™ tasks, you can copy the systems manuals and train new personnel with ease but you need to complete cashflow projections and credible market research to know if the new location is feasible. There is also the potential for cannibalizing sales from your first location if the stores are too close together.

Acquiring the competition is the same but you're investing in an on-going concern not new equipment and personnel. Obtaining an accurate value for the businesses is an essential step so you will not be laboring under an unreasonable debt burden with low profits. See **Appendix G** for valuation methods.

You can easily track profit performance and compare your two locations by using "classes" in Quickbooks. Each transaction is designated as either the class of Location 1 or Location 2. You can then obtain a Profit and Loss Statement total, or Profit and Loss by "class" that gives you a side-by-side comparison.

Vertical Integration

Vertical integration means owning the inputs or outputs to your current business. You can look up or down the supply chain for opportunities including:

- Materials
- Manufacturing
- Distribution
- Retail

Vertical integration is difficult for small businesses because the input and output processors are usually large market entities such as a mill providing lumber to many retail locations or manufacturers receiving raw material from extraction experts. Do not make the mistake of working beyond your expertise without research, planning, and training. I had a manufacturing client who opened a retail location for their luxury boats and failed terribly because their expertise in manufacturing did not provide the skills they needed for retail sales.

Strategic Partnerships

A close association with other providers in the supply chain can increase your competitive advantage. I called my private practice Douglas Hammel and Associates because I formed relationships with preferred experts in technology, psychology, manufacturing, and law that helped me provide full-service consulting. Find the partnerships that enhance your competitive offerings.

Tools and Analysis

<u>Differential Analysis</u>

Differential analysis is a tool you will use many times in your expansion and is simply the activity of comparing an alternative to the status quo. You may compare going to a new trade show with not going, eliminating a profit center, or keeping it, or any number of activities you are considering with the alternative.

You only need to use the revenue and expense items that change. Anything that remains the same can be left out. Determine the revenues and costs, then subtract the Status Quo from the Alternative. See Figure 46 for an example.

	Alternative	**Status Quo**	**Result of Changing to Alternative**
Revenue	5,000	6,000	(1,000)
Expenses	4,000	5,500	(1,500)
Net Income	1,000	500	500

Figure 46: Differential Analysis

Revenue and expenses for the Alternative are less than the Status Quo, but net income is better so the Alterative is the best choice. Fewer resources have been used to create a more profitable result.

Break Even for Expansions

Unlike a cashflow projection that outlines month by month cashflow, a breakeven for expansion shows you profitability at various levels of production for an average month. This is a visioning exercise that points you to the right goal and avoids stairsteps of expenses.

BREAK EVEN ANALYSIS AT VARIOUS LEVELS OF PRODUCTION
(Average Month)

Unit Price	$10						
Units Sold		100	300	500	700	900	1,100
Sales in Dollars		1,000	3,000	5,000	7,000	9,000	11,000
COGS	35%	350	1,050	1,750	2,450	3,150	3,850
Gross Profit		650	1,950	3,250	4,550	5,850	7,150
Operating Expenses							
Rent		1,800	1,800	1,800	1,800	1,800	1,800
Heat		50	50	50	50	50	50
Phone		50	50	50	50	50	50
Employee		2,000	2,000	2,000	2,000	5,000	5,000
Insurance		50	50	50	50	50	50
Total Operating Exp		3,950	3,950	3,950	3,950	6,950	6,950
Profit/(Loss)		(3,300)	(2,000)	(700)	600	(1,100)	200

Figure 47: Breakeven at Various Levels of Production

From your accounting system and your cashflow projection you should have a clear idea of your profitability at your current level of production. If you are in an expansion, you must choose the next best level that is profitable. Many entrepreneurs make the mistake of believing profitability is scalable in small increments and that if you are profitable now, any increase in production will make you more profitable. This is not true.

Figure 47 shows profit and loss statements for production levels between 100 and 1,100 units. GOGS and operating expenses are estimated for each level. Let's assume you are currently producing less than 100 units and you are profitable. When you envision other production levels you find some are profitable and some are not. Operating expenses remain flat until 900 units when an increase in employee expense incurs a stairstep that creates a loss.

If you had faith in your analysis, which level would you choose? Clearly 700 units is the most profitable level and all your efforts in marketing, finance, operation, and human resources need to be focused on achieving that goal in the shortest time possible and at the least expense. This requires building cash reserves and loan applications, creating all the marketing, creating any new systems, and training employees *before* you implement the expansion. Without this level of planning, you may fall short of your goal and must contract to the previous profitable level. Some expenditures are revocable, and some are not. You can shed employees, but you may not be able to get out of the lease for your increased square footage. Expansions become turnarounds when executed poorly.

TASK: Create your Breakeven spreadsheet at Various Levels of Production

Staging Each Strategy

All the possible expansion strategies available to you cannot be implemented at the same time. You will have to choose the first best strategy that you can afford before moving on to the next. Implementing multiple strategies at the same time can tax your employees beyond their ability to learn new skills and create effective systems. Focusing on one major goal at a time will allow you and your employees to solve unforeseen problems and acclimate to the new level without burning out.

Status Quo

Standing still can sometimes be the best option if you are profitable and have created the life you want. There is no purpose to expansion if you are happy and making enough money, but the market is dynamic and you should always be watchful for new threats: competition, cost changes, and new technologies making your skills and equipment inefficient or obsolete. Complete yearly strategic planning and assess market changes.

Contraction Strategies

In the life of your business, you will face recessions, market downturns, pandemics, and new competition and you need to ready yourself with a contraction plan. The objective is to stay competitive and profitable as you shed costs but maintain core:

- Skills
- Equipment
- Employees
- Square footage

When the threat has passed you will be able to expand easily because you have maintained essential infrastructure, the infrastructure that is most difficult to replace.

Your contraction strategy begins with improving your cashflow projection with a toggle switch for sales/volume. Write a formula for each month on your total sales line that key to a cell that is formatted as a percent. The formula might look as below:

=SUM(B3:B10)*(1+G2)

B3:B10 sums all the sales in that range. G2 is the cell with the percent you want to change. The dollars signs mean always go to that single cell, no matter where you copy the formula. You can then copy the formula for total sales across your cashflow for each month. When you change cell G2 to 10%, all your sales sums will increase. When you change cell G2 to -10%, all your sales sums will decrease. If you have automated COGS as a percent of total income, COGS will also change. You can now test the result of various price/volume increases of decreases by changing a single cell and plan your contraction appropriately.

Other expenses not automated to change with sales may have to be accomplished by hand. You should create separate spreadsheets for best, medium, and worst-case scenarios and have a preplanned set of tasks to implement for each. You can also build in trigger points to your plan to stage your solutions such as:

- At -10% of sales, terminate Staff Member 1
- At -20% of sales, rent out excess square footage
- At -30% of sales, sell unusable but easily replaced assets

The key is that you have thought through the entire contraction process, so you are solving your downturn immediately while your competition flounders and uses up their cash and debt capacity.

TASK: Create your Contraction Strategy Cashflow with triggers and tasks identified

PRINCIPLE:
Prepare for the next recession with your contraction plan.
WHY:
You have already solved the recession while your competition flounders.

All of Us

The Clean Corporation had made a basic mistake, believing that once they got beyond their first breakeven point, profits were incrementally scalable, but they expanded up under a stairstep of expenses and began using up cash trying to understand what had happened. With a quick analysis of breakeven at various levels of production they quickly focused on the most profitable number of units to produce and succeeded in their expansion.

Moving Forward

If you continue with an expansion strategy, you may need new systems. **Chapter 6** begins with scalability and reminds you that systems need constant attention.

CHAPTER 6: Develop New Systems

Planning Document
Scalable Systems
- **Marketing**
- **Office**
- **Production**
- **Human Resource**

ALL of Us

Superior Control Systems Inc. was an industry innovator and preferred provider of control systems design for manufacturing, but they had a problem. The partners had never resolved how to end their association if they could not agree how to run the company. They had avoided this system/contract in their rush to succeed and now it threatened the future of their work.

One partner wanted out, and they had to decide how to accomplish this delicate task and remain friends.

Develop New Systems

Planning Document

- Your Plan
- Loan Proposal Template

Scalable Systems

- Marketing
  - Research
  - Communication
  - Sales Training
- Office
  - Software
  - Workflow
  - Filing
  - Workspace
- Production
  - Capacity
  - Space Plan
  - Inventory
  - Accounting
  - Shipping
- Human Resources
  - Training
  - Compensation/Incentives
- Ownership

Figure 48: Develop New Systems

If you have become a skilled systems designer, you may have already completed the activities in this chapter by addressing systems issues through oversight and continuous improvement. You may have completed all the systems you need to effectively operate your business and finished most of your development tasks, but if you are pursuing an expansion, you will be changing your products, services, and volume and will probably need some new or improved systems to sustain your business at a higher level.

This chapter is a reminder not to leave systems incomplete in the demanding endeavor of expansion.

Develop activities focus on:

- Your planning document
- Loan proposal/investment prospectus
- Systems

Completing them will:

- Identify and create new systems
- Fix any lingering inefficiencies in old systems

Planning Document

The essential system that keeps you on track and stores all your work is your planning document.

Your Plan

If you have been diligent in placing your finished tasks in your plan, you have slowly completed a business systems manual that can be used for multiple purposes. If you have not, you have made your work more difficult when you must find or recreate information. All or parts of your planning document can be used to:

- Organize strategy
- Set goals
- Track progress
- Document systems
- Have systems oversight
- Support a loan proposal

I prefer a single computer file replicated in a physical notebook. The computer file makes it efficient to edit your document while the notebook is an easy access resource used for jotting down ideas and corrections. Detailed systems manuals can be stand-alone files and notebooks. Keep printed copies as backups.

Loan Proposal Template

Your planning document is also your loan proposal template or should have covered all the sections of a loan proposal, so you can cut and paste the appropriate sections into a loan document. If you are creating a loan proposal from scratch, you have missed the opportunity to simplify something that should be easy to accomplish.

Scalable Systems

Are your systems scalable, that is, can they produce higher or lower levels of output without redesigning? I am reminding you again about systems because managers tend to ignore time-consuming activities when they are faced with complex problems. Expansion is the most complex endeavor you may ever approach and requires new skills and a well-defined process including oversight on systems. Consider the following example.

Service Organization

AAA Mechanical installed complex systems in the maritime industry, but they had grown beyond the capabilities of their customer relationship management system (CRM) and their project costing system did not accurately define costs for labor, materials, overhead and profit. They worked with an advisor for several counseling sessions to create both systems.

Results:

Profits:	$204,000 in new Profit in the first year
Profit Margin:	Increase from 2% to 30% in three months
Customers:	Customers accepted the pricing changes

AAA Mechanical had left old systems in place without oversight even in the face of low profits and dwindling cash reserves. A lack of understanding in accounting and project costing systems led them into the trap of creeping profit reductions. They needed new skills to understand that the old approach was not working. If you find yourself baffled by your low profits, get help from your EDC, SBDC, or a private consultant.

So, you have questions to answer:

- Are your systems scalable?
- Are your employees trained to use them effectively?

Marketing

If you have changed your strategic focus, you may need newer more efficient systems in:

- Research
- Communication
- Customer relationship management software (CRM)
- Sales Training

Office

Office systems may be the easiest to upgrade because you can buy them off the shelf. Office Suites like Microsoft Office and other opensource systems are economical even paying a yearly subscription fee because all the hard work has been done for you. Systems to consider include:

- Office productivity software
- Accounting (getting off spreadsheets and implement a real accounting system)
- Workflow
- Computer file nomenclature (naming things logically so you can find them later)
- Paper files
- Workspace design for efficiency

Production

In production, sometimes the quickest way to systems efficiency and increased profit is the purchase of new equipment. This can be upgrades or creating a new profit center by in-house production of what you formerly paid others to produce. You can also gain information and efficiency through the following:

- Accounting: Using "classes" to track profits at multiple locations
- Electronic control systems for machinery

- Sizing capacity to the production level with the highest profits
- Space Planning
- Inventory/Shipping

Human Resources

Human resource systems have been covered in-depth already but remember you can gain efficiency through:

- Training
- Compensation/Incentives

Ownership

Ownership agreements are a contract system that business owners leave out because they never think it will be a problem and other activities seem more important. Don't forget to finish the following:

- Buy/sell agreement between partners
- Subscription agreement for new shareholders
- Agree upon valuation models for share price

PRINCIPLE:
Make systems oversight and redesign a continuous process.
WHY:
Systems become inefficient and obsolete over time as new employees are hired, and oversight is ignored. Lingering systems issues will reduce your profits.

TASK: Complete all unfinished systems

All of Us

In the rush to create sales and an industry reputation, Superior Control Systems had forgotten they needed a buy/sell agreement between the partners, a new system. They were fortunate that each of the partners wanted the best result for the other. Their agreement stated that at any time one partner could offer to sell his shares to the other. If the partner refused to buy, the one who wanted to leave had the right to buy him out. This was a forced sale model that broke any 50-50 deadlocks. The valuation model had been identified and the selling partner did sell his shares and even offered a discounted price if the remaining partner could complet3e the deal in 30 days. They both walked away happy.

Moving Forward

You have planned, studied, and improved your business but now you need to finance your plan and implement your strategy. **Chapter 7** will help you find the right financing, avoid implementation problems and complete your business development.

CHAPTER 7: Finance Alternatives/Implement Expansion Strategy

Long-term Financing

- **Revise Cash Flow Projections**
- **Sources of Capital**
- **Loan Types**
- **Loan Proposals**
- **Bankers**

Implement Expansion Strategy

- **Timeline**
- **Tracking Progress**
- **Adjusting**

When to Sell Your Business

<u>ALL of Us</u>

Treble Music School had begun with two musicians and bloomed into a school of the arts with ten music teachers and a building with rehearsal space and practice rooms. They had never had cash reserves and expanded using internal cashflow. The regular banking system viewed them with skepticism, and they did not have collateral to pledge against a loan. In small increments they used credit cards to fund short-falls and the purchase of equipment. New credit cards were used when credit limits were reached. They remained profitable but suffered under the burden of excessive debt and wondered what mishap might sink them.

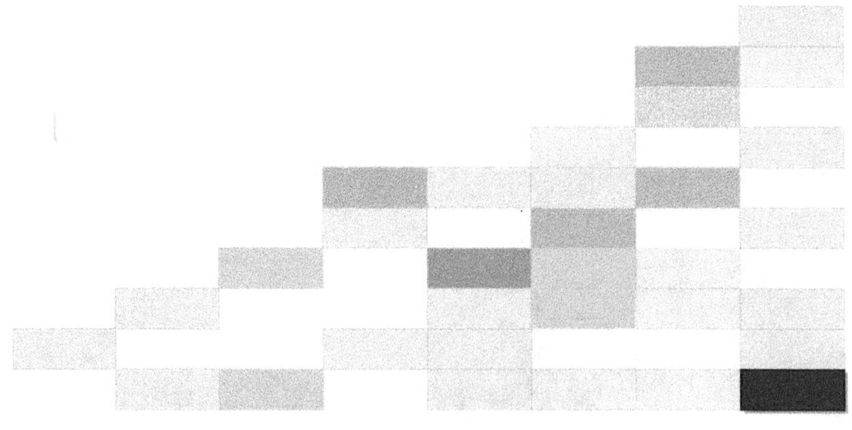

Finance Alternatives

<u>Long-term Financing</u>

Revise Cash Flow Projections
Sources of Capital
Loan Types
Loan Proposals
Bankers

Implement Expansion Strategy

Timeline
Tracking Progress
Adjusting

When to Sell Your Business

The Right Time
The Right Price

Figure 49: Finance Alternatives/Implement Expansion Strategy

Financing is being covered late in this book because it is typically not the best solution in the early stages of your business development. Receiving financing before addressing pricing, efficiency, and volume places you in the position of throwing dollars at problems without enough planning. You will ask for the wrong amount, use it up and then ask for more without proving to your funding source that you effectively managed their first loan.

Finance/Implement activities focus on:

- Sources of capital
- Loan types
- Loan proposals
- Bankers
- Timelines
- Tracking Progress
- Adjusting
- Selling Your Business

Completing them will:

- Help you understand financing alternatives
- Get you the right financing
- Build credibility with funding sources
- Avoid costly mistakes in timing
- Allow you to create interventions at the earliest opportunity
- Value your business for a potential sale

Long-term Financing

Now that you have improved cash flow and efficiency, and created a market strategy, you have an organization that is lean enough and smart enough to finance the activities that will bring you additional sales. Your marketing plan has identified these activities.

Long-term financing can only come from two places: your own cash flow or an outside source. Perhaps you have found that with all the improvements you have made that you no longer need outside financing and can adequately plan for your expenditures by using internal cashflows. You may also have found that it will be impossible to expand without additional debt. Whichever case you have identified, the next thing you must do is revise your cash flow projects to incorporate costs for your market plan and systems development.

Revise Cash Flow Projections

Hopefully, you have gained skill at using computer spreadsheets and incorporated your cashflow projections as a valuable tool and revised it many times as you uncovered pertinent information in the development process. This revision should just be the next step, but with long-term goals in mind. If you have not updated your initial cash flow projection and used it continually to manage your business, now is the time to start. Make it a habit.

Go over your latest revision item by item and insert changes based on the following to make sure you get beyond the next breakeven point:

1) Estimated savings from changes made in the development process.
2) Estimated sales from implementing the marketing plan with reasonable stepwise increases.
3) Estimated costs for the new marketing plan and systems development.
4) Estimated financing required and the monthly payment if you should need to finance with a loan.

Be thorough in your revision. You are eliminating risk every time you make reasonable, thoughtful estimates. The result is your Most Likely Case Scenario. Make this the first tab in your Excel Workbook. Create a new tab and copy this Most Likely Case onto it. Reduce the sales estimates by 30%. The result is your Worst-Case Scenario. Check to see if additional financing is required and for how long. If you have written formulas that reduce variable costs as sales go down, you will have a better model of reality. Next, create another tab and again copy the Most Likely Case onto it. Increase sales by 30%. This is your Best-Case Scenario. Check again to see if any additional financing is required. You may be surprised to find a lump sum in additional financing required to support the increased sales level. Rapidly expanding businesses gobble up cash quickly. Be careful not to expand beyond your ability to finance this scenario or you will be back in the development process again.

Creating the Worst Case and Best-Case Scenarios brackets your risk, that is, they show you how much financing is required at the extremes.

Sources of Capital

Internal Cashflow

Internal cashflow is sometimes the only source of money for a business in its early stages of expansion and makes it essential that you maximize those cashflows before going to the bank. You avoid the expense of interest and know exactly how much you can spend.

Home Equity Loan

Your personal residence is the greatest source of wealth for the average citizen, and you can access your equity through a home equity line of credit (HELOC.) It gives you flexibility to use and pay back and a reasonable interest rate. In a regular bank loan, most small businesses do not have enough assets to cover a loan default and so use their homes as collateral.

Equity Investors

Family and friends are the traditional sources of capital for a startup but can also be useful in an expansion if you sell a portion of your business to them or another investor. Many states offer an avenue to issue a private stock offering without the burden of regulations for a public offering. Both you and your investors need a business valuation to understand the value of the business and what percentage is being sold. See **Appendix G** for business valuation methods.

The Banking System

Banks have a set of rules and ratios from which they gage the health of your business and its readiness for financing. Most new businesses fall outside of these parameters and are forced outside of the banking system for funding. Debt ratios (total liabilities divided by total assts) beyond 43% are not viable. You must improve your profitability to qualify for a bank loan. The bank will also want your home as collateral. Even if you are an LLC or S-corporation, you will have to pierce your corporate veil and pledge your house against default. Also keep in mind that loan officers are not financial experts. They use ratios and computer programs to judge your fitness for a loan, but they are not managers who can delve beyond your financial statements to see value.

State Programs

Many states have programs to assist businesses and focus support on specific areas of a state's economy. The following are just a few examples:

- Job Retention Dollars
- Gap Financing
- Manufacturing grants
- State Department of Commerce programs

Federal Programs

Federal programs are likewise created to support federal economic goals such as:

- SBA Guarantee Loans (bank loans with a small business administration guarantee by the government.)
- SBIR grants (small business innovation research grants specifically set aside for small business.)

- Export Line of Credit

Other Organizations

LION (local investment opportunity network) is an informal network of local investors focused on supporting their community through private loans to business. This group functions only in Jefferson County, Washington but there may be similar groups in your area. Check with your local Economic Development Council (EDC.)

Craft 3 is a community lending organization that focusses on entrepreneurs falling outside the banking system. They have a social mandate and fund daycares and other socially important community projects.

EDC

Your local Economic Development Council may administer grants that provide critical support at no cost to you, freeing your cashflow for other uses.

Crowd Funding

Kick Starter and other entities provide an internet forum to connect entrepreneurs with individuals interested in donating to startup businesses. This requires a well-crafted campaign to catch the interest of private donors.

Credit Cards

Credit cards are the worst form of financing for a business, and you should not use them except in an emergency. Their interest rates are extremely high, and they are not meant to act as term loans or lines of credit.

Factoring

Factoring is selling your accounts receivable at a discount to a factoring company. You get the cash now but the accounts receivable are paid to the factoring company when they come in. The implied interest rate is high.

Debt Consolidation

Debt consolidation may be an avenue for reducing your monthly debt payments and freeing up internal cash, but the interest rates are high.

Loan Types

There are two types of loans, term loans and lines of credit, and you should ask for the appropriate combination of both when submitting your loan proposal to the funding source.

Term Loans

Term loans are large lump sum loans meant for equipment, renovations, working capital, construction, relocation, expansion, inventory purchases, or any other large purchase that will take longer than one year to pay off. The monthly payment is determined by the interest rate and the term (how many years you must pay it off.) Reducing the interest rate and lengthening the term will lower the monthly payment. Bank loans for most businesses have a term of three to five years. The interest rate will probably be set by the bank but the term may be negotiable, so get the best deal you can.

Lines of Credit

Lines of credit are loans meant to cover short term cash needs like seasonal inventory, payroll, and unexpected purchases. They are meant to be paid to zero at least once a one year, but too often small business owners establish a line of credit and then use it like a term loan. Determine the kind of loan you need first and ask for the right one. Interest rates on lines of credit can be four to eight points higher than a term loan and there is no reason to bear this additional expense.

You may need a combination of a term loan for your development/expansion and a line of credit for seasonal variations in cash flow. Get the right amount of each.

Loan Proposals

See "Writing a Winning Loan Proposal," **Appendix H**.

Bankers

There are some wonderful loan officers who are highly skilled, know their business, and will be essential partners in the success of your business but most have very little training or skill in finance, especially in determining the viability of your business. They work from formulas and computer programs created by management underwriters who change loan criteria to suit the interests of the bank.

You may remember the Great Recession of 2008 was caused by bankers who granted billions in subprime loans to consumers who could not afford them, then fraudulently sold the loans as top-quality financial instruments to unsuspecting investors. Their activities were not based on sound financial management but on creating unreasonable profits and passing the risk on to someone else. The scheme crushed our economy and the entire country suffered. These same bankers will hold you to a higher standard, but you still need to impress them with your diligence.

Be prepared to answer tough questions but expect that your loan officer will not have read your loan proposal. I have had bankers ask for Balance Sheets, personal financial statements, and use of funds sections that were already prominently featured in my client's proposal. Walk the banker through the whole document in a face-to-face meeting so they really understand it. Be cordial in the face of low skill and point out the information they ask for. They may still misinterpret your document. I had one loan office who thought the Trust left to my client by their mother (a $300,000 asset) was a debt they owed someone else (a liability.) Not all bankers are bad. Most are qualified professionals. I sincerely hope you will be fortunate and be assigned a qualified professional who wants to help you succeed.

Prepare and rehearse before you present your loan proposal to bankers. Also shop for the right bank. I have had very good luck with this approach. When one bank thought my client was wrong for them, another thought they were perfect. Don't be shy about changing all your accounts to the bank that will fund you.

Implement Expansion Strategy

You have been implementing strategy all along but now we are speaking of the implementation of a major expansion and it needs additional thought and oversight. Intro…

Timeline

Your timeline is a schedule of critical events and should be incorporated into your cash flow projection as a Gant Chart above the actual numbers so you can match costs to events (see below.) Comments can be added to cells to clarify details. Refer to Figure 50 as I explain the timeline.

For this client, the timeline began with planning and was extended according to the time it would take to complete each task: planning, renovations, equipment installation, and training. The timeline was then placed under a chart for the sales season with planning starting on the current date. Arrows were added to indicate the flow of time. and color coded to match the sales season.

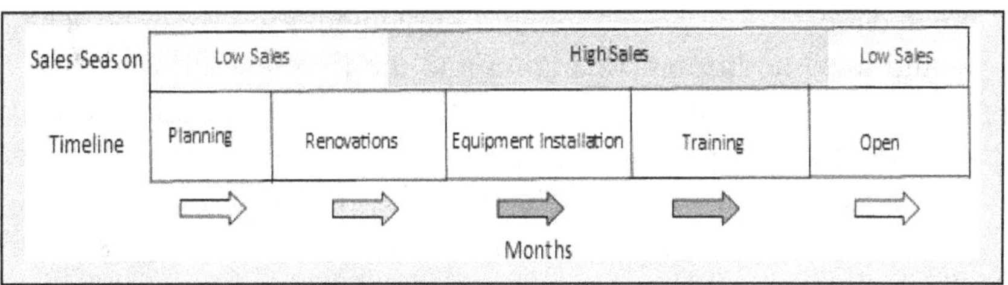

Figure 50: Implementation Timeline

Problems were immediately apparent. There was not enough time to complete the whole renovation before the high sales season and efficiency would be disrupted. The decision to wait until the beginning of the next slow sales season seemed reasonable, economical, and effective. The clients had to adjust their desire to fulfill their dream in favor of financial stability.

Timelines can be simple or complex, but the same principles apply.

Avoid mistakes by:

- Placing critical events in the right order
- Buy equipment after the renovation
- Test equipment before production
- Train employees before you need them
- Begin at the right time of year if you have a seasonal business

The following example is illustrative:

Timeline

Katcher's Kitchen had been successful for two years at a local farmer's market but had inefficiencies imbedded in their old kitchen. They could get by and still make a good profit, but their excess cash tempted them to begin the renovation immediately. They had poured over catalogues of new equipment and were ready to realize their dream.

They still had three months in the season for the market to be open but were nervous enough about the expenditures to want another opinion and went looking for qualified advice.

They sought the advice of their local EDC business advisor and created a cashflow projection and implementation timeline. They would need additional financing and the timeline showed that it would take a full five months for renovation, installation of new equipment, testing, and training of employees. To begin now would mean they carried debt for eight months before the new sales season and disrupt sales at the end of the current high season.

Their business advisor convinced them to wait and start their renovation at the beginning of the slow season and finish one week before the market opened again. They saved thousands of dollars in interest expenses and did not disrupt sales. Waiting had been a strategic decision.

Tracking Progress

You need to invest in a monthly financial analysis, with an understanding of the profit and loss, statement of cashflows, and balance sheet. You cannot move blindly into the future without becoming an expert at analyzing these documents. If you skipped this skill development, as many do, now is the time to correct your mistake. Get free instruction at your EDC or SBDC or take a class. Your objective is to compare the budget versus actual results. Most managers compare their cashflow projection with their Quickbooks financial reports. Finding variances will save you time and money if you can make corrections early.

Adjusting

As you track your progress against your financial statements and implementation timeline, you may find you are behind or ahead of your projected target dates. Adjust costs in the cash flow due to delays, inefficiencies, additional training, and unexpected events in the marketplace and question assumptions that lead to the current result. You may find you need additional financing.

When to Sell Your Business

Improving a business is difficult work, rewarding for some and punishing for others. If you have gotten this far in your development process you may have a clearer picture of the life you want to create and whether your business is a part of that picture. You may have several reasons to sell your business because you:

- No longer enjoy the work
- Want more time for other pursuits
- Want to capitalize on your high profits
- Know it is unprofitable

The Right Time

The right time to sell your business is *after* you have made it profitable again. If you have no profits to value, all you will get for it is the liquidation value (assets minus debts) — unless you find an unsophisticated buyer. In the unlikely case where you have made a diligent development effort and the business is still failing, the time to sell is immediately. Don't wait and incur more debt. Sell everything you can at cost and get out of your location so you can eliminate your overhead. If you haven't sold everything by the time your lease is up, offer it to your competition or store it and advertise in the classifieds.

If you have succeeded in your development, there may be seasonal considerations that influence the right time to sell. Try to pick the slowest sales season or a time before new capital purchases for inventory or equipment must be made. You will have more time to spend facilitating the sale and spending time with the new owner to orient him/her to the operation.

The Right Price

Some business owners conclude during the development process that they really do not like being in business and want to sell. I applaud you if you have made this decision because not everyone really has an interest in becoming an entrepreneur. As stated earlier, most entrepreneurs start a business because they have a technical skill or an interest in something they want to develop into a living but are unaware of the business skill required to create a *profitable* business. If you have found the "business" part of business a nightmare, then get out. You will be much happier pursuing a lifestyle and career that suits you.

You have, however, done yourself a great favor by improving your business, because now it is worth something. You may be counting the days when you will be free but do not be rash. Just as you have taken the time to invest in the development of your business, take the time to sell the business at the right time and at the right price.

Valuation Method

The only valid methods supported by financial theory are the Liquidation Value and the Discounted Cashflow. See **Appendix G** for a complete explanation. You need help to value your business. Hire someone credible.

The Right Help

Many individuals will claim to know how to place a value on your business, some have no background in finance and others will charge you too much for unnecessary and questionable methods.

Business brokers rarely have the expertise to value your business. They may do a good job of marketing the sale, but they use ad hoc methods such as three times the net income that have no basis in financial theory.

Certified Public Accountants (CPAs) understand the financial theory and use liquidation value and discounted cashflow methods, but they add other methods such as Common Size to show due diligence. These additional methods are not valid in my experience, but you get charged for them. Common Size states that there are businesses like yours that have recently been purchased and that your business should be approximately the same price. This ignores the fact that each business has a different profit margin, management, market demographic, asset utilization, and buyers with various required rates of return on the investment. There is nothing common in common size.

A CPA may want to charge you $5,000 for a complete valuation. I believe it should cost $1,500. If you use a CPA, tell them you want only the liquidation and discounted cashflow values.

All of Us

Treble Music School was like many small businesses experiencing growth: not bankable. Their six credit cards were maxed out and they could not attract a regular bank. Their local investment network, composed of citizens interested in supporting their community, were interested in their diligence and creativity and supplied them with a term loan for debt consolidation and a line of credit for summer music festivals. The term loan reduced their monthly cash outflow for debt, and the line of credit allowed them to invest in teaching summer classes and paying the cost back with tuition fees. With their finances in order, they continued to operate profitably.

Moving Forward

The following Chapter places your business in the larger framework of our global and domestic economies and will help you understand the difficulties and solutions available to you as an entrepreneur.

CHAPTER 8: Our American Economic System

Global and Domestic Systems
Solutions

<u>ALL of Us</u>

Don and his family ("All of Us", Chapter 1) had solved their cash crisis and gained much skill in managing their business. Sales were expanding every year and new products were well received by their loyal customer base. Then in the fall of 2008 the Great Recession unexpectedly overwhelmed the economy and they lost 30% of their monthly sales. Two months later they lost another 10%. For all manufacturers in their industry this was a business killing event. The family was better prepared than most, but they had low cash reserves and did not look bankable due to lingering debts. The recession had hit at exactly the wrong time but what could they do to save their business?

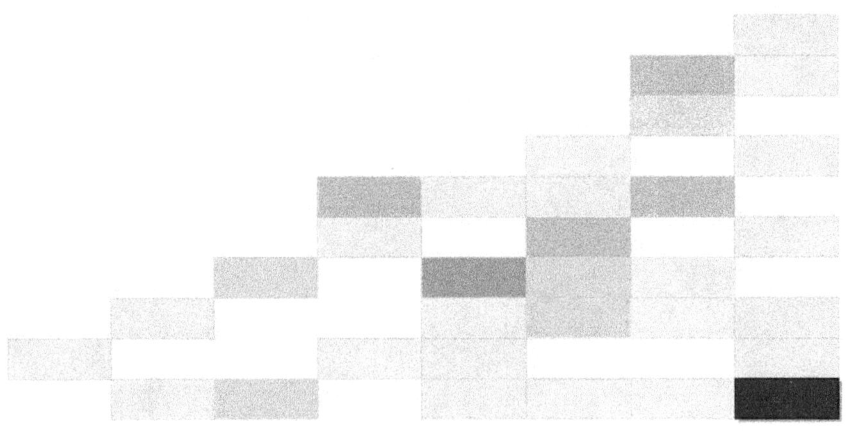

Global and Domestic Systems

You may have wondered why it is so hard to make a living in our contemporary culture and the answer is it is not your fault. Our current economic system is weighed against the middle class and in favor of the wealthy and corporations. The stagnation of wages over the last fifty years and unfavorable tax policies have driven the middle class almost out of existence. Productivity has soared due to computers and the skill level of employees, but the additional profits were taken by shareholders and not passed on to the work force. While CEOs take home millions in compensation, the average family can no longer save for retirement or send their kids to college. Few solutions are available to wage earners but *are* still there for entrepreneurs.

The Tyranny of Wealth

Wealth creates a kind of tyranny because the wealthy and the corporations they own can buy influence in Congress through political donations. This tyranny creates extreme wealth in a small part of our population and has a corrosive effect on democracy. Negative effects including:

- Defending the status quo to maintain an economic advantage
- Decreased social mobility
- The spread of misinformation concerning cause and effect
- Using professed values to hide real values
- Selling democracy to the highest bidder
- The politics of ignorance and fear: the fear of "socialism" (helping each other) is camouflage for favoring the wealthy
- Intolerance
- Income disparity and taxation
- The transfer of wealth from the middle class to the wealthy (recession of 2008)

You will hear arguments for why the wealthy should enjoy these benefits, but they are all economic nonsense.

Old Argument: Give the wealthy and corporations a tax break and they will create a job for you (trickle-down economics.)
Reality: Most jobs are created by small businesses. Congress creates corporate welfare by reducing corporate taxes. Taxes then fall on the middle-class and small businesses, eroding their savings.

Old Argument: Social systems such as the Affordable Care Act (healthcare) are socialist and are a drain on our country's resources.
Reality: Health insurance is beyond the means of many people. The wealthy do not want to pay taxes to support the average citizen and create an equitable society even though healthy people create a wealthy society.

Institutionalizing Inequality

Noam Chomsky in his documentary *Requiem for the American Dream* outlines ten principles of the concentration of wealth and power that the wealthy use to influence and warp our economic system.[7] The concentration of power creates a vicious cycle in which power creates favorable policies for the wealthy, that increases their wealth, and then gives them more power.

The ten principles include:

1) Reduce democracy so the average citizen has less political power.
2) Shape ideology so people believe in policies that do not benefit them.
3) Redesign the economy to:
   - Increase the role of financial institutions to 40% of corporate profits.
   - Deregulate risky investments. Eliminate separation of investment and commercial banking so taxpayers pay for bad investments when banks collapse.
   - Send production of goods offshore to reduce the income of working people and increase the profits of investors.

---

7 Noam Chomsky, *Requiem for the American Dream*, Seven Stories Press, New York 2017.

4) <u>Shift the burden of taxes</u> so:

- The wealthy pay less.
- The middle class pays more.

5) <u>Attack solidarity</u> to:

- Create a culture of self-interest not sympathy.
- Destroy Social Security.
- Create private schools.
- Increase tuition burden on students.

6) <u>Run the regulators</u> so:

- Corporations influence or control regulators.
- Deregulation of industry benefits shareholders. Creates economic crashes.
- Bank bailouts are paid with tax dollars to benefit shareholders.

7) <u>Engineer elections and funding rules</u> so:

- Wealth can buy elections.
- Give the right of personage to corporations so money becomes a right of speech.

8) <u>Keep the Rabble in Line</u>

- Undermine unions.
- Taft Hardly Act.
- McCarthyism.
- Strike breaking.

9) <u>Manufacture Consent</u>

- Media abuse
- Trapping consumers in the superficial.
- Fabricating consumers.
- Uniformed consumers.

10) <u>Marginalize the Population</u>

- Focus anger on each other.

The American Cause and Effect System

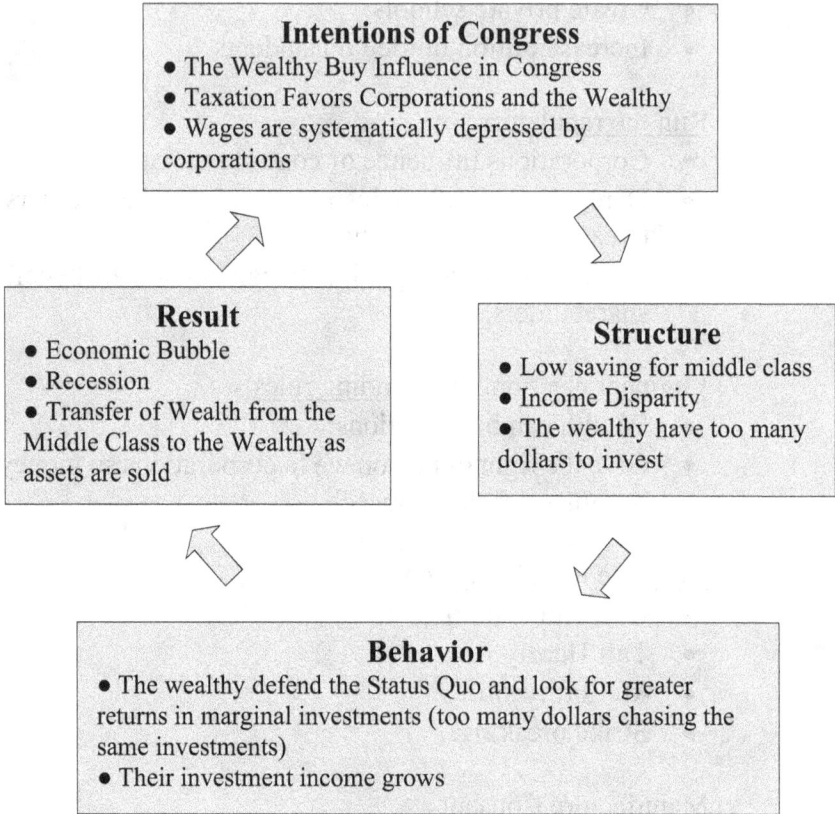

Just as management Intentions create Structures and Behaviors in your business (**Chapter 2**), so do the Intentions of our Congress create Structures and Behaviors in our economic system. The American Cause and Effect Systems is represented in Figure 51.

This is a reinforcing loop that gets worse over time.

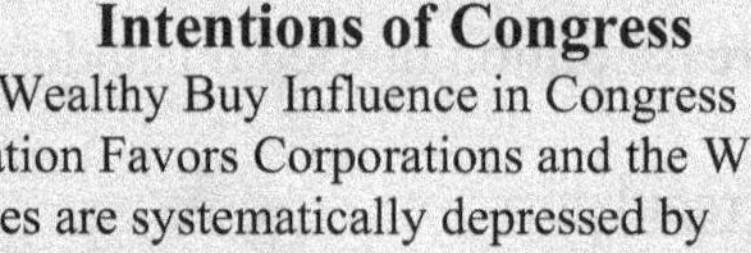

Intentions of Congress
• The Wealthy Buy Influence in Congress
• Taxation Favors Corporations and the Wealthy
• Wages are systematically depressed by corporations

Result
• Economic Bubble
• Recession
• Transfer of Wealth from the Middle Class to the Wealthy as assets are sold
Structure
• Low saving for middle class
• Income Disparity
• The wealthy have too many dollars to invest

Behavior
• The wealthy defend the Status Quo and look for greater returns in marginal investments (too many dollars chasing the same investments)
• Their investment income grows

Figure 51: American Cause and Effect System

The wealthy, looking for greater returns, invest in marginal investments and inflate those assets. The middle class invest in houses, washing machines, cars and other durable goods and expand the economy.

Results of the system include:

- The transfer of wealth from the middle class to the wealthy
- Further income disparity
- Lower standard of living
- A culture of scarcity, meanness, anger, and frustration
- Increasing crime
- The wealthy have income from investments even in a recession, the middle class do not
- Savings for the middle class decrease each year and each generation
- Down-sizing
- Violence

In an extreme recession like the one beginning in 2008 the wealthy had their assets devalued but still maintained great wealth. The middle-class lost everything: their jobs, houses, and sometimes their families. The wealthy buy the assets that the middle class have lost, and income disparity becomes more extreme. The national debt would not exist if corporations and the wealthy paid their share of taxes, especially on foreign earnings.

The intentions of Congress are to keep the status quo for the wealthy out of fear, ignorance, and self-interest. The inevitability of imbalance follows their intentions.

Solutions

To create a better society, we must create economic equity. By that I mean more income must flow into the hands of the middle and lower classes through adequate compensation. Changing tax laws that favor the wealthy and corporations would be a start but that is treating the symptoms, not the fundamental solution.

The real solution is a change in culture, a way of valuing people that is absent at the highest levels of business and government. Changing our culture is difficult and takes generations to achieve. We have already seen much of this change in our attitudes toward new minorities, racial injustice, and gender issues but the crisis of our time is income disparity. Cultural and legal change will come slowly so you, the entrepreneur, must apply the solutions available to you in *this* generation.

Political Solutions

If the intention of Congress was fair, there might be a political solution, but it is unlikely. Congress is ruled by greed, fear, power, and ignorance but you can vote out of office any politician who uses the tired old arguments of trickle-down economics and undermines real solutions.

Trickle-down economics sets forth the idea that if you do not tax the wealthy, they will create jobs. This is false. The largest creator of jobs in our nation is small business, but you as a middle-income business owner never get the personal and business tax breaks the corporations and the wealthy receive.

Regulation, criminal consequences, and taxation can solve a part of the problem but only organizing into powerful donor groups can influence congress. The AARP organizes on behalf of retired people and has great influence. You can join or start entrepreneurial groups or associations to gain influence locally and nationally.

Entrepreneurial Solutions

Entrepreneurship is one of the few solutions any person can apply to counteract the pernicious effects of an unfair economic system. You don't have to be a doomsday prepper or survivalist to see the importance of creating and storing value. Your business is one of these. It is a productive asset that can be managed to move *with* the market through pricing, efficiency, and volume. You can grow your skill and knowledge to match the changing economy and not get stuck with minor pay increases in a paycheck job that slowly erodes your purchasing power. If you treat your employees well, they become a part of your success team and contribute to solving difficult problems, but the value you have created can be destroyed by forces outside of your control including unfair taxation, government and corporate corruption, recessions, bank failures, rising costs, and globalization.

So, in addition to running your business, you must diversify assets away from it. Don't expect to sell your business to fund your retirement. Make the highest profits you can now and then use those profits to make investments in other assets.

Other assets include:

- Stock index funds
- Bonds
- Cash
- Rental properties

Prepare yourself for a secure future by:

- Eliminating debt. There is no such thing as a cash back credit card. It is *all* debt, and you pay for it.
- Constructing a modest, zero net energy house with solar panels to charge your electric car
- Placing your assets in a living trust

Do not buy:

- A big house
- A vacation home
- Time share property
- Expensive cars
- Big travel

All of Us

Don and his family were well along in the *SUCCEED!*™ Process when the recession hit. They had built resources and capabilities (Chapter 2,) maximized productivity and cash flow except for some production systems (Chapter 3,) and invested in strategic planning each year for two years (Chapter 4.)

Don called a strategic planning meeting with all the key personnel including his business advisor. In a five-hour session cash flows were revised, a recession action plan was mapped out, and an implementation schedule created. The focus was on creating new profit centers for the current products.

The business returned to prerecession sales levels within nine months and then expanded at 18% per year from 2009 to 2012. Other manufacturers did not recover as quickly and 50% of the industry went bankrupt. It was not as easy as it sounds but the results are true and exceptional.

In 2012 additional savings accrued because the business advisor became obsolete. Don knew everything his advisor knew and could manage his business without assistance.

Conclusion

Through the examples of real entrepreneurs presented here and your own hard work completing each *SUCCEED!*™ task, you should now be able to see that real skill applied to real problems is the only effective means for running a profitable business. Wishful thinking, avoidance, and investing in management fads leads to false hope and eventual failure.

As an entrepreneur, your education and skill development is a lifelong process and the techniques covered in this manual are only a portion of the available information on business management. But you have gained a framework in the Problem-Solving Sequence to place your new information. I urge you to read widely, learn as much as you can and tailor the information to your individual needs.

Remember you are not alone. Private consultants, the Small Business Development Center, and Economic Development Councils are there in your state ready to help you. Community Colleges offer many weekend workshops on business subjects, and The Small Business Administration has programs and Resource Centers available to you for free.

Please refer this book to your friends in business. I believe it to be, and I hope you believe it to be, a valuable resource for all entrepreneurs. I would also like to know what you think. Your feedback is of great value because you are an entrepreneur with knowledge and skill that I and others can benefit from. You can send your thoughts to me at www.douglasjhammel.com.

Please consider writing a positive review on Amazon or your favorite book related website. With your help, *SUCCEED!*™ will continue to grow and improve.

The best of luck to you in all your endeavors.

APPENDIX A: The *SUCCEED!*™ Outline

The complete outline that begins each chapter follows below.

Build Resources/Capabilities

Information:

- Financial Review/Embezzlement
- Project Costing System (Bid Sheet)
- Cash Flow Projections
- Price Increases/Retail (Merchandising)
- Collections/Construction Liens
- Software/Information System
- Accounting/Planning Notebook/Cash Management

Profit:

- Cost/Profit/Volume
- Price Ceiling/Higher Profit Margin Products & Services
- Overhead Allocation to Profit Centers/Product Strategies
- Up-selling/Easy Cost Reductions/Clutter

Risk:

- Timeliness in Invoicing/Contracts
- Insurance/Legal Structure/Control/Ownership
- Intellectual Property/Handling Procedures/Image

Leadership Lesson 1

- Personal Goals/Educating the Whole Organization
- Facilitation/Making Transitions
- Communication/Training/Delegation

Intentions

- Intentions/Assumptions
- The Entrepreneurial Problem
- Thinking Patterns/Personality Types
- Wellness Issues/Commitment to Change

Practical Point of Attack: Tasks for This Section

Maximize Cash Flow/Productivity

Leadership Lesson 2

Balance/Expertise/Honesty/Integrity/Availability

Problem Solving

Vetting Existing Employees
Problem Solving/Learning Organizations
The Systems Dialogue
Group Problem Solving
Facilitation of Systems Redesign
Conflict Resolution

Efficiency

Types of Systems
Systems Redesign
Capacity: Space Planning

Strategic Compensation

Skill Blocks
Market Pay Line
Internal Consistency
Personnel Policy Manual

Productivity Measures and Incentive Pay

Beyond the 20% Profit Margin
Productivity Measures
Benchmarks and Goals
Incentives

Practical Point of Attack: Tasks for This Section

Evaluate Your Market

Set New Goals

Mission/Values

- The Mission Statement
- The Value Statement

Leadership Lesson 3

- Transformational Leadership

Expansion Strategies

- Profit Centers
- Horizontal and Vertical Integration
- Strategic Partnerships
- Tools and Analysis
    - Differential Analysis
    - Break Even for Expansions
    - Staging Each Strategy

Status Quo

- Threats

Contraction Strategies

- Skills
- Equipment
- Employees
- Square Footage

Develop New Systems

Planning Document
- Your Plan
- Loan Proposal Template

Scalable Systems
- Marketing
  - Research
  - Communication
  - Sales Training
- Office
  - Software
  - Workflow
  - Filing
  - Workspace
- Production
  - Capacity
  - Space Plan
  - Inventory
  - Accounting
  - Shipping
- Human Resources
  - Training
  - Compensation/Incentives
- Ownership

Finance Alternatives

Long-term Financing

- Revise Cash Flow Projections
- Sources of Capital
- Loan Types
- Loan Proposals
- Bankers

Implement Expansion Strategy

- Timeline
- Tracking Progress
- Adjusting

When to Sell Your Business

- The Right Time
- The Right Price

Staff Meeting Agenda

(Planning for Change, a Competitive Strategy)

Reports

Restatement of the Mission
Succeed! Progress Report/Tasks
Department Reports

- Production/Work Efficiency
- Benchmarks
- Problems
- Potential solutions

Threats/Opportunities: assess according to the Chart below

Area of Concern	Information Item Only	Potential Market Trend	Developing Threat	Direct Market Threat
Systems				
Competition				
Industry				
Economy				
Customers				
New Products				
Technologies				

Prioritize and place as an activity in your task table.

Training

Succeed! Management Reading/Discussion
Other Training

Systems Redesign Work

Continue Current Systems Redesign
Oversight on Other Systems

APPENDIX B: Internal Control Questionnaire

Answer each question “Yes” or “No”. Address “No” answers thoroughly.

General

1. Are accounting records kept up-to-date and balanced monthly?
2. Is a chart of accounts used?
3. Does the owner use a budget system for watching income and expenses?
4. Are cashflow projections created and used as a decision-making tool?
5. Are adequate monthly financial reports available to the owner?
6. Does the owner appear to take a direct and active interest in the financial affairs and reports which should be or are available?
7. Are the personal funds of the owner and his personal income and expenses completely segregated from the business?
8. Is the owner satisfied that all employees are honest?
9. Is the bookkeeper required to take annual vacations?
10. Is the accounting system passworded so employees have access to only the features they need?
11. Are checks and credit cards secured in a locked cabinet?

Cash Receipts

1. Does the owner open the mail?
2. Does the owner list mail receipts before turning them over to the bookkeeper?
3. Is the listing of receipts subsequently traced to the cash receipts journal?
4. Are receipts deposited intact daily?
5. Are over-the-counter receipts controlled by cash register tapes, counter receipts, etc.?
6. Are employees who handle funds bonded?

Cash Disbursements

1. Are all disbursements made by check?
2. Are pre-numbered checks used?
3. Is a controlled, mechanical check protector used?

4. Is the owner's signature required on checks?
5. Does the owner sign checks only after they have been properly completed?
6. Does the owner approve and cancel the documentation in support of all disbursements?
7. Are all voided checks retained and accounted for?
8. Does the owner review the bank reconciliation?
9. Is an impress petty cash fund used?

Accounts Receivable and Sales

1. Are work orders and/or sales invoices pre-numbered and controlled?
2. Are customers' ledgers balanced regularly?
3. Are monthly statements sent to all customers?
4. Does the owner review statements before mailing them himself?
5. Are account write-offs and discounts approved only by the owner?
6. Is credit approved only by the owner?

Notes Receivable and Investment

1. Does the owner have sole access to notes and investment certificates?

Inventories

1. Is the person responsible for inventory someone other than the bookkeeper?
2. Are the periodic physical inventories taken?
3. Is there physical control over inventory stock?
4. Are perpetual inventory records maintained?

Property assets

1. Are there detailed records available of property assets and allowances for depreciation?
2. Is the owner acquainted with property assets owned by the company?
3. Are retirements approved by the owner?

Accounts Payable and Purchases

1. Are purchase orders used?
2. Is someone other than the bookkeeper in charge of purchasing?
3. Are suppliers' monthly statements compared with recorded liabilities regularly?
4. Are suppliers' monthly statements checked by the owner periodically if disbursements are made from invoice only?

Payroll

1. Are the employees hired by the owner?
2. Would the owner be aware of the absence of any employee?
3. Does the owner approve, sign, and distribute payroll checks?
4. Does the owner check to make sure pay rates for each employee are correct in the payroll system?

APPENDIX C: Accounting Explained

Understanding Financial Statements

Financial statements like the Balance Sheet and Income Statement, also known as the Profit and Loss Statement, seem to confuse many entrepreneurs. The Statements look complex and the logic behind them appears convoluted or "twisted" as one of my clients put it. I think this perception persists for two reasons:

- The first time through any new subject can be difficult and most entrepreneurs avoid this difficulty because they are already busy trying to *run* the business
- Accounting instructors seem to explain it in the most difficult way. I want to explain it to you the most effective way.

Because I have had many small business clients I had to develop a quick but effective way to explain accounting. I created a graphical method that avoids all the confusing jargon of debts and credits and reveals the simple logic underneath. I can accomplish this with most clients in 40 minutes while a college accounting class confuses students for many weeks before the logic becomes clear.
I will explain accounting in this order:

- The Balance Sheet
- The Income Statement (Profit & Loss)
- How they fit together
- Individual transactions on paper
- Individual transactions in an accounting system like Quickbooks

Refer to Figure 52 as I explain the Balance Sheet.

Balance Sheet			
Assets		**Liabilities and Equity**	
		Liabilities	
Current Assets		Current Liabilities	
Cash	10	Accounts Payable	5
Accounts Receivable	5	Accrued Taxes	5
Inventory	10	Credit Cards/LOC	10
Fixed Assets		Long-term Liabilities	
Equipment	25	Term Loan	5
Land & Buildings	50		
		Total Liabilities	25
		Equity	
		Opening Balance	15
		Investment	0
		Net Income	50
		Retained Earnings	10
		Total Equity	75
Total Assets	100	Total Liab & Equity	100

Value (Assets side) — Who Owns the Value (Liabilities and Equity side)

Figure 52: The Balance Sheet

The Balance Sheet

The Balance Sheet is a document that keeps track of the value of assets used in the business and who owns them and is divided into two sections. Sometimes you see these two sections placed top to bottom and sometimes you see them placed side by side. I like to place them side by side because it is easier to explain how they relate to each other.

Value. The left side of the Balance Sheet is called Assets and lists everything of value. What is of Value? Everything you would expect: Cash, Inventory, Accounts Receivable (money that customers owe you), Equipment, Fixtures, Buildings, Land, and more. This seems very intuitive, and it is! Add up everything on the left side and you have the value of your Total Assets, in this case $100. Do not confuse this value with the price you would sell the business for if you had a buyer. That is a different calculation covered in **Appendix G**.

Who Owns the Value? The right side of the Balance Sheet is called Liabilities and Equity and represents who owns the value. You might say that you own all the value — it is your business — but that is not quite true. If you receive inventory from a vendor and do not pay her in cash, she owns a piece of your business and what she owns, or has a claim on, is listed as Accounts Payable. You may have bought a computer with a credit card and still owe the credit card company. You might owe payroll taxes to the IRS for work completed by your employees and would be accounted for as Taxes Payable. These transactions would all be listed as Current Liabilities because you intend to pay them off within a year.

A bank loan would be listed as a Long-term Liability because it will take longer than one year to pay it off.

You cannot say, necessarily, that the cash you have in Assets came from the bank loan, or that the Accounts Payable is for the inventory that is still on the shelves, but you do owe these amounts and the people you owe them to have a claim on that much value from your business. Add all the Liabilities on the right side of the Balance Sheet and you have Total Liabilities, in this case $60.

But if there is value, someone must own all of it, so now something is wrong. You have $100 of value but only $60 of whom owns it. So, who owns the other $40. You do! What you own of the business is a special category on the right side called Equity or Net Worth. If you add together everything on the right side, Liabilities plus Equity, you get $100, and all the value on the left side is accounted for.

Remember that Equity is always the "plug" figure that makes both sides equal. If you were accomplishing this on paper the process would:

- List everything of value on the left side and find your Total Assets by adding everything together.
- List everything you owe other people on the right side and find Total Liabilities by adding all this together.
- Find your Equity (Net Worth) by subtracting Total Liabilities from Total Assets.
- Check to make sure that Liabilities plus Equity equals Total Assets.

Where does the information come from to create the balance sheet?

From your monthly record keeping for income and expenses, your check book, your monthly inventory count, and worksheets you have created to keep track of the value of various assets and liabilities; but accomplishing this on paper would be tedious and time consuming. It is much easier to use an accounting system like Quickbooks that recalculates all financial statements after each transaction.

How can you use the information in the Balance Sheet? As a red flag to tell you whether you are making any progress (covered in detail in **Appendix D:** Financial Analysis.) The way you do this is to create percentages by dividing each item on the Balance Sheet by Total Assets. From Figure 52, if you divide Accounts Receivable by Total Assets you get 20/100 = .20, which is 20%. You can see I made the numbers easy to understand by making Total Assets equal to 100. What if you calculated these percentages each month and found that Accounts Receivable went from 20% to 30% to 45% over a three-month period. You would know something was wrong with your collections or credit policy. The same would be true for the percentages for Debt, Equity, or any other item on the Balance Sheet. You would see the problem coming and do something about it before it became a crisis.

<u>The Income Statement</u>

The Income Statement, also known as the Profit and Loss Statement (P&L), is a document that lists sales, and the expenses incurred to generate those sales. Figure 53 shows a typical P&L. This document seems very intuitive, and it is. You subtract all expenses from sales and get Net Income, which is either a Profit or a Loss (in accounting, negative numbers appear in parentheses). But there are a few wrinkles that seem to confuse business managers. Notice that under expenses only the interest from a loan appears, whereas the principle for the same loan is recorded after the Net Income. This is for two reasons:

- The government wants to tax you on Net Income and will only allow the interest on a loan as a deduction
- The interest really is the *expense* of using the bank's money, and you are trying to find out what your expenses are.

Think of this interest as the rent you pay the bank to use their money. The principal payment on the loan is taken out of Net Income. When you pay the bank loan every month you make only one payment, but the bank divides this payment into interest and principal. The interest and principal may be printed on your payment coupon. If it isn't, you can ask the bank for a loan amortization schedule that will show the interest and principal for each payment.

Income Statement	
Income	
Sales	100
Cost of Goods Sold (COGS)	25
Gross Profit	75
Operating Expenses	
Rent	5
Wages	5
Phone	5
Depreciation	5
Interest	5
Total Operating Expenses	25
Net Income	50

Figure 53: The Income Statement (P&L)

The other wrinkle is depreciation. This is a tax deduction that allows you to take off a portion of the expense of large equipment each year. You are trying to find out how much of the equipment you use up each month or year in creating the sales for that month or year. Consider a machine that costs $10,000 but will be useful for 10 years. It would not be reasonable to say that you used up $10,000 of that machine to create the sales just for one month because the machine will contribute to sales in every month for the next ten years. But it would be reasonable to say that $1,000 of the machine was used up every year. That is depreciation. It is sometimes confusing because you *have* spent the $10,000 in cash, but it is showing on your P&L only $1,000 at a time.

Small businesses do have the option of taking the entire cost of large equipment purchases as an expense up to $17,500 per year and not depreciate. This is called a 179 Deduction and can be found on your Schedule C Tax Form under depreciation. In the example above you could take the full $10,000 as an expense for the machine in the first year you use it. Doing this does not give you an accurate P&L but it does reduce your taxes.

You may now be confused about why certain expenses items are cash deductions, others are non-cash depreciation, and still others don't even show up on the P&L. Keep in mind that an Accrual P&L shows sales, whether or not you received the cash for the sales; and expenses, whether or not you actually paid for the expenses.

In this very simple example, a business owner had a sale of $100. The product he purchased to sell to his customer cost him $25, leaving a Gross Profit of $75. Let's assume the customer left the store without paying for the product and the business owner got the product from his supplier without paying for it. No cash has changed hands, but he still wants to know if what he charged for the product and what it cost him, left him a profit. In Accrual P&L, we are talking about sales and expenses, not necessarily cash. The Cash Flow Statement, covered in the next appendix, tracks cash.

You can use the P&L just like the Balance Sheet: as a red flag to point out problems (covered in detail in **Appendix D:** Financial Analysis.) Again, create percentages but this time divide every item on the P&L by Total Sales. Compare these percentages month to month and look for changes. If your materials expense goes from 25% to 30% to $40% over a three-month period, you have a problem to solve such as embezzlement. You can look at every expense item and head off bad trends as soon as you notice.

How They Fit Together

Balance Sheet			
Assets		**Liabilities and Equity**	
		Liabilities	
Current Assets		Current Liabilities	
Cash	10	Accounts Payable	5
Accounts Receivable	5	Accrued Taxes	5
Inventory	10	Credit Cards/LOC	10
Fixed Assets		Long-term Liabilities	
Equipment	25	Term Loan	5
Land & Buildings	50		
		Total Liabilities	25
		Equity	
		Opening Balance	15
		Investment	0
		Income Statement	
		Sales 100	
		Expenses 50	
		Net Income	50
		Retained Earnings	10
		Total Equity	75
Total Assets	100	Total Liab & Equity	100

Figure 54: The Balance Sheet Expanded

The Balance Sheet and Income Statement are one document. As you can see in Figure 54, the whole P&L is imbedded in the Balance Sheet (shadowed box.) In Figure 52 you saw only the Net Income listed on the Balance Sheet because it would make the report very large and difficult to read if all the P&L items were included. Figure 54 shows that all the items on the P&L are present.

The Chart of Accounts is the list of Balance Sheet items beginning with cash and listing all the assets in order, then moving over to the liabilities and equity side and listing those accounts in order, including all the item in the P&L and finishing with Retained Earnings.

Individual Transactions in a Chart

If we simplify the balance sheet to its most basic form, it will appear as it does in Figure 55. You can see the left side representing assets, the right-hand side representing the liabilities and equity sections, and the box for the P&L. We can now graphically represent any transaction by placing them in the appropriate spaces. Follow along as I explain accounting in six transactions.

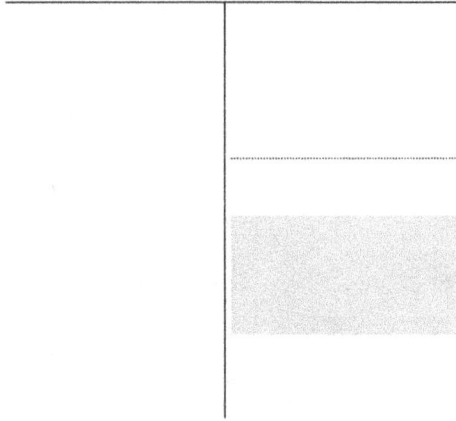

Figure 55: The Balance Sheet Simplified

Figure 56 shows the bank account being used to pay an expense. The bank balance goes down and equity goes down due to the expense. Both sides of the balance sheet have decreased by the same amount, so the balance sheet stays in balance. Remember any transaction on the P&L affects equity because the P&L is inside the equity section. Sales make equity increase. Expenses make equity decrease.

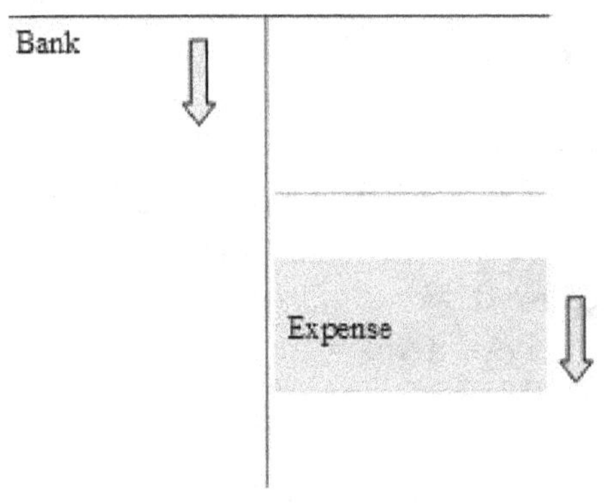

Figure 56: Use Bank to Pay Expense

The next transaction, Figure 57, shows the credit card being used to pay an expense. The credit card balance increases due to the charge, and equity decreases due to the expense. The credit card has increased by the same amount that equity has decreased, and the right side of the balance sheet has not changed. All examples are called balancing transactions because they keep the balance sheet in balance. In the first transaction, the balancing was across the center line, in the second the balancing was on the right side only.

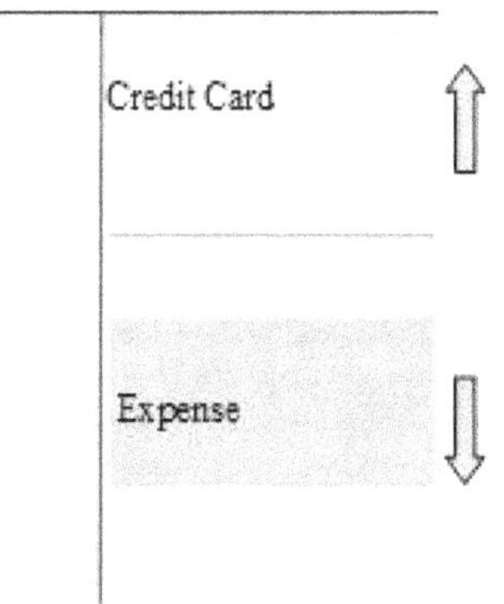

Figure 57: Use Credit Card to Pay Expense

The third transaction, Figure 58, shows the bank account being used to pay down the credit card. The bank balance decreases and the credit card balance decreases. The balancing transaction is across the center line.

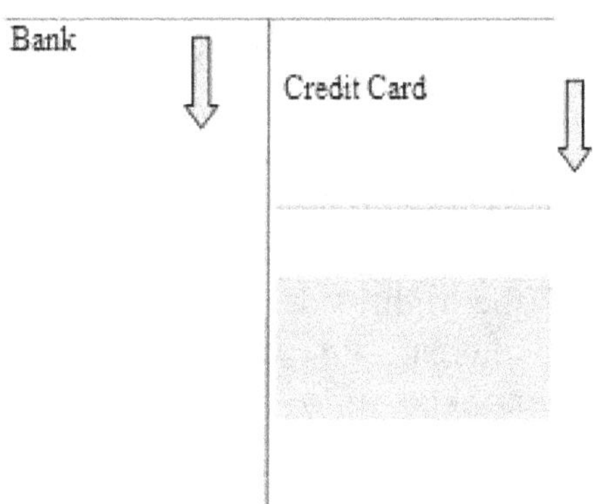

Figure 58: Use Bank to Pay Credit Card

The fourth transaction, Figure 59, shows the bank account being used to buy equipment. Equipment is an asset, not an expense, and can be found on the left side of the balance sheet. The bank balance decreases and the equipment account increases. The balancing is on the left side.

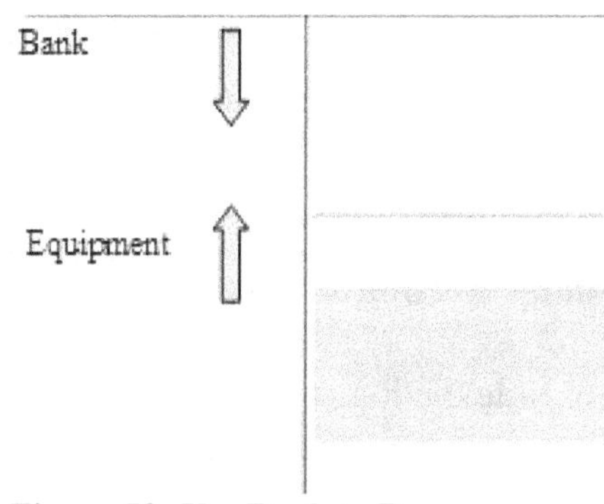

Figure 59: Use Bank to Buy Equipment

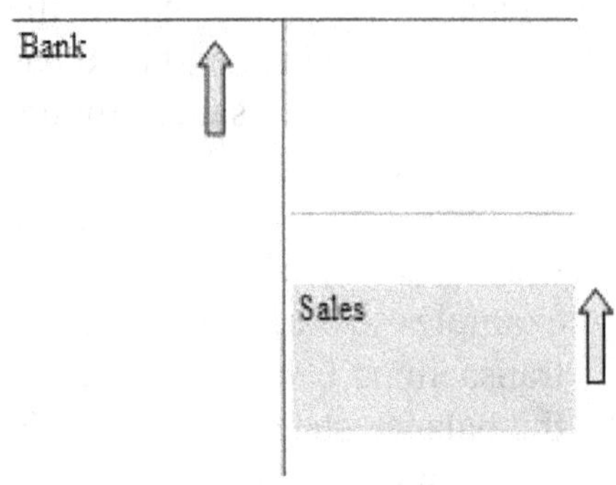

Figure 60: Sales Are Deposited into the Bank

The fifth transaction, Figure 60, shows a sale being made on the P&L and the funds being deposited in the bank. Equity increases due to the sale and the bank account increases due to the deposit. The balancing transaction is across the center line.

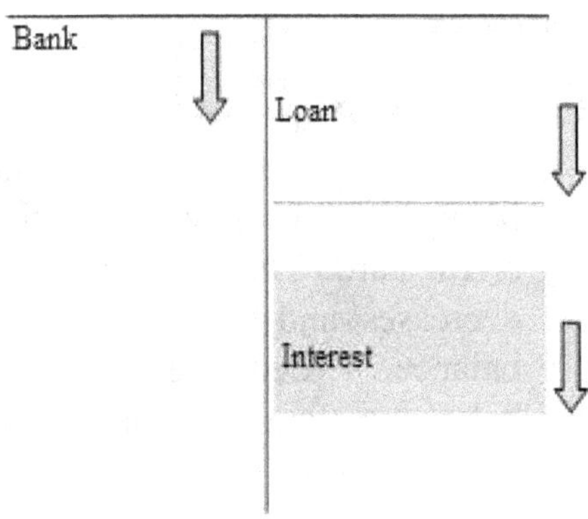

Figure 61: Loan Split

The last example, Figure 61, is the most complex transaction you may encounter and shows what is called a loan split. The bank decreases by the full amount of the loan payment on the left side. On the right side, principal and interest are split apart and booked into the approriate item. The principal part of the loan payment decreases the loan balance and the interest part of the loan payment decreases equity.

The totals at the bottom of the balance sheet for Assets (left side) and Liabilities & Equity (right side) may have changed in some transactions but they are always equal and in balance if the transaction is entered correctly.

Individual Transactions in an Accounting System

In an accounting system they try to hide the logic of the transaction rather than explain it but if you have understood the logic, you are more likely to input the transaction correctly and not corrupt your accounting data. In Quickbooks, you begin any new input by pressing the "New" button on the top left of the start page. For booking an expense, you choose Expense on the next page. The input page for an expense transaction, Figure 62, looks like you are writing a check, and you fill in each box according to the information needed. You choose the vendor who you are paying to, your payment account (bank or credit card,) the date, the payment method, and a reference number (check number.) At the bottom, on Line 1, input information into each window. You choose the balancing transaction in the dropdown window under "Category," create a description, and input the amount. The dropdown window under "Category" has the entire chart of accounts in it, so you must choose the correct account to accurately balance your balance sheet. When you hit "Save" the transaction is completed and your balance sheet is rebalanced.

The Inputs Paths for each transaction with Payment Account identified appears in column 1. The Balancing Transaction Category appears in column 2. Credit Card is abbreviated CC:

Column 1 Input Path	Column 2 Balancing Transaction Category
New > Expense > Bank	Expense Account
New > Expense > CC	Expense Account
New > Expense > Bank	Credit Card
New > Expense > Bank	Equipment
New > Deposit > Bank	Sale Income
New > Expense > Bank	Line 1: Loan Line 2: Interest

If you would like to view tutorials for Quickbooks Online, search YouTube for *The Quickbooks Dude*. He has posted many useful instructional videos.

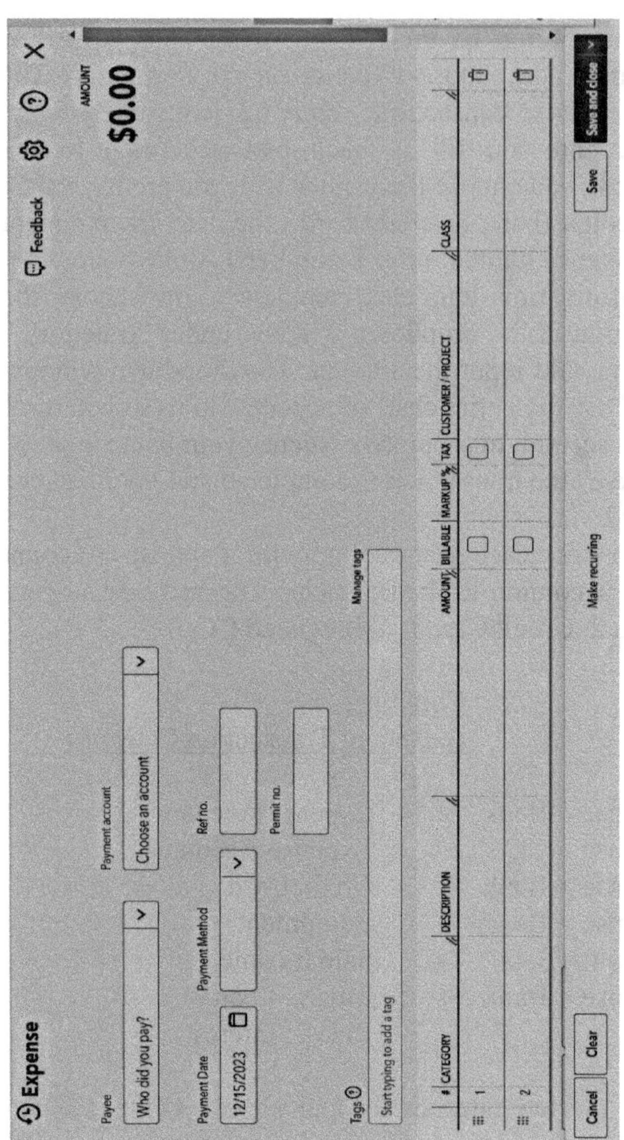

Figure 62: Quickbooks Expenditure Transaction

APPENDIX D: Financial Analysis

Financial Analysis is best accomplished by reviewing financial statements in this order:

- Income Statement (Profit & Loss)
- Statement of Cash Flows (Sources and Uses of Funds)
- Balance Sheet

The reason for this sequence is that the last number on the P&L, Net Income, is the first number on the Statement of Cash Flows. The last number on the Statement of Cash Flows, Cash Balance, is the first number on the Balance Sheet. Each financial statement is connected to the previous statement and is organized as a logical flow of information. The following abbreviations will be useful as we proceed.

Abbreviations

A/R:	Accounts Receivable
A/P:	Accounts Payable
CA:	Current Assets
CL:	Current Liabilities
COGS:	Cost of Goods Sold
INV:	Inventory
NI:	Net Income
OE:	Operating Expenses (same as Overhead, OH)
PM:	Profit Margin
ROA:	Return on Assets
ROI:	Return on Investment
TA:	Total Assets
TD:	Total Debt

The Income Statement (P&L)

Refer to Figures 63 and 64. Figure 63 is the P&L and Figure 64 is the financial analysis. The data for analysis could be by month or year. This spreadsheet shows data for the years 2002-2006. In all financial analysis we are looking for trends both in dollars and percentages.

<u>Dollars Trends</u>

- Sales are increasing but is it trouble or not? Without any other information it does not look like a problem but be cautious. Increased sales usually incur increased expense.

- Cost of Goods Sold (COGS) is also increasing, and you would expect it to with sales also increasing but it is difficult to tell if it is reasonable without looking at it as a percentage of sales.

- Operating Expenses (OE) are increasing and it is clear that there has been a significant increase since 2005 and is probably a bad trend.

- Net Income (NI) tells a more complete story with sales, GOGS, and operating expenses combining to first increase net income then decrease it in a bad trend. The dollar trends should point you to investigate further with percentage trends to confirm your suspicions and give you additional insight.

<u>Percentage Trends</u>

Divide every item on the P&L by total sales to get a percentage. Quickbooks can do this for you. Look for month by month or year by year trends that indicate trouble:

- COGS % has increased from 35% to 50% of sales and is a significantly bad trend. Prices in the marketplace for goods may have increased due to supply chain shocks or you may have just lost track of your costs. It could also indicate embezzlement where an employee is writing checks to fictitious companies and cashing them for their own profit.

- Gross Profit (GP) is a mirror image of COGS and can be seen decreasing as a percentage of sales as COGS increases. This means you have fewer dollars available to cover operating expenses.

- Increases in expense item percentages shows a mixed story. First, as sales increased wages dropped to 25% but then almost doubled to 44% when wages made a dramatic jump in 2005.

- The Profit Margin (PM) tells you how well your combined income and expenses are working to create profits. I believe a 20% profit margin is what all businesses need and can achieve. This business had an increasing PM and then a decreasing PM. The causes are clear: higher COGS, and a jump in wages. Here is where you apply solutions in pricing, efficiency, and volume but, if you could only manipulate volume, you would always choose to produce $3,000 in sales as in 2004, which resulted in the highest PM and highest dollar value in profits.

INCOME STATEMENT
(P&L)

	2002	2003	2004	2005	2006
SALES	1,000	2,000	3,000	3,500	4,000
COGS	350	720	1,200	1,338	2,000
GROSS PROFIT	650	1,280	1,800	2,162	2,000
OPERATING EXPENSES					
Rent	400	400	400	400	400
Wages	200	200	200	1,500	1,200
Phone	50	50	50	50	50
Depreciation	20	20	20	20	20
Interest	80	80	80	80	80
TOTAL OP EXP	750	750	750	2,050	1,750
NET INCOME (NI)	(100)	530	1,050	112	250

Figure 63: P&L Statement

FINANCIAL ANALYSIS

	2002	2003	2004	2005	2006
Dollar Trends					
Sales	Increasing: Trouble or Not?				Not.
COGS	Increasing: Good or Bad? Reasonable or Not?				Bad Trend
Op Exp	Increasing: Good or Bad?				Bad Trend
Net Income (NI)	Increasing or Decreasing?				Bad Trend
Always ask the question: Why is the trend occuring?					
Percentage Trends (% of Sales)	2002	2003	2004	2005	2006
COGS	0.35	0.36	0.40	0.38	0.50
Gross Profit (GP)	0.65	0.64	0.60	0.62	0.50
Operating Expenses	0.75	0.38	0.25	0.59	0.44
Profit Margin (PM)	(0.10)	0.27	0.35	0.03	0.06
Break Even (BE)	1,154	1,172	1,250	3,319	3,500

Figure 64: P&L Financial Analysis

The Statement of Cash Flows

Another useful report beyond the Balance Sheet and the P&L is the Statement of Cash Flows. Do not confuse the Statement of Cash Flows with a Cash Flow Projection, they are completely different documents. The Statement of Cash Flows, also known as Sources and Uses of Funds, shows you how cash was made available (sources) or was used (uses) through changes to your balance sheet that do not show up on your P&L. Positive numbers provide cash and negative numbers use cash. Only dollar data is useful in the Statement of Cash Flows. Negative numbers are in parentheses. Refer to Figure 65 and 66 as I explain.

Dollars Trends

The report begins with Net Income for 2002 as the first source of cash. A profit (positive number) adds cash. A loss (negative number) subtracts cash. Let's look at each item and how it added or subtracted cash from the statement of cashflows.

- Net Income (NI) is negative in 2002 and subtracted cash. NI from 2003 through 2006 is positive and increased cash but it is variable and has a bad downward trend.
- Accounts receivable (A/R) in every year is a negative number and subtracted cash by getting larger, that is, your customer did not pay you and used your cash, making A/R larger. The actual A/R on the Balance Sheet could be any value but between Jan 1, 2002, and Dec 31, 2002, got larger by 100. This is the same for all years, showing an ever-expanding A/R.
- Inventory is a negative number and subtracted cash by getting larger, that is, you used cash to purchase inventory and inventory got larger by 200 in 2002.
- Accounts payable (A/P) is a negative number and subtracted cash by getting smaller, the is, you used cash to pay down A/P and A/P got smaller.
- Credit Cards seem to have had a minor effect on cash until 2006 when $950 was provided by using the card.

- Bank Loans provided $1,000 in both 2005 and 2006, increasing overall Debt.
- Equipment is a negative number and used cash by getting larger, that is, you used cash to purchase equipment and equipment got larger.
- The Owner's Investment is a positive number in 2002 and added cash, that is, the owner invested cash into the business and investment got larger. You can see that if this investment had not been made, there would have been a negative Ending Cash.

Each year shows its own sources and uses of cash. In general cash is being used by increasing A/R, and Inventory and being provided by owner's investment, credit card, and bank loans. Net cash has increased due to increasing debt, not net income. This is overall a bad trend. You can see that you would be missing information if you only looked at the P&L and might not understand why your cash balance is different than expected.

Percentage trends are not relevant to the Statement of Cash Flows.

STATEMENT OF CASH FLOWS

Additional sources and uses of cash NOT on the P&L

Additional Source of Cash: Positive Numbers
Additional Use of Cash: Negative Numbers

	2002	2003	2004	2005	2006
Net Income	(100)	530	1,050	112	250
Operating Activities					
A/R	(100)	(100)	(100)	(200)	(500)
Inventory	(200)	(200)	(400)	(400)	(300)
A/P	100	100	100	(100)	(100)
Depreciation	20	20	20	20	20
Accrued Taxes	0	20	10	10	10
Credit Cards	0	0	50	0	950
Fianncing Activ-ites					
Equipment	(300)	0	0	0	0
Buildings	(500)	0	0	0	0
Bank Loan	0	0	0	1,000	1,000
Investing Activites					
Owner's Investment	1,100	0	0	0	0
Owner's Draw					
Net Cash for the Period	20	370	730	442	1,330
Beginning Cash	0	20	390	1,120	1,562
Ending Cash	20	390	1,120	1,562	2,892

Figure 65: Statement of Cash Flows

FINANCIAL ANALYSIS

		2002	2003	2004	2005	2006
Dollar Trends						
A/R	Are A/R continually using up cash i.e. are they growing?					Yes.
Inventory	Is Inventory growing unreasonalby or being depleted?					Growing.
A/P	Is A/P continually being used as a source of cash?					No.
Accrued Taxes	Are Taxes continually being used as a source of cash?					Yes.
Credit Cards	Are Credit Cards continually being used as a source of cash?					Maybe.
Bank Loan	Are Bank Loans being used to create Profit Margin and Productivity or as a substitute for poor profits?					Substitute
Net Cash						
	What is the real source of Net Cash?					Debt.

Figure 66: Statement of Cash Flows Financial Analysis

The Balance Sheet

From **Appendix C**: Understanding Accounting, you understand that the Balance Sheet shows you the Value in your business (Assets) and Who Owns the Value (Liabilities and Equity.) Trend analysis on the Balance Sheet can point out concerns you may need to address. Items will change over time and some of the changes may indicate a bad trend developing. Refer to Figures 67 and 68 as we analyze the balance sheet.

Dollar Trends

- Cash is growing and would normally be a positive trend, but we know that cash came from debt without contributing to higher profits, so here cash indicates a bad trend.
- A/R is increasing but it is difficult to understand if it is a bad trend until you calculate the percentages, I would suspect that it is a bad trend simply because all the data indicates that the business is in trouble.
- Inventory is similar. It is increasing but it is difficult to see the bad trend.
- Debt (Total Liabilities) is increasing rapidly and is probably a bad trend.

Percentage Trends

Percentage trends are calculated by dividing every balance sheet item by Total Assets (TA.) The real story on the balance sheet becomes clear when reviewing percentages.

- A/R as a percent of TA has grown from 9% to 16% and is a bad trend because sales are not flowing through to the cash balance.
- Debt Ratio has increased from 9% to 52% and is a bad trend because the debt has not created new sales and is so high that banks will no longer want to lend this business money.
- Equity is a mirror image of the Debt Ratio and has fallen from 91% to 48%. That is, the portion of the business the

owner owns has decreased and is a clear sign of unresolved profit issues.

- Return on Equity (NI/Equity) has decreased from a high in 2003 of 35% to a low of 8%. The owner is making less of a return on their investment due to low profits.

Ratios

Ratios between balance sheet items can tell you about the health of your business and point out issues you may need to address. Find below standard ratios with acceptable values.

- The Current Ratio is a liquidity ratio that tells you if you have sufficient current assets to run your business. Divide current assets by current liabilities:

$$\frac{CA}{CL} \qquad \text{2:1 is good}$$

The current ratio is above 3:1 but remember that cash came from debt, not NI.

- The Quick Ratio is a liquidity ratio but removes inventory from current assets and tells you if you have sufficient cash to run your business. Divide current assets minus inventory by current liabilities:

$$\frac{CA-INV}{CL} \qquad \text{1:1 is good}$$

The quick ratio is higher than 1:1 but, again, the cash came from debt, not NI.

BALANCE SHEET

	2002	2003	2004	2005	2006
ASSETS					
Cash	20	390	1,120	1,562	2,892
A/R	100	200	300	500	1,000
Inventory	200	400	800	1,200	1,500
Equipment	300	300	300	300	300
Buildings	500	500	500	500	500
Depreciation	(20)	(40)	(60)	(80)	(100)
TOTAL ASSETS	1,100	1,750	2,960	3,982	6,092
LIABILITIES & EQUITY					
Curent Liabilities					
A/P	100	200	300	200	100
Accrued Taxes	0	20	30	40	50
Credit Cards	0	0	50	50	1,000
Total Current Liab	100	220	380	290	1,150
Long-term Liabilities					
Bank Loan	0	0	0	1,000	2,000
TOTAL LIABILITIES	100	220	380	1,290	3,150
Equity					
Opening Balance	1,100	1,100	1,100	1,100	1,100
Net Income	(100)	530	1,050	112	250
Retained Earnings	0	(100)	430	1,480	1,592
Total Equity	1,000	1,530	2,580	2,692	2,942
TOTAL LIAB & EQUITY	1,100	1,750	2,960	3,982	6,092

Figure 67: Balance Sheet

FINANCIAL ANALYSIS

	2002	2003	2004	2005	2006
Dollar Trends					
Cash	Increasing: Good or Bad?			Bad (not from NI.)	
A/R	Increasing: Good or Bad?			Bad.	
Debt	Increasing: Good or Bad?			Bad.	
Percentage Trends					
A/R (AR/TA)	0.09	0.11	0.10	0.13	0.16
Debt Ratio (Debt/TA)	0.09	0.13	0.13	0.32	0.52
Equity (Equity/TA)	0.91	0.87	0.87	0.68	0.48
Return on Equity (NI/Equity)	(0.10)	0.35	0.41	0.04	0.08
Ratios					
Current Ratio (CA/CL)	3.20	4.50	5.84	11.25	4.69
Quick Ratio (CA-Inventory/CL)	1.20	2.68	3.74	7.11	3.38
Inventory Turnover (Annual COGS/ Ave Monthly Inv)	1.75	1.80	1.50	1.12	1.33

Figure 68: Balance Sheet Financial Analysis

- Inventory Turnover tells you if you are moving enough products off your shelves every year. You have a limited amount of space in retail and must move product through every square foot several times to make a profit. Your industry has its own standard, so do some research. Divide annual sales by average inventory at retail prices:

  $$\frac{\text{Annual Sales}}{\text{Ave. Inv. at Retail}} \qquad \text{4 is average}$$

  The inventory turnover is consistently less than two and confirms that there is too much inventory for the level of sales.

- The Average Collection Period (not shown in the analysis) tells you if your credit policy is working. If your average collection period goes beyond 30 days, you are unreasonably financing your customer's purchases. You do not have the capacity to be a bank. Divide average payments received per month by average daily sales:

  $$\frac{\text{Ave. Received}}{\text{Ave. Daily Sales}} \qquad \text{30 days is good}$$

APPENDIX E:

SERVICE AGREEMENT[8]

This Independent Contractor Agreement (this "Agreement") is made as of this _____ day of _____________, 20_____, (the "Effective Date") by and between:

Company: ______________located at_____________[Address] ("Client") and

Contractor: _____________ located at____________ [Address] "Contractor").

Client and Independent Contractor may each be referred to in this Agreement as a "Party" and collectively as the "Parties."

1. Services. Independent Contractor shall provide the following services to Client (the "Services"):

____

____

_______________________________________. In addition, Independent Contractor shall perform such other duties and tasks, or changes to the Services, as may be agreed upon by the Parties.

2. Compensation. Inconsideration for Independent Contractor's performance of the Services, Client shall pay Independent Contractor: (Check one)

☐ A Periodic Fixed Wage. Client shall pay Independent Contractor $__________ (Check one) ☐ per hour ☐ per week ☐ per month ☐ per year ☐ other: __________. Independent Contractor will be paid: (Check one)

> ☐ Every week. Independent Contractor will be paid on __________ [Day of the week] of every week.
>
> ☐ Every month. Independent Contractor will be paid on the __________ [Day of the month] of every month.
>
> ☐ After Independent Contractor sends an invoice. Independent Contractor will be paid within __________ days after receiving Independent Contractor's invoice. Independent Contractor will submit

8 Free download from http://legaltemplates.net

invoices for payment (Check one) ☐ at the end of every week ☐ on the __________ of every month ☐ within __________ days after completion of the Services ☐ other: ______________.

☐ Other: ____

☐ <u>A Set Fee.</u> Client shall pay Independent Contractor $__________: (Check one)

☐ After the Independent Contractor completes the services.

☐ Within __________ days after receiving Independent Contractor's invoice. Independent Contractor will submit invoices for payment (Check one) ☐ at the end of every week ☐ on the __________ of every month ☐ within __________ days after the completion of the Services ☐ other: ______________.

☐ Other: ____

☐ <u>After Completing Certain Milestones.</u> Client shall pay Independent Contractor according to the following schedule:

- $__________ for ____ [Milestone description]
- $__________ for ____ [Milestone description]

Independent Contractor will be paid: (Check one)

☐ After the completion of each milestone.

☐ Within __________ days after receiving Independent Contractor's invoice. Independent Contractor will submit invoices for payment (Check one) ☐ at the end of every week ☐ on the __________ of the month ☐ within __________ days after completion of the Services ☐ other: ______________.

☐ <u>Other.</u> ____

3. Expenses. (Check one)

☐ Independent Contractor will be reimbursed. Except as otherwise specified in this Agreement, Client shall reimburse Independent Contractor for all pre-approved, reasonable and necessary costs and expenses incurred in connection with the performance of the Services.

☐ Independent Contractor will NOT be reimbursed. All costs and expenses incurred by Independent Contractor in connection with the performance of the Services shall be the sole responsibility of and paid by Independent Contractor.

4. Term and Termination. Independent Contractor's engagement with Client under this Agreement shall commence on ________________, 20_____.

Termination (Check one)
☐ After all of the Services are completed. The Parties agree and acknowledge that this Agreement and Independent Contractor's engagement with Client under this Agreement shall terminate upon the completion by Independent Contractor of the Services.
☐ After a fixed period of time. The Parties agree and acknowledge that this Agreement and Independent Contractor's engagement with Client under this Agreement shall terminate after (Check one)
☐ __________ days ☐ __________ months ☐ other: _______________.
☐ On a specific date. The Parties agree and acknowledge that this Agreement and Independent Contractor's engagement with Client under this Agreement shall terminate on ________________, 20_____.
☐ At will. Independent Contractor acknowledges and agrees that the engagement with Client is at will, subject to being terminated at the discretion of Client at any time, (Check one) ☐ without prior notice ☐ upon __________ days prior written notice to Independent Contractor. In addition, this Agreement may be terminated by Independent Contractor upon ___________ days prior written notice to Client.

At the time of termination, Independent Contractor agrees to return all Client property used in performance of the Services, including but not limited to computers, cell phones, keys, reports and other equipment and documents. Independent Contractor shall reimburse Client for any Client property lost or damaged in an amount equal to the market price of such property.

5. Independent Contractor. The Parties agree and acknowledge that Independent Contractor is an independent contractor and is not, for any purpose, an employee of Client. Independent Contractor does not have any authority to enter into agreements or contracts on behalf of Client, and shall not represent that it possesses any such authority. Independent Contractor shall not be entitled to any of Client's benefits, including, but not limited to, coverage under medical, dental, retirement or other plans. Client shall not be obligated to pay worker's compensation insurance, unemployment compensation, social security tax, withholding tax or other taxes or withholdings for or on behalf of the Independent Contractor in connection with the performance of the Services under this Agreement. Nothing contained in this Agreement shall be deemed or construed by the Parties to create the relationship of a partnership, a joint venture or any other fiduciary relationship.

6. Confidentiality. (Check one)

☐ Independent Contractor will NOT be exposed to confidential information.

☐ Independent Contractor will be exposed to confidential information.

a. Confidential and Proprietary Information. In the course of performing the Services, Independent Contractor will be exposed to confidential and proprietary information of Client. "Confidential Information" shall mean any data or information that is competitively sensitive material and not generally known to the public, including, but not limited to, information relating to development and plans, marketing strategies, finance, operations, systems, proprietary concepts, documentation, reports, data, specifications, computer software, source code, object code, flow charts, data, databases, inventions, know-how, trade secrets, customer lists, customer relationships, customer profiles, supplier lists, supplier relationships, supplier profiles, pricing, sales estimates, business plans and internal performance results relating to the past, present or future business activities, technical information, designs, processes, procedures, formulas or improvements, which Client considers confidential and proprietary. Independent Contractor acknowledges and agrees that the Confidential Information is valuable property of Client, developed over a long period of time at substantial expense and that it is worthy of protection.

b. Confidentiality Obligations. Except as otherwise expressly permitted in this Agreement, Independent Contractor shall not disclose or use in any manner, directly or indirectly, any Confidential Information either during the term of this Agreement or at any time thereafter, except as required to perform the Services or with Client's prior written consent.

c. Rights in Confidential Information. All Confidential Information disclosed to Independent Contractor by Client (i) is and shall remain the sole and exclusive property of Client, and (ii) is disclosed or permitted to be acquired by Independent Contractor solely in reliance on Independent Contractor's agreement to maintain the Confidential Information in confidence and not to use or disclose the Confidential Information to any other person. Except as expressly provided herein, this Agreement does not confer any right, license, ownership or other interest in or title to the Confidential Information to Independent Contractor.

d. Irreparable Harm. Independent Contractor acknowledges that use or disclosure of any Confidential Information in a manner inconsistent with this Agreement will give rise to irreparable injury for which damages would not be an adequate remedy. Accordingly, in addition to any other legal remedies which may be available at law or in equity, Client shall be entitled to equitable or injunctive relief against the unauthorized use or disclosure of Confidential Information. Client shall be entitled to pursue any other legally permissible remedy available as a result of such breach, including but not limited to, damages, both direct and consequential. In any action brought by Client under this Section, Client shall be entitled to recover its attorney's fees and costs from Independent Contractor.

7. Ownership of Work Product. (Check one)

☐ Client has ownership. The Parties agree that all work product, information or other materials created and developed by Independent Contractor in connection with the performance of the Services under this Agreement and any resulting intellectual property rights (collectively, the "Work Product") are the sole and exclusive property of Client. The Parties acknowledge that the Work Product shall, to the extent permitted by law, be considered a "work made for hire" within the definition of Section 101 of the Copyright Act of 1976, as amended, (the "Copyright Act") and that Client is deemed to be the author and is the owner of all copyright and all other rights therein. If the work product is not deemed to be a "work made for hire" under the Copyright Act, then Independent Contractor hereby assigns to Client all of Independent Contractor's rights, title and interest in and to the Work Product, including but not limited to all copyrights, publishing rights and rights to use, reproduce and otherwise exploit the Work Product in any and all formats, media, or all channels, whether now known or hereafter created.

☐ Independent Contractor has ownership. The Parties agree that all work product, information or other materials created and developed by Independent Contractor in connection with the performance of the Services under this Agreement and any resulting intellectual property rights (collectively, the "Work Product") are the sole and exclusive property of Independent Contractor. Independent Contractor grants to Client a limited, non-exclusive license to use the Work Product. The Work Product is to be used only by Client, and Client may not assign, transfer, lease or sublicense any Work Product to any person or entity without Independent Contractor's prior written consent.

8. Insurance. (Check one)

☐ For the term of this Agreement, Independent Contractor shall obtain and maintain a policy of insurance, with appropriate and adequate coverage and limits, to cover any claims for bodily injury, property damage or other losses which might arise out of any negligent act or omission committed by Independent Contractor or Independent Contractor's employees or agents, if any, in connection with the performance of the Services under this Agreement.

☐ For the term of this Agreement, Independent Contractor is NOT required to obtain and maintain a policy of insurance for injuries or damages.

9. Non-Compete. (INITIAL if you want to include this clause. CROSS OUT if you do not.)

______ Independent Contractor agrees and covenants that during the term of this Agreement, and for a period of __________ months following the termination of this Agreement, Independent Contractor will not, directly or indirectly, perform or engage in the same or similar activities as were performed for Client for any business that is directly or indirectly in competition with Client.

10. Non-Solicit. (INITIAL if you want to include this clause. CROSS OUT if you do not.)

______ Independent Contractor agrees and covenants that for a period of __________ months following the termination of this Agreement, Independent Contractor will not, directly or indirectly, solicit any officer, director or employee, or any customer, client, supplier or vendor of Client for the purpose of inducing such party to terminate its relationship with Client in favor of Independent Contractor or another business directly or indirectly in competition with Client.

11. Mutual Representations and Warranties. Both Client and Independent Contractor represent and warrant that each Party has full power, authority and right to execute and deliver this Agreement, has full power and authority to perform its obligations under this Agreement, and has taken all necessary action to authorize the execution and delivery of this Agreement. No other consents are necessary to enter into or perform this Agreement.

12. Independent Contractor Representation and Warranties. Independent Contractor represents and warrants that it has all the necessary licenses, permits and registrations, if any, required to perform the Services under this Agreement in accordance with applicable federal, state and local laws, rules and regulations and that it will perform the Services according to the Client's guidelines and specifications and with the standard of care prevailing in the industry.

13. Indemnification. (INITIAL if you want to include this clause. CROSS OUT if you do not.)

______ The Independent Contractor shall indemnify and hold harmless Client from any damages, claims, liabilities, loss and expenses, including reasonable attorney's fees, arising out of any act or omission of Independent Contractor in performing the Services or the breach of any provision of this Agreement by Independent Contractor.

14. Governing Law. The terms of this Agreement and the rights of the Parties hereto shall be governed exclusively by the laws of the State of __________________, without regarding its conflicts of law provisions.

15. Disputes. Any dispute arising from this Agreement shall be resolved through: (Check one)

☐ Court litigation. Disputes shall be resolved in the courts of the State of __________________.

☐ If either Party brings legal action to enforce its rights under this Agreement, the prevailing party will be entitled to recover from the other Party its expenses (including reasonable attorneys' fees and costs) incurred in connection with the action and any appeal.

☐ Binding arbitration. Binding arbitration shall be conducted in accordance with the rules of the American Arbitration Association.

☐ Mediation.

☐ Mediation, then binding arbitration. If the dispute cannot be resolved through mediation, then the dispute will be resolved through binding arbitration conducted in accordance with the rules of the American Arbitration Association.

16. Binding Effect. This Agreement shall be binding upon and inure to the benefit of the Parties and their respective successors and permitted assigns.

17. Assignment. The interests of Independent Contractor are personal to Independent Contractor and cannot be assigned, transferred or sold without the prior written consent of Client.

18. Entire Agreement. This Agreement constitutes the entire agreement between the Parties hereto with respect the subject matter hereof, and supersedes all prior negotiations, understandings and agreements of the Parties.

19. Amendments. No supplement, modification or amendment of this Agreement will be binding unless executed in writing by both of the Parties.

20. Notices. Any notice or other communication given or made to either Party under this Agreement shall be in writing and delivered by hand, sent by overnight courier service or sent by certified or registered mail, return receipt requested, to the address stated above or to another address as that Party may subsequently designate by notice, and shall be deemed given on the date of delivery.

21. Waiver. Neither Party shall be deemed to have waived any provision of this Agreement or the exercise of any rights held under this Agreement unless such waiver is made expressly and in writing. Waiver by either Party of a breach or violation of any provision of this Agreement shall not constitute a waiver of any subsequent or other breach or violation.

22. Further Assurances. At the request of one Party, the other Party shall execute and deliver such other documents and take such other actions as may be reasonably necessary to effect the terms of this Agreement.

23. Severability. If any provision of this Agreement is held to be invalid, illegal or unenforceable in whole or in part, the remaining provisions shall not be affected and shall continue to be valid, legal and enforceable as though the invalid, illegal or unenforceable parts had not been included in this Agreement.

IN WITNESS WHEREOF, this Agreement has been executed and delivered as of the date first written above.

______________________________	______________________________
Client Signature	**Client** Full Name
______________________________	______________________________
Independent Contractor Signature	**Independent Contractor** Full Name

APPENDIX F: LEAN Principles

LEAN Thinking

LEAN is a set of principles that can be applied to any system but is incredibly powerful when applied to creating and assembling products. It is an essential concept you will employ in Systems Redesign, **Chapter 3**. Its goal is to eliminate unnecessary expenses and minimize waste: anything your customer is not willing to pay for or reduces your competitive advantage.

Definitions

"**LEAN**" stands for the Lean Education Academic Network. "**Sigma 6**" (S6) stands for: Sort, Safe, Straighten, Scrub, Standardize, and Sustain. The titles seem academic, but the concepts are straightforward.

Philosophy

The Pillars of LEAN thinking include:

- Continuous Improvement.
- Respect for People.

This means that you are never finished with a system and must work continuously to maintain and improve efficiency. Employees are trained in systems redesign and LEAN Thinking to improve their own work environment. It is essential to include everyone who "touches" the system and work in teams.

LEAN Goals

The four goals of LEAN Systems are to:

- Eliminate Waste
- Improve Quality
- Reduce Time
- Reduce Total Costs

Eliminate Waste

LEAN identifies eight types of waste:

- Defects
- Over Production
- Waiting
- Non-utilized talent
- Transportation
- Inventory
- Motion
- Over-processing

In Systems Redesign you will draw a flow chart and space diagram of each existing system and identify waste, so let's talk in more detail.

The key question is: does each activity in the system create value the customer is willing to pay for? If they are willing to pay for the activity, it is Value Added; if they are not willing to pay for the activity or it is irrelevant to their concept of value, it is Non-Value Added. Your task is to eliminate all the Non-Value-Added activities.

When you begin your systems redesign with your team and draw your diagrams, you will discuss each step/activity in detail and eliminate all the following wastes.

<u>Defects</u>

Defects create costs from wasted materials, reworking products, and overproduction to make up for products that cannot be sold. You can eliminate defects by building reliability into your systems and inspecting quality at each step.

<u>Over Production</u>

Over production means using more resources than necessary to produce the system outcome. Producing more than you can sell creates many down-stream costs such as: purchase of unnecessary parts and materials, interest on loans, storage space for inventory, and personnel to manage it. Solutions include smaller batch sizes and fewer tasks per production station.

Waiting

Anytime employees, materials, machines, or products sit still, there is a cost. Minimizing waiting saves dollars.

Non-utilized Talent

Every one of your employees has a very big brain, better than the best supercomputer. By not educating them, including them in group problem solving, and incentivizing their commitment, you have wasted this incredible resource. One of them may have the answer that saves you thousands of dollars and creates a competitive advantage so take the lessons in **Chapter 3** seriously.

Transportation

Unnecessary transportation of products or materials does not create any value and may damage, lose, or delay what is being moved. It exposes the material to theft or alteration and requires additional management time. Shipping a product somewhere to have it processed and then shipping it back to finish the manufacturing is a waste when you can buy the machinery to process it yourself.

Inventory

Inventory uses cash but does not create income. You do need a certain amount of inventory to provide timely fulfillment of orders, but it is at a level that supports sales without creating waste. If you have inventory on the shelf for more than 30 days, you have waste. Just-in-time ordering of material makes inventory management efficient, but it requires reliable communication with your sources and may require them to adopt LEAN principles.

Motion

The motion of employees, tools, and materials must be minimized to maximize profit. This requires a system that is simple, with the fewest number of moving parts and moving employees. The placement of workstations with point of use storage for tools and materials must minimize all motion. Small batch sizes are easier to process and creating process stations with fewer tasks in each step reduces motion.

If you must process a piece of wood with six different router cuts, it is better to have six routers, each dedicated to a single cut rather than change and calibrate the router blade six times.

Over-processing

Over-processing means applying more work to a process or item than is required or using overly complex tools or methods than necessary. This can also include using highly qualified employees to accomplish low level work. The owner of a small business who fails to delegate jobs is using his/her management skill to over-process an elementary task.

Improve Quality

Continuous improvement is a key concept in LEAN. After you have created a system, you are not done. Every employee needs to be conscious of opportunities to improve the quality and efficiency of the system. This requires oversight, measurement, and group problem solving to regularly improve each process.

Here is your opportunity to transform your management style to create and nurture teams that imbedded quality in the function of their jobs. It is easy to kill the motivation in individuals and teams and you must be the one protecting quality by protecting the process of change in systems redesign and quality improvement. It is a continuous process with no end point, only the goal of improvement.

Reduce Time

Reducing all types of waste results in a reduction in time spent assembling and transporting parts and inventory. Small batch sizes create continuous flow and you may be able run machines faster.

Reduce Total Costs

Taken together, reducing waste will reduce your total costs and it can be measured through production metrics. Figure 69 shows a comparison between mass production principles and LEAN Thinking (adapted from MIT materials.)

Item	Mass Production	LEAN Thinking
Focus	Product	Customer
Operation	Batch and Queue	Synchronized Flow
Aim	Reduce Cost/Increase Efficiency	Eliminate Waste/Add Value
Quality	Inspection after Production	Built in by Design
Strategy	Economies of Scale	Productivity/Adaptability
Improvement	Expert-driven Periodic Improvement	Worker-driven Continuous Improvement

Figure 69: Mass Production vs LEAN Thinking

LEAN Process

The LEAN Process is outlined below but you can see an example of a real business under Systems Redesign in **Chapter 3**. To complete the process of redesigning a system using LEAN you must:

10) Form the Redesign Team
11) Understand how the systems works now
12) Draw a process map
13) Draw a value stream map
14) Draw a spaghetti diagram and current space plan
15) Redesign the process with new space plan
16) Document the system
17) Avoid implementation problems
18) Maintain oversight

With the system in place, you can create continuous improvement through daily system meetings and track goals and changes on whiteboards or computers.

APPENDIX G: Valuing Your Business

A large portion of your wealth as an entrepreneur is imbedded in your business. Many entrepreneurs plan to sell their business and use the proceeds as part of their retirement, so it is important to understand valuation methods.

First you need to know that there are two values for any business:

- The Liquidation Value
- The Discounted Profit Value

You need to use both to obtain an accurate value. There are supposedly many ways to value a business, but these are the only two supported by financial theory. If someone offers to value your business using a method other than the Liquidation Value and the Discounted Profit Method, be skeptical. They do not know anything about finance.

Don't use Common size or Triple the Net. Common Size assumes there is a business just like yours that has already been sold, so your business should be worth the same. It is a false assumption. Local markets are different, profit margins are different, and data bases used in this method are flawed. Some CPAs use several methods to confirm the price range and common size is one of them. It's expensive and useless.

Triple the net is a rule of thumb method that has no basis in fact. It states that your business is worth three times your annual Net Income. If you have $1.00 in Net Income, your business is supposedly worth $3.00, even if you have a million dollars in assets in your warehouse.

Let's begin with the first credible method. The Liquidation Value of any business is the value left over after selling all the assets and paying off all the liabilities. It is the *only* value of a business without profits because there is nothing else to value other than the assets. But this is not the real value of a business creating profits. Consider a business that has a machine worth $10,000 if it was sold today, but that machine produces $1,000,000 in profits each year. Is the business worth only $10,000? Of course not! It is worth far more. What creates value in a profitable business is the *profits* it generates.

In the Discounted Profit Valuation method, you are valuing the profits, but not just this year's profits. You are trying to determine what the next ten years of profits are worth TODAY. Some professionals will use Discounted Cash Flow instead of Discounted Profit because the cash is what is useful and real, but I use Profit because you can compare the Return on Invest for your business with *all* other Investments. The stock market uses Return on Investment (ROI) and you and your buyer should too. Refer to Figure 70 as I explain how this is accomplished.

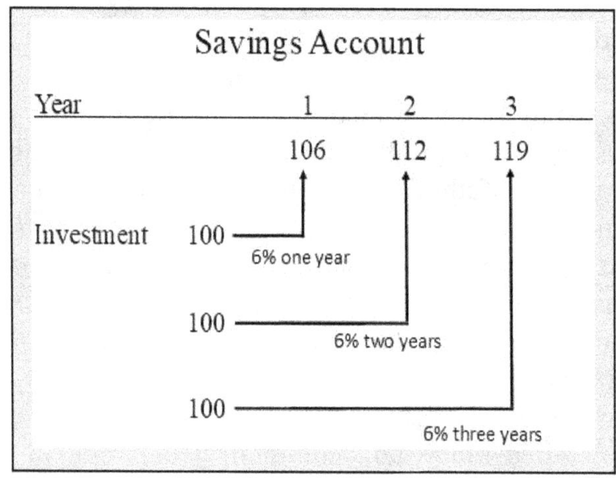

Figure 70: Savings Account

First imagine that you have a savings account and that you deposit $100 for one year at 6%. You would expect to withdraw $106 at the end of the year. What you are really doing is buying that future $106 from the bank for $100. You pay $100 today but agree not to pick up your $106 until the year is over.

A buyer for your business is doing the same thing. They are looking out into the future at the profits they are likely to acquire (the $106 in this case) and deciding what to pay for them today. If you decide to pay $100 now for $106 in profits next year, you will make a 6% return on your investment. $100 is the discounted value of $106 (discounted back one year to the present at 6%). But when you are buying a business, you are not just buying next year's profits, you are buying many future years of profits; so you have to value the profit in each future year and then add them all together. How do you do this? By making cash flow projections, finding out what the future profits are likely to be, and then discounting the profits back in time to the present at the rate of return the buyer and seller agree on. Figure 71 shows a business with each of three years of profit discounted backward to the present at 6%. If you wanted only a 6% return, the total value of this business would be $300.

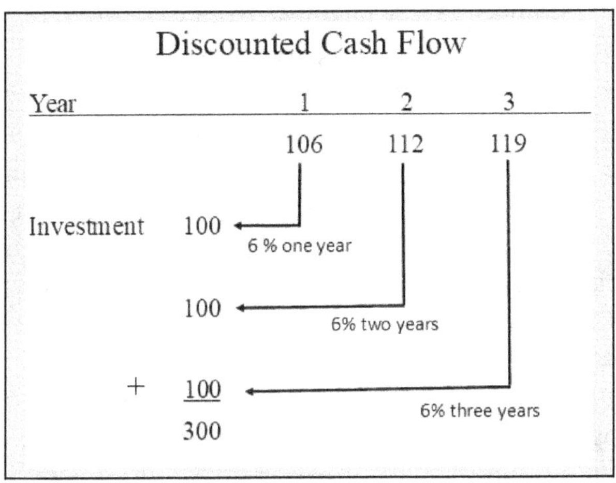

Figure 71: Discounted Cashflow Value

I use ten years of future profits because no one's crystal ball goes out farther than that, but the rate of return you use, your Return on Investment (ROI,) is not going to be 6%. The rate of return has to reflect the level of risk you are taking by being in business. Consider that a savings account has no risk, so a bank may only pay 1-3%. There is absolutely no risk that you will lose your money, so you do not need to be compensated beyond the minimum return. The stock market has more risk and on average pays 10-11% because there *is* a chance you could lose your money. Small business is probably riskier than the stock market so the rate of return you use in your Discounted Cashflow should be 12-14% or greater. How much more? That depends on how much risk the buyer perceives. (Do not confuse this rate of return with your Profit Margin, they are two numbers with very different meanings.)

$$\textbf{Profit Margin} = \frac{\text{Net Income}}{\text{Sales}}$$

$$\textbf{ROI} = \frac{\text{Net Income}}{\text{Investment*}}$$

*"Investment," is the agreed-on purchase price of your business.

When you purchased your business from the previous owner, you should have projected ten years' worth of profits and discounted them backward in time to the present at the rate of return *you* wanted on the investment. You can still do that now and determine what a reasonable price should have been. One caution: you must place a reasonable expense for the previous owner's salary in your cash flow projections. That means deciding what you would have to pay someone else to do the same job. That way the profits that are left to value in the Discounted Cashflow reflect what is left after *all* expenses have been considered.

The right price is the price that the buyer and seller agree on after first valuing the business with the method outlined above. The buyer will want to get a higher rate of return for themselves by reducing the price, the seller will want to get a higher rate of return for themselves by raising the price. Both buyer and seller should determine their upper and lower limits by knowing what rate of return they are getting for the price they are discussing. You will probably need to get help from a consultant to do the valuation calculation.

There is one major caution to be aware of in valuing a business. If land or a building is being sold as part of the business, you must get a real estate appraisal. There is the possibility that the land and building may be worth more than the Discounted Cashflow if real estate prices have risen dramatically or if the seller has held the property a long time. In this case the Liquidation Value would be higher than the Discounted Profit Value.

The value of buildings and land should be calculated *separately* and sold separately from the business.

APPENDIX H: Writing a Winning Loan Proposal

Clients often ask me how long it takes to receive a loan and the answer is only a few days *if* you are prepared when you go to the bank. It takes a banker a relatively short amount of time to decide on your loan, but it takes a good deal of time to construct a credible loan proposal. How long it takes then really depends on you. You must address four major issues in any proposal to be considered a good candidate for a bank loan — or any other form of financing. How well you address these issues will determine the outcome. Being concise but also thorough in your approach will shorten the loan process and make a favorable impression on your loan officer. The four major issues to consider are:

- Cash Flow
- Character
- Collateral
- Net Worth (Equity)

It is very common for the entrepreneur to cover each critical area piecemeal; having gone to the bank with a few scattered documents and finding they need to be coached through the process by the banker. It is far better to complete all the preparations beforehand and appear well versed when you sit down to ask a financial institution for money. Let's cover each area in a little more detail.

<u>Cash Flow</u>

Banks are cash flow lenders not collateral lenders. That means they want the loan paid back through the profitable cash flow of the business not through the sale of assets. Cash flow usually can be proven by your historical accounting data from your Income Statement (Profit & Loss) and your Balance Sheet. In addition, you will have to make cash flow projections for at least two years into the future to show the bank that the loan will contribute to future success.

If you are starting a new business, you will have only the projections with which to make this point. In this case, or if your historical cash flows are marginal, you may need to show a secondary source of cash flows that could be used to repay the loan, such as: a job, interest income, or a cosigner.

Character

Character is a nebulous issue that hopefully demonstrates you behave like a person who is likely to repay a loan. This can be indicated by your longevity in business, your management/technical experience, and your credit rating. Any black marks in these areas will cast doubt on your ability to manage the bank's money — particularly in the credit area. A bankruptcy within the last ten years will probably eliminate you from consideration. Keep in mind that the bank is loaning you their depositor's savings and has the responsibility to make a reasonable return.

Collateral

Collateral is simply something the bank can take away from you if you default on the loan. The bankers favorite form of collateral is residential real estate, in most cases your home. Other forms of collateral like inventory, accounts receivable, business property, and equipment with a ready secondary market may be considered. Tools and fixtures are usually not good forms of collateral.

Net Worth (Equity)

Net worth, or equity, is what is left when you subtract all the liabilities of the business from all the assets and represents the portion of the business you own. Banks are typically looking for a debt-to-equity ratio of one to three, one to two on the outside. This means that you would be eligible to increase your total debt to $30,000 if your net worth was currently $10,000. If you are starting a new business and need $40,000 to get it off the ground, the bank will lend you $30,000 and you will have to invest $10,000 of your own money in cash or other assets.

How you arrange all this information is also important. It should follow a logical order, be clear and concise, and have a professional appearance.

A suggested outline:

Title Page: Loan Proposal, WYZ Company
Table of Contents
Summary of the Loan (1 page)
Description of the Business/Short History
Description of the Market
Management Resumes
Use of Funds (Listed item by item)
Accounting Data: P&L and Balance Sheets for Three Years
Aging of Accounts Receivable
Aging of Accounts Payable
Schedule of Long-term Debt
List of Collateral
Cash Flow Narrative/Assumptions
Cash Flow Projections for Two Years
Projected P&L and Balance Sheet for Two Years
Appendix
- Tax Returns for Three Years
- Personal Financial Statement

With all your information in good order, placed in a readable format, and well presented, the banker should be able to acquire a clear picture of your business and make a decision within a week or two. But beyond that, *you* will also have a better understanding of your business and be able to discuss and clarify for the loan officer any additional concerns.

APPENDIX I: Resources

Free Downloads
www.douglasjhammel.com

Spreadsheets
Amortization Schedule.xls
Breakeven for Expansions.xls
Cash Flow – simple.xls
Cash Flow – units and personnel.xls
Differential Analysis.xls
Markups and Margins
Open to Buy
Project Costing System.xls
Retirement

Business Advising Resources

Douglas J. Hammel Business Advising in person in Jefferson County, WA, and by Zoom in other locations. Contact me through www.douglasjhammel.com for an appointment

Center for Inclusive Entrepreneurship (CIE) Washington State: Free startup advising, support, training, financing, and networking.
360-230-8082
https://www.cie-nw.org/

Small Business Development Centers (SBDC): Free business advising in every state, information, and training. SBA and local funding.
https://www.sba.gov/local-assistance/resource-partners/small-business-development-centers-sbdc

Economic Development Council (EDC): May include free business advising. County funded.

Information Resources

CIE, SBDC, EDC: as above.

Department of Commerce: Your state.

Legal Documents
Legal Templates: http://legaltemplates.net

U.S. Patents and Trademarks Office
www.uspto.gov

Management Reading List

William Bridges, *Transitions: Making Sense of Life's Changes*, (Cambridge: Da Capo Press, 2004)

John Carver, *Boards That Make a Difference: A New Design for Leadership in Nonprofit and Public Organizations*, (San Francisco: Josey-Bass, 1997)

Phillip Kotler, *Principles of Marketing*, (Upper Saddle River: Prentice Hall, 2010)

Cheryl Hamilton, *Communicating for Results*, (Boston: Wadsworth: Cengage Learning, 2011)

Joseph J. Martocchio, *Strategic Compensation*, (Boston: Pearson, 2015)

Imai Masaki, *Gemba Kaizen* (complete set of LEAN tools)

Peter M. Senge, *The Fifth Discipline: The Art and Practice of the Learning Organization*, (New York: Doubleday, 2006)

J. Thomas Wren, Ed, *The Leader's Companion: Insights on Leadership Through the Ages*, (New York: The Free Press, 1995)

INDEX

About the Author:

Douglas J. Hammel has owned and operated successful businesses in wholesale produce, the performing arts, electronics, business consulting, and publishing. He previously served as the Director of the Small Business Development Center in Olympia, Washington, the Business Services Director for the Jefferson County EDC in Port Townend, Washington, and as a Professor of Business and Entrepreneurship at several colleges. He has assisted more than three thousand entrepreneurs since 1988 with improving their business practices. He received his B.S. from Michigan State University and his M.B.A. from Washington State University. He continues to advise business managers, write, and present workshops and seminars in support of entrepreneurs through all phases of business development.

Forthcoming books by Doulgas J. Hammel:

SUCCEED!™ for Exceptional Business Advising

www.ingramcontent.com/pod-product-compliance
Lightning Source LLC
Chambersburg PA
CBHW071730270326
41928CB00013B/2623

* 9 7 9 8 2 1 8 3 4 9 6 6 0 *